SoJourn Volume 7

A journal devoted to the history, culture, and geography of South Jersey

Autumn 2023

SoJourn is a collaborative effort. Local historians contribute the articles; Stockton students—in this issue, the editing interns of fall 2022, spring 2023, and fall 2023—edit the articles, set the type, and design the layout; the directors of the South Jersey Culture & History Center at Stockton University oversee the publication.

Editors
Kyle Annassenz, Mariah Ayala, Ashley Baker, Anthony Bastos, Travis Finley, Evelyn Hunt, William King, Cory Krause, Zophia Krause, Juliana Long, Olivia Murawski, Cassius Navarro, Victoria Orlowski, Lauren Parks, Therese Reidy, Mary Reitmeyer, Sofia Rossi, Amanda Sciandra, Gabrielle Shockley, Sheisa Tapia, Randi Ward, Alice Watt, Lisa Weck, Frank Wendling, Rachel Wronko.

Supervising Editors
Tom Kinsella and Paul W. Schopp

ISSN: 2474-6665
ISBN: 978-1-947889-22-4
A publication of the South Jersey Culture & History Center
at Stockton University
www.stockton.edu/sjchc/

© 2023, the authors, South Jersey Culture & History Center, and Stockton University. All rights reserved.

Filler images, at the conclusion of articles, courtesy of the Paul W. Schopp collection unless otherwise noted.

To contact SJCHC write:
SJCHC / School of Arts & Humanities
Stockton University
101 Vera King Farris Drive
Galloway, New Jersey
08205

Email:
Thomas.Kinsella@stockton.edu
Paul.Schopp@stockton.edu

SoJourn 2023

In early November 2023, I joined a festive group on a prohibition cruise down Tuckerton Creek, through Tuckerton Cove, and into Little Egg Harbor. On the two-hour voyage, our guide Paisley Blair, dressed as a 1920s flapper, recounted the history of prohibition in the United States, spicing the details with local stories of rum running, and introducing sayings and drinks from the period that have cultural resonance to this day: bootleggers and teetotalers, the bee's knees, the real McCoy, and Mary Pickfords. Along the way we paused to admire many great blue herons posing on anchored boats and docks, flying cormorants, and a single loon. We also passed a great deal of history.

Slipping slowly down the creek, we motored by wild stretches and built-up areas, with red cedars adjacent to old docks, and new housing huddled close together, most built on stilts to mitigate the inevitable flooding. In the harbor we saw the skyline of Long Beach Island to the east and Atlantic City to the south. Someone pointed out Parker Island. Paisley described Tucker's Island as "the Atlantis of New Jersey."

A colleague and I had been invited on this voyage as a thank you for Stockton's collaboration with the Tuckerton Seaport and its new exhibition, "Taste Traditions of South Jersey." Thanks to the good work of Cynthia Anstey, the South Jersey Culture & History Center had made available some of Marilyn Schmidt's cookbooks, preserved in Stockton's Special Collections, and maple syrup produced from Stockton's stand of red maples. Several other individuals and organizations contributed to this cooperative exhibit of local foodways as well.

Reflecting upon the culture of drinking in the 1920s and 1930s, and the broader traditions of local cuisine, prompted me to ponder the ways local historians cope with the inevitability of change. How do *we* honor what has come before? Tucker's Island flourished for a time; now it is gone. The rum runners are gone, too.

As our cruise ship reentered Tuckerton Creek, making for home, the passengers—some perhaps lubricated by their byob refreshments—began to point out family sites: "Look! That was my grandmother's house" and "Those lights show where my family's business stood." Grandma's house is gone; so is the seafood business. In their place stand expensive, new, and sometimes beautiful houses. The conversation drifted from the bayman's lifestyle of yesteryear to life on the bay today.

We did not disembark with answers, though we knew more than when our voyage began (thanks to our wonderful guide Paisley and Captain Dick). It was clear, though, that history surrounds us. *SoJourn* and publications like it record this history. We attempt to document it with completeness and fidelity, but the result can never reproduce the past. We record snapshots, and we hope that they are well chosen and skillfully made.

I apologize for the delay in the publication of this issue of *SoJourn*. Thank you for your patience. Our little student-staffed local history press is working as industriously as possible. While I write these words I am sitting in an outdoor gazebo on the shore of Stockton's Lake Fred. It is a warm November afternoon and I sit thirty feet from the site of what was once a colonial sawmill. History is all around us.

Tom Kinsella

Director
South Jersey Culture & History Center
Stockton University

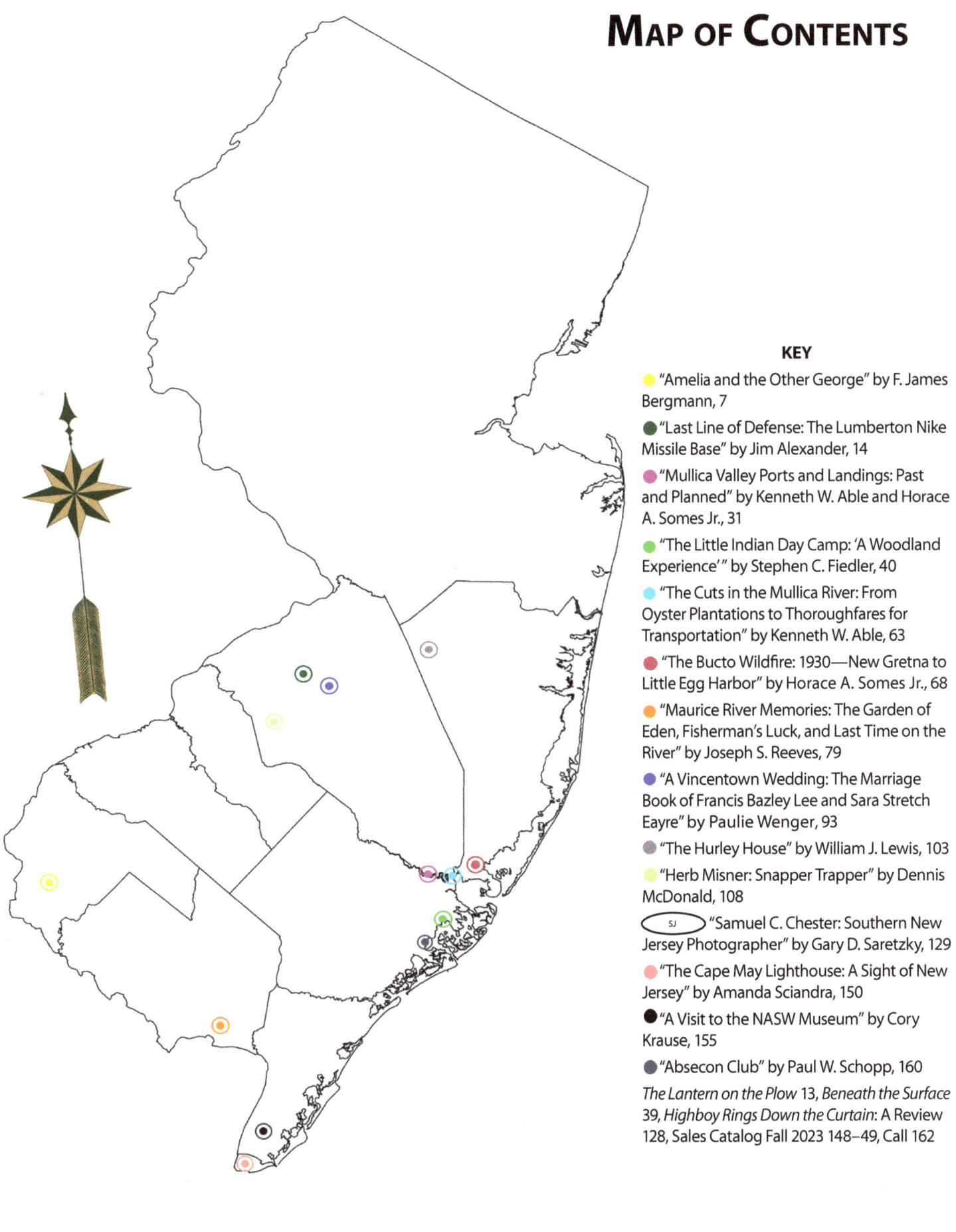

MAP OF CONTENTS

KEY

- "Amelia and the Other George" by F. James Bergmann, 7
- "Last Line of Defense: The Lumberton Nike Missile Base" by Jim Alexander, 14
- "Mullica Valley Ports and Landings: Past and Planned" by Kenneth W. Able and Horace A. Somes Jr., 31
- "The Little Indian Day Camp: 'A Woodland Experience'" by Stephen C. Fiedler, 40
- "The Cuts in the Mullica River: From Oyster Plantations to Thoroughfares for Transportation" by Kenneth W. Able, 63
- "The Bucto Wildfire: 1930—New Gretna to Little Egg Harbor" by Horace A. Somes Jr., 68
- "Maurice River Memories: The Garden of Eden, Fisherman's Luck, and Last Time on the River" by Joseph S. Reeves, 79
- "A Vincentown Wedding: The Marriage Book of Francis Bazley Lee and Sara Stretch Eayre" by Paulie Wenger, 93
- "The Hurley House" by William J. Lewis, 103
- "Herb Misner: Snapper Trapper" by Dennis McDonald, 108
- (SJ) "Samuel C. Chester: Southern New Jersey Photographer" by Gary D. Saretzky, 129
- "The Cape May Lighthouse: A Sight of New Jersey" by Amanda Sciandra, 150
- "A Visit to the NASW Museum" by Cory Krause, 155
- "Absecon Club" by Paul W. Schopp, 160

The Lantern on the Plow 13, *Beneath the Surface* 39, *Highboy Rings Down the Curtain*: A Review 128, Sales Catalog Fall 2023 148–49, Call 162

Windle W. Hollis reputedly began the Jersey shore craze of Salt Water Taffy. Born in the Manayunk section of Philadelphia during 1838 to Jacob and Mary Hollis, by 1870 he resided in Chicago, Illinois, and worked as a confectioner. He formed the W. W. Hollis Candy Company but lost everything in the great Chicago fire of 1871. Windle and his family relocated to Cleveland, Ohio, where the loss in Chicago caught up with him, forcing him to assign all his goods and chattels to an administrator for the benefit of his creditors. Shortly after 1880, he relocated to Wilmington, Delaware, where he operated a confectionery shop at 807 Market Street and boarded at the Lafayette Hotel and later at the Delaware House. During the summer months, he hawked his candy creations on the Atlantic City boardwalk near Arkansas Avenue. Working at the seaside resort, it was not a stretch to think that he named small taffy candies wrapped in waxed paper "salt water taffy." On his application to obtain a trademark for his taffy label, he claimed he began using the logo (and the term "salt water taffy") in 1883. No confirmation has been found that Hollis actually resided full time in Atlantic City. By 1904, Windle had moved to Westbrook, Maine, where he continued his work as a confectioner. On July 14, 1910, his body was found lying on the commons in Portland, Maine, with a bullet in his brain. He had been going blind for some time and likely committed suicide. His son Harry, who resided in Lafayette, Indiana, declared that his mother had died without knowing the whereabouts of her husband Windle. A sad ending for the man who many credit with originating Salt Water Taffy.

Amelia and the Other George

F. James Bergmann

What do a famous aviatrix, a successful New York City publisher, and an oft published author have in common with South Jersey? To better understand we start with the aviatrix, Amelia Earhart.

Amelia Earhart was a household name world-wide in the first half of the twentieth century. She remains a well-known figure to this day. Most know that Earhart was the first female aviator to fly solo across the Atlantic Ocean and most know that she met her tragic and mysterious end while crossing the Pacific Ocean in 1939.

Born in Kansas in 1897, Earhart's quest for flight began when she was a young girl. She saw her first airplane at the Iowa State Fair in 1908 and the sight of it sparked her desire to take to the skies. In 1920, Earhart took her first plane ride, piloted by Frank Hawks in California. The ride was exhilarating, but she wanted to be pilot rather than passenger, and, in 1921, she began taking flight lessons with Neta Snook, a pioneering female flight instructor. Shortly afterwards, Earhart purchased her first airplane, a Kinner Crackerbox, which she soon replaced with a Kinner Airster that she dubbed "The Canary."

Earhart first gained public attention in 1927, when Captain Hilton H. Railey invited her to be the first woman to fly across the Atlantic, but only as a passenger. Though she was disappointed by her flight status, Earhart could not pass up this monumental opportunity. She accompanied pilot Wilmer Stultz and copilot/mechanic Louis Gordon on the flight, nominally as a passenger, but with the added duty of keeping the flight log. The team departed from Trepassey Harbor, Newfoundland, in a Fokker F.VIIb/3m, named "Friendship" on June 17, 1928. Earhart thus became the first woman to fly across the Atlantic.

In August 1928, Earhart flew solo coast to coast. In Pittsburgh, Pennsylvania, she was involved in a "ground loop" accident when unbalanced wings caused the plane to drag one wing along the ground, the other skyward. After repairs, Earhart completed the flight. Determined to execute a solo transoceanic flight, Earhart succesfully crossed the Atlantic in 1932. Again, she was the first woman to do so. This flight propelled Earhart into the spotlight, solidifying her status as the daring pilot she is known as today.

On this trip, Earhart landed in England and met Lady Mary Heath, an Irish pilot. From her, Earhart purchased an Avro 594 Avian III, SN: R3/AV/101, called the G-EBUG, which replaced her Canary. She had it shipped to America.

Amelia Earhart's favorite photograph of herself, c. 1930–1931.

SoJourn

On July 2, 1937, Earhart, accompanied by navigator Fred Noonan, began a Pacific leg of her attempt to circumnavigate the globe. While the flight ended in tragedy, Earhart remains one of the most influential figures of the twentieth century.

The Two Georges and Amelia

George Putnam, a well-known New York City publisher, met Earhart in 1928, during the period of her first transatlantic flight as passenger. A year earlier Putnam had published *We*, Charles Lindbergh's best-selling autobiography. Probably because of this, and Putnam's friendship with Captain Railey, he was invited to be a promoter of Earhart's transatlantic

(Left) Always adventurous, Amelia Earhart atop the dome of Low Memorial Library at Columbia in 1920. Earhart recalled in a 1933 interview that "The first adventure I had at Columbia was in the air. I climbed to the top of the Library."[2]

Los Angeles, California, USA, August 1929. Some of the nineteen participants before the start of the First National Women's Air Derby, often referred to as the "Powder Puff Derby," between Santa Monica and Cleveland, Ohio. Standing in front of a plane at the Breakfast Club (from left to right): Louise M. Thaden (eventual winner of the "heavy flight class"--Earhart was third), Bobbie Trout, Patty Willis, Marvel Crosson, Blanche W. Noyes, Vera Dawn Walker, Amelia Earhart, Marjorie Crawford, Ruth Elder, and Florence Lowe Barnes. Courtesy of Wikipedia.

Amelia and the Other George

flight. Putnam soon became well acquainted with Earhart. As a promoter, he saw marketing potential in her independent nature, as well as her then-unusual position as a female aviator. Believing he could profit off her image as the champion of female aviation, he began to promote Earhart. As their interactions continued, Earhart and Putnam fell in love with each other and married in 1931.

GEORGE A. CHAMBERLAIN

Here is where the South Jersey connection comes in. A few years before Putnam met Earhart, Putnam's publishing company, G. P. Putnam's Sons, began publishing novels by George Agnew Chamberlain, who was then an up-and-coming author based in Salem and Cumberland counties. Chamberlain joined the likes of Ben Hecht, author of *Erik Dorn* (1921), A. A. Milne—Putnam published *Once on a Time* (1922) but not *Winnie the Pooh*—and popular author Lord Dunsany (Edward John Moreton Drax Plunkett). By 1925 Chamberlain and Putnam were in constant contact about upcoming novels and potential movie deals.

Though the Georges' relationship started as a professional one, they became fast friends who held a deep respect for each other. In a 1950 letter to his sister Margaret, Putnam described, "George [Chamberlain]'s 'terrific courage' as something he constantly admired."[1]

CHAMBERLAIN AND EARHART

Thanks to their mutual friendship with Putnam, Earhart and Chamberlain met in the late 1920s. At this time Chamberlain traveled frequently between New York City, Paris, and Bridgeton, New Jersey. On Earhart's visits to Bridgeton, she flew into Buck Airport on Parvin's Mill Road in Upper Deerfield Township. Chamberlain entertained both Amelia and George Putnam at Lloyd's Landing, his estate in Alloway Township.

Like Earhart, Chamberlain took an interest in aviation. His attraction dates from his time as a WWI Consul General to Lorenco Marques, Portuguese East Africa. While there, on July 14, 1915, he wrote to his mother about possibly buying an airplane.

Ultimately, Chamberlain did not purchase a plane, nor join the aviation corps, but his interest continued after the war. While staying at the Seymour Hotel in New York City (likely between the late nineteen teens and early nineteen twenties), he purchased a pair of

Amelia Earhart and husband George Putnam, April 2, 1931. Courtesy of International News Photos/Wikipedia.

Letter from George Agnew Chamberlain to his mother, dated July 14, 1915. "If we go into the war dear mother, your honorable will not remain here; just because this place will remain quiet throughout as far as I can predict. I have already made my plans. I shall prepare myself, buy myself a machine, and join the aviation corps."

aviation goggles, which were a part of the Chamberlain collection at the Alloway Historical Museum.

Proof of Earhart and Chamberlain's friendship exists in the physical records they left behind. In an undated letter to Chamberlain, Earhart writes, "GP has some handsome pictures of thee and me. He probably sent you some already. If I can do anything for you sometime let me know."

Chamberlain, as well, wrote letters to Earhart and Putnam. The Purdue University Archives hold two messages Chamberlain sent to the couple after Earhart's 1932 solo flight across the Atlantic. A Western Union Telegram sent to Putnam in New York City reads, "I am sharing your relief and joy and have cabled congratulations to AE." This telegram is dated May 21, 1932. The same day Chamberlain sent a Western Union Cablegram from Salem to Earhart at 14 Princes Gate, London. It read, "Heartfelt congratulations." Chamberlain obviously cared a great deal for Earhart's safety and took pride in her achievements.

Chamberlain held frequent parties for friends and associates at Lloyd's Landing. Visitors included authors, artists, entertainers, and of course Amelia Earhart and George Putnam. All visitors apparently signed Chamberlain's guest book, often commenting on the occasion (and sometimes, if artistically inclined, drawing pictures of the visit).

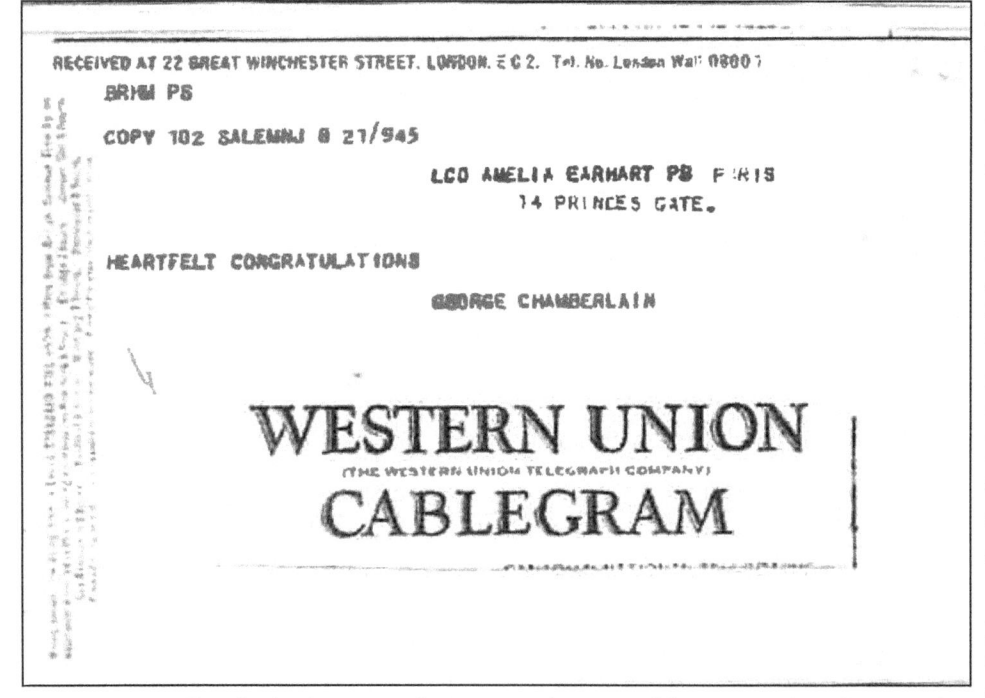

Mention of Amelia and George Putnam's visit to Lloyd's Landing, *Salem Sunbeam* (Salem, New Jersey), April 15, 1931.

On a visit on April 13, 1931—surely the visit mentioned in the *Salem Sunbeam* above—Earhart signed the guest book, writing "Dry" under her name. Though this was the era of Prohibition, local lore has it that Chamberlain would receive shipments of spirits, brought up Alloways Creek and deposited on his dock, from time to time. "Dry" meant that he was temporarily out of alcoholic drinks, while "Wet" or "Very wet" meant that he had enough alcohol to go around. Though it was nominally illegal to possess alcohol during the Prohibition era, Chamberlain defied the law with his parties, as did Earhart by attending them. Chamberlain and Earhart, a dauntless pair, broke the rules and had fun doing it.

Earhart and Chamberlain regularly visited local South Jersey establishments, especially in Quinton and Bridgeton. Chamberlain, who was a member of the Cohanzick Country Club in Fairton, Fairfield Twp., could often be seen playing golf at the club, sometimes with Earhart by his side.

Though both famous, the pair enjoyed the company of many local people. I have written previously about Earhart and Chamberlain's interaction with Frank Hankins, son of the

George Agnew Chamberlain's congratulations to Earhart on safely crossing the Atlantic on her solo flight in 1932.

Amelia and the Other George

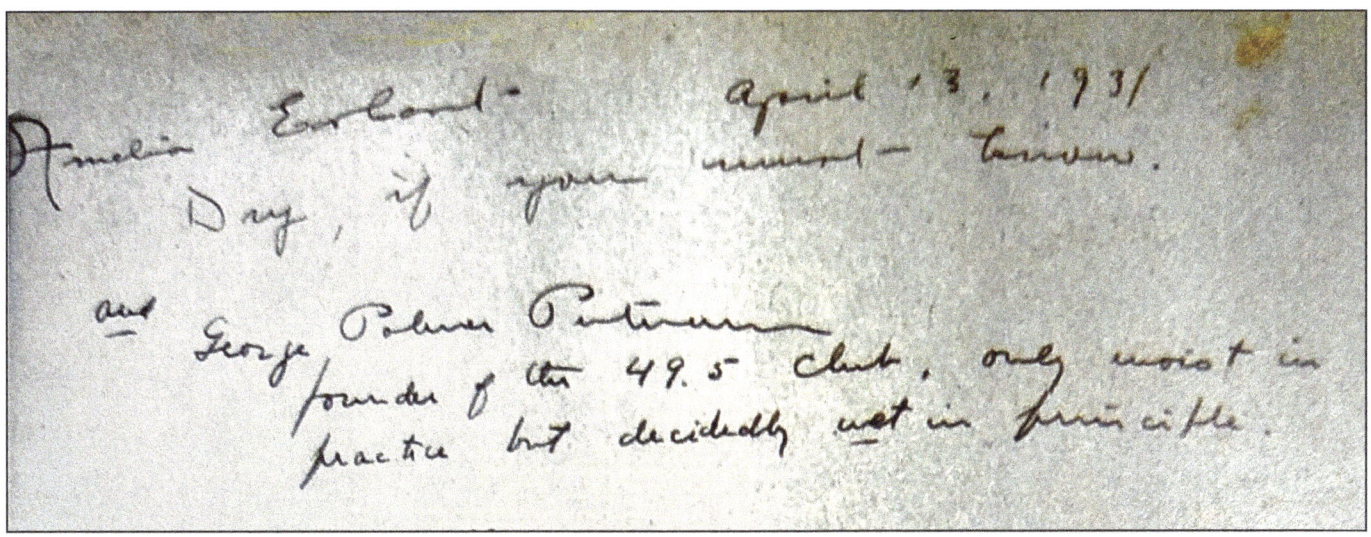

A copy of page eight of Chamberlain's guest book at Lloyd's Landing, Alloway Township. (Top) "Amelia Earhart April 13, 1931. Dry, if you must know." (Bottom) "and George Palmer Putnam founder of the 49.5 club, only moist in practice but decidedly wet in principle."

owner of a lumberyard in Bridgeton (*Bridgeton Evening News*, March 20, 2012). Frank kept a pony in a livery stable near the current county jail. As he saddled up his pony one day, a man and a woman, there for a leisure ride, invited Hankins to ride with them. The trio left the stable and rode to Broad St. and from there on to the city park entrance. They rode throughout the park and then back to the stable. When Hankins relayed this story to his father, his father was sure the mysterious pair was Amelia Earhart and George Chamberlain.

Admiral Jesse Gearing Johnson, another former Bridgeton resident, spoke to Earhart in 1935 when she was in Honolulu preparing to fly from there to Oakland, California. Admiral Johnson had grown up in Bridgeton, joined the Navy during WWI, and was stationed in Honolulu in 1935.

In a June 1963 article in *The American Philatelist* magazine Johnson wrote, "During some of my 23 years as a Naval Aviator I met Miss Earhart several times. At Honolulu, while she was preparing for her flight to the mainland, it was my pleasure to look over her charts. They were on a great circle course from Honolulu to San Francisco." For the uninitiated, a great circle course to sailors is a straight line on the rounded earth's surface.

Johnson went on to write, "Her chart was properly prepared and stood her in good stead when she was doing her own navigating from Honolulu to Oakland. I tried to get her to use a sextant to check her course during the night of her flight with a very simple check of the North Star. But she had [such] great confidence in her new radio compass, which was installed on her plane, that I had no success in this respect."

These visits to South Jersey came to an end in 1939 when Earhart and her navigator, Fred Noonan, disappeared somewhere over the Pacific. Chamberlain's

George Agnew Chamberlain, c. 1940.

(Left) Chamberlain went to China in 1937 to write a serial for *This Week* of the *New York Herald Tribune* and twenty-three other newspapers. The trip resulted in the story "All Blood is Red," about four Americans in China who for a day held history in their hands. Here Chamberlain is standing in his grape arbor at Lloyd's Landing wearing a traditional Chinese men's robe acquired on this trip. (Right) Amelia Earhart in 1932. Courtesy of the Library of Congress.

friendship with Putnam continued until Putnam's death in 1950 (Chamberlain would die in 1966), and one must wonder how the friendship between Earhart and Chamberlain would have evolved had she lived. Earhart brought renown to the South Jersey area and plenty of stories for local residents.

Earhart's presence can still be felt in South Jersey. On March 26, 2012, *The Daily Journal* posted a photo of two girl scouts posing with a life-like Earhart and her airplane. The photo was taken at Schalick High School in Centerton, Salem Co., New Jersey. Though Earhart is with us no longer, the mark she, George Putnam, and George Chamberlain left on South Jersey will remain for years to come.

About the Author

Jim Bergmann grew up in Glassboro, New Jersey, attended Glassboro High School, Glassboro State College (now Rowan University), Temple and Rutgers. He taught Special Education and Alternative Education classes and was the first principal of Cumberland County Vocational-Technical Center. He relocated to Maine, where he lived in Alna for sixteen years; he is the author of the book *The Narrow Gauge Railroad in Alna Maine* (2009). Since his retirement in 2000, he has been able to collect and write about various subjects. He resides in Upper Deerfield Township and is currently working on a biography of George Agnew Chamberlain.

Amelia and the Other George

References

Bergmann, Jim. *Bridgeton Evening News* (Bridgeton, New Jersey), March 23–26, 2012.

Loper, George. "George Agnew Chamberlain." *Bridgeton Evening News* (Bridgeton, New Jersey), March, 1991.

Mary S. Lovell, *Sound of Wings: the Life of Amelia Earhart* (St. Martins Press, 1989.

Guest Book, George Agnew Chamberlain, 1929. From a copy in possession of the author.

Salem Sunbeam (Salem, New Jersey), April 15, 1931.

Endnotes

1. Mary S. Lovell, *Sound of Wings: the Life of Amelia Earhart* (St. Martins Press, 1989), 331.
2. "Climbing Dome of Main Library is Ambition of Amelia Earhart, Former Columbia Student," *Columbia Daily Spectator*, May 2, 1933. Reference found via Wikipedia.

The Lantern on the Plow
a novel by George Agnew Chamberlain

The 100th-anniversary edition, published by the South Jersey Culture & History Center.

George Agnew Chamberlain was a successful American writer during the first half of the twentieth century. He wrote dozens of novels, with seven made into motion pictures. *The Lantern on the Plow*, set in Salem and Cumberland counties, follows the tribulations and ultimate triumph of the Sherborne family as they struggle to find their way in a changing landscape.

Available through Second Time Books in Mount Laurel, Amazon, or directly from SJCHC.

ISBN: 978-1947889194
338 pages. $19.95

stockton.edu/sjchc

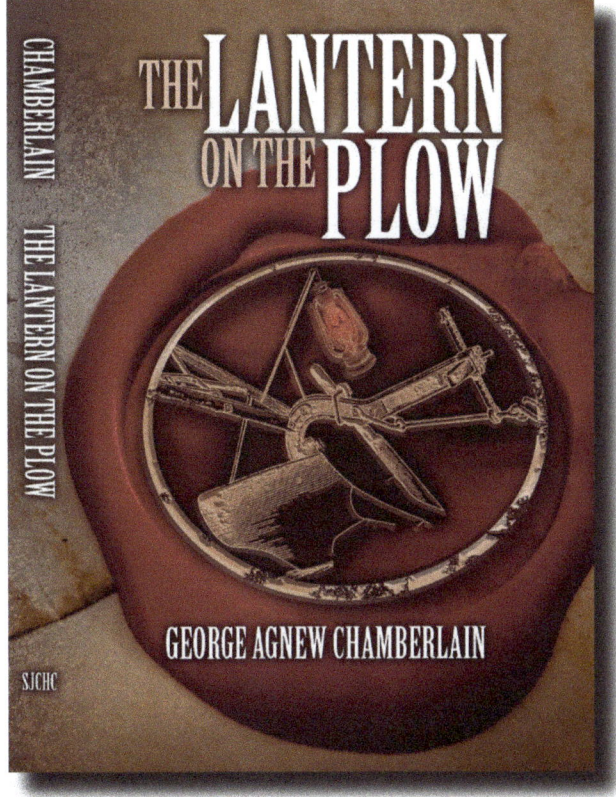

As seen in 2015 just before being dismantled to allow a housing development, this steel structure in Lumberton was the platform for a high-powered Nike Missile radar system. The actual antenna was mounted atop the structure, allowing it to scan out into the Atlantic, watching for incoming bombers; it would have been protected from weather by a fabric golf-ball-appearing radome. The adjacent building housed electronic equipment; other support buildings are in the distance. Photograph courtesy of Richard Lewis.

Last Line of Defense:
The Lumberton Nike Missile Base

Jim Alexander

Some 40 years after the Lumberton Nike Missile Base was taken out of service, photographer Richard Lewis shot a series of stunning photographs of its radar control area, which was by then being demolished to make way for housing. The vitality of the base's operations during its years of operation between 1955 and 1974, which included radar towers, nuclear-armed anti-aircraft missiles and underground storage magazines, was never preserved with such skilled photography.[1]

The jarring click of a round being chambered in an Army rifle prior to being fired in the spring of 1960 is a sound one Lumberton resident in Burlington County will never forget. It all happened when one of Doris Barton's high school girlfriends suggested they sneak a visit to the back part of the Reid family farm that had been sold to the government.[2] At that time, Lumberton was almost all farmland, and there wasn't much excitement. The arrival of the United States Army a few years earlier was a matter of curiosity.

Some 60 years later, married and now widowed, Doris Priest sat in her living room thinking back over the decades, occasionally crossing the room to check an old friend's number for follow-up, and a story emerged. As one of the small number of people who grew up in Lumberton before postwar suburban growth consumed much of the farmland, she has a keen sense of history,

This 1951 aerial photograph detail shows the agricultural nature of Lumberton. With Newbolds Corner Road (now Municipal Drive) running across the map, and Eayrestown Road on the right, the only concentration of houses is at the lower left, along Landing Street.[54]

having later been a township official herself and a leader of the Lumberton Historical Society.

She recalled that day when she and her friends jumped in a car and drove up an old dirt path off of what is now Municipal Drive, heading toward the back of the old apple farm by Bobby's Run. They had hardly turned the engine off, when they were startled by the loud click, followed by an Army sentry ordering them to leave immediately—no discussion about the old family farm, or that they didn't realize they were on the part that had been sold, just move on!

Most residents of Lumberton were never allowed access behind the barbed wire fencing that surrounded what had become the Lumberton Nike Missile Base, although a few recalled venturing to play in the fields surrounding the launch area.[3] Doris was to have more encounters on the property several decades later.

The Last Line of Defense

The story really begins in the final years of World War II. Fearing German air raids on America's homeland, our cities had been ringed with anti-aircraft batteries to fend off incoming bombers. The problem, as the military learned from its European experience, was that they would not have offered very much protection. Seized records showed that when the Germans fielded their feared "88" artillery guns against incoming waves of American B-17s, they had to fire over 2,800 shots to bring one down.[4] Fast-moving planes at varying altitudes were just too hard to hit, even using flak.

So, in 1945, the federal government commissioned New Jersey's Bell Laboratories to design a defensive missile for use against incoming enemy bombers.[5] As Bell continued their efforts, the Russians tested a nuclear bomb in 1949, and soon Soviet TU88 bombers were flying off the American coast.[6] School children began participating in Civil Defense drills, in which their teachers instructed the students to get under their desks or go into basements, where officials had stockpiled emergency supplies. People listening to the radio became acquainted with CONELRAD, a system through which the government could seize control of commercial radio transmissions to confuse incoming bombers.[7]

Fears grew that Navy and Air Force interceptors would not be able to halt incoming waves of bombers headed for American cities.

By the early fifties, Bell Labs, conducting most of the developmental work at its Whippany labs in New Jersey, had designed and tested a new radar-controlled system whose missiles could soar 30 miles toward incoming Soviet bombers, carrying warheads that could down the approaching planes. It came to be known as the Nike Ajax missile system.[8] Douglas Aircraft built the missile frames and Bell system's Western Electric assembled the control components. Missile construction took place in Burlington, North Carolina, at the Western Electric Tarheel Army Missile Plant.[9]

Acting with urgency, the Army Corps of Engineers oversaw the construction of over 250 missile bases that ringed major cities and military installations in the United States. Similar construction occurred overseas to protect European allies. The Corps' Philadelphia Office issued requests for contractor proposals to construct bases in the Philadelphia area in early 1954.[10]

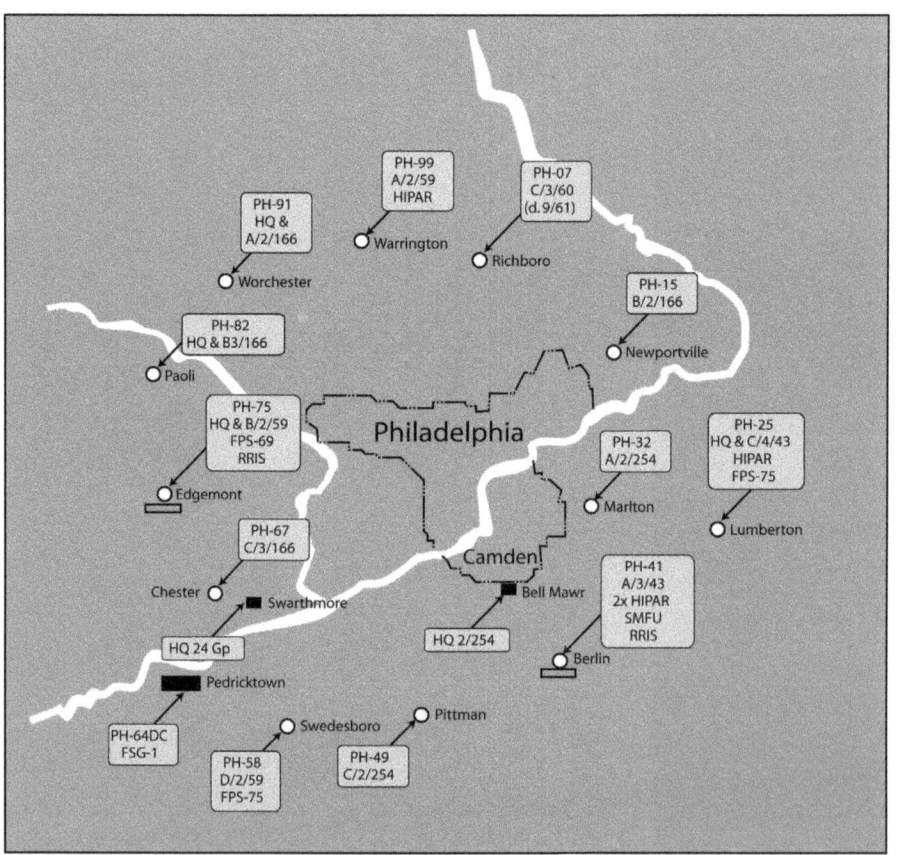

Nike bases protecting Philadelphia area.[55]

Last Line of Defense

Soon, the Philadelphia area was ringed by twelve such bases, with five located in Burlington and Camden counties. A massive concrete bunker in Salem County's Pedricktown provided the command-and-control facility for those twelve bases ringing Philadelphia.[11]

Each missile base consisted of two separate sections: the radar (officially called the IFC, or Integrated Fire Control) area, and the missile Launch Area,[12] and each included barracks, generator buildings, administrative and support facilities, and their own water and sewer systems.[13] Most prominent to those looking over the barbed wire fences that surrounded them were the multiple radars, typically covered by protective "golf-ball" domes, but the missile launch area had underground storage magazines that could not be seen from the road. Typical construction of the magazines can be seen in the sketch below.[14]

To build one, the contractor excavated a large pit, and then assembled a reinforced concrete structure below ground level. The main level served as missile storage. In the center, a deeper pit housed a massive elevator that would carry the missiles up to ground level. A thick steel double door at ground level opened to allow the missiles to rise or descend.

As constructed, a separation existed between the radar and the launch areas relative to the radar tracking the launched missiles as well as incoming aircraft. The missiles rocketed into the sky so fast that some distance was needed to make sure the radar did not lose contact. The two sections at Lumberton, roughly sixteen acres each, were about 4000 feet apart, connected by the gravel-covered portion of Newbolds Corner Road.[15] The Army reportedly paid $65,100 to acquire the land.[16]

Most Nike bases followed a similar plan,[17] with some adjustments for local terrain or nearby development. While storing the missiles underground did afford some protection from attack, the primary reason stemmed from those bases sited in locations adjacent to real estate development, where costs were high, and safety regulations would have required larger, more expensive, protective buffer lands if the missiles had been stored above ground.[18] The missiles had to be raised to a firing position; they were not fired from underground.

LIFE ON THE BASE

At Lumberton, eight officers and 100 enlisted soldiers occupied the site in March 1955,[19] while construction remained ongoing. Initially, they lived in tents while waiting for proper facilities to be assembled. Early aerial photographs disclose that construction required several phases. The base constituted one of the few facilities known as a double base, meaning that it had six underground missile storage/launch areas, rather than the usual three, and double the radar capability to control them. A captain commanded the base, with lieutenants in charge of each part. In its early years, the majority of the soldiers were as young as eighteen, having been intensively trained and constantly tested, with surprise and demanding inspections.

Local residents knew of the base, but the locked gates prevented access without specific authorization.

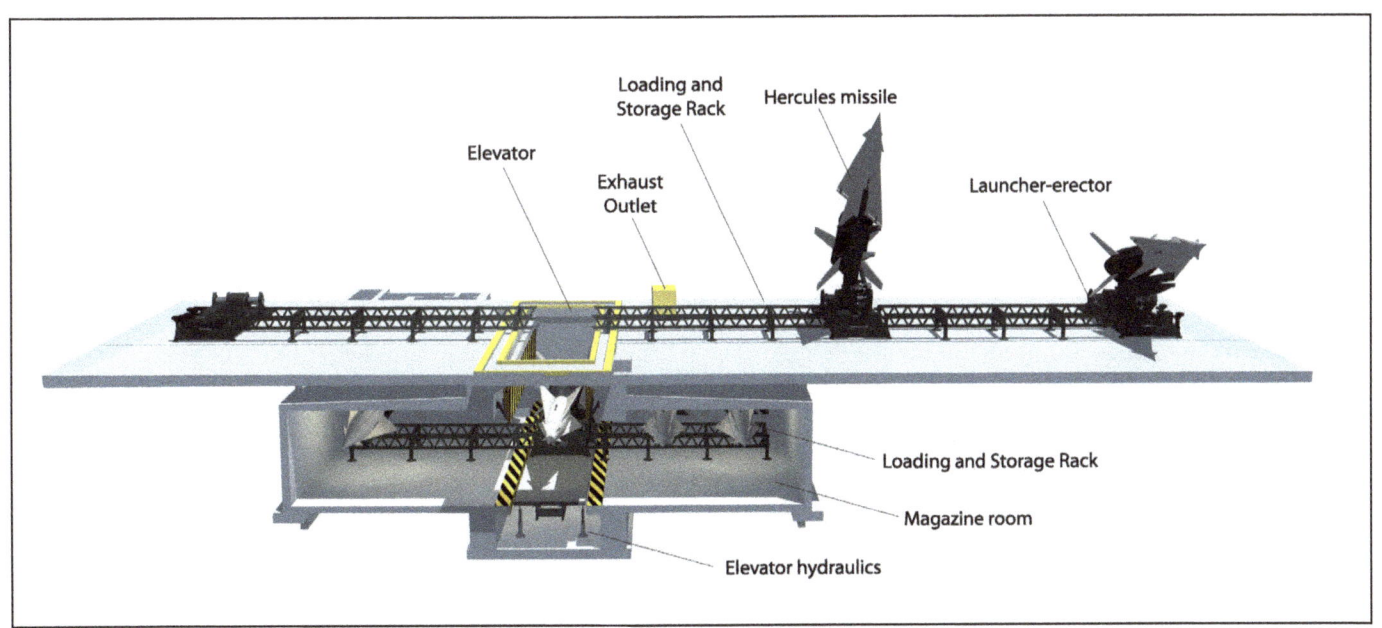

As a result, while the local people could see through the fences, and even see the missiles when raised for drills, much of what was remembered was the sounds of trucks, of lights and sirens, but little understanding of the complex work inside.[20] On occasion, helicopters would land for transporting supplies or bringing the brass for surprise inspections.[21]

Exceptions to the tight security occurred on occasion. In May 1960, a photograph of Miss Burlington County appeared in the local papers, standing in front of raised missiles at Lumberton.[22] This was in preparation for one of several tightly controlled "open houses" that took place in conjunction with Armed Forces Day programs. She was there in preparation to crown Miss 43rd Artillery. The Nike missile forces were part of that Army artillery unit.

The following year, the base briefly opened to the public again for missile raising demonstrations, "cartoons for children, sentry dog demonstrations, helicopter displays," and other presentations. Those present for the event included that year's Miss Burlington County, a Philadelphia TV personality, and a retired US Secretary of Labor.[23]

The military deemed good public relations especially helpful in the missile system's early years around the country, where in some areas, especially urban, opposition arose. A second reason stemmed from the Air Force's development of its BOMARC Missile system (with a prototype base installation at McGuire Air Force Base), and that service branch pressed Congress to shift funding from the Nike program to its own.[24]

At Lumberton, there was little to occupy the soldiers' off-time, despite the presence of a chapel, a PX, and exercise and recreation facilities. So, it was not unheard of for a few soldiers to head for the bright lights of nearby Mr. Holly on their time off, where, on occasion, some excess libation led to arrests.[25] With one exception that involved a private becoming involved with a local waitress and an ensuing murder/suicide attempt,[26] very little real friction developed with the locals.

"We really didn't know that much about what went on inside the base," Doris noted. The two worlds lived side by side, but apart. Internal base records did not survive,[27] yet some comments collected years later from soldiers stationed at Lumberton[28] give some clues:

> "I didn't appreciate being located in the middle of a cabbage field," one obvious city boy recalled. Indeed, the base was surrounded by farmland.

> "A lot of local girls would drive along the roads looking for the guys." Whether this was a wishful recollection cannot be determined, but at least one soldier did marry a local girl.

Typical Hercules Missiles as seen at Ft. Hancock base at Sandy Hook. The missile at right is in upright firing position on its launcher, while the other missile is only partly raised. Each missile was 41 feet long with its booster, 31.5-inches in diameter, 6-foot wingspan, and weighed of over 10,000 pounds.[56]

Last Line of Defense

"I used to sign out a shotgun and shoot squirrels along the gully behind the barracks in the main IFC area." This would have been by Bobby's Run, a small tributary to the Rancocas Creek, where Doris had gotten the scare of her life.

"The drilling was very intense. There were constant alerts."

"A kind Sergeant's wife who provided Thanksgiving dinner at his home." Doris had recalled such kindnesses from other locals.

How it worked

While the base initially housed six missile storage magazines underground, two years into its operation the Nike Hercules system replaced the Nike Ajax missiles.[29] The new missiles had several advantages over the Ajax: these 5-ton missiles could fly for 96 miles, in this case allowing intercepts out over the ocean; they could climb to 100,000 feet, with a speed of 3.65 times that of sound. Most significantly, in addition to conventional explosives, they could carry nuclear warheads with optional explosive yields of either 2, 20, or 40 kilotons.[30]

The added nuclear capability enhanced the ability to destroy a fleet of bombers rather than just one plane, and in so doing, it immobilized any atomic bombs within the planes. By way of comparison, the atomic bomb dropped on Hiroshima was 15 kilotons. The Army was convinced that unleashing such devastation above the homeland was a reasonable tradeoff to prevent the bombers from dropping even higher payloads directly on the cities; it was also argued that explosions high in the air would have less effect on the ground. The missiles would only be fired if naval and air force efforts had failed to stop the incoming bombers. Thus, the system was known as the last line of defense. Such were the dilemmas of the Cold War. Subsequent defensive missile systems, being more precise, did not carry nuclear warheads.

The military command structure that operated the Nike missile program evolved from the Army's Artillery organization and changed over the years. Initially, the program was part of the Army Anti-Aircraft Command (ARAACOM), which was formed in 1950. By 1957, it was the Army Air Defense Command (ARADCOM), whose patch is shown below at left.[31] Several years later, to allow the regular Army to focus on other emerging challenges, operating responsibility shifted to various state National Guard units.

As is the case with many other military units, an unofficial mascot known as the Oozlefinch, seen at right below, developed from earlier versions for the Nike soldiers.[32]

The Lumberton base was one of the first in the country to be converted from Ajax to Hercules missiles. Base commander Captain Fletcher E. Newland had been involved in test firings at another base that validated the system's effectiveness, and his soldiers were among the first trained to operate the system, which also involved a more complex and capable radar system.[33] Thus, newspaper photographs of the rollout at Lumberton, with troops lined up for inspection, appeared in October 1958. The increased capability of the Hercules led to the abandonment of two older Ajax magazines, leaving four in operation. By 1963, with the greater capability of the Nikes, the Army closed the bases at Pitman and Marlton.

While the public never learned the specifics, a review of general documentation suggests that each of the four underground magazines then held six Hercules missiles, for a likely total of 24, of which at least 20 may have been armed with nuclear warheads of varying kiloton yields, and perhaps four with conventional warheads.

Most local residents were unaware that the Hercules missiles would be lobbed from their launchers by a solid-fuel booster rocket consisting of four of the earlier-designed Ajax boosters assembled together, and that after a few seconds of flight, the expended booster would fall off. Contrary to some belief, the missiles were not "shot at the plane," but controllers guided them from the ground control area, which used one radar to track and guide the missile and another to follow the incoming planes. When the trajectories converged, the blast command was sent from the ground.

Missiles would be fired one at a time, following a choreographed, intensely rehearsed, series of manual ground actions.[34] Depending on local circumstance, one missile every one or two minutes might be launched, mainly limited by the radar system's tracking ability.[35]

Specific designs for each base included calculations for where the boosters might fall, with the plan that they would land in unpopulated areas. In the case of Lumberton, the missiles, when lifted to the surface, pointed generally eastward, the direction from which the military expected the bombers to come, but when raised almost vertical for firing, they never stood straight up, lest the boosters fall back to the launch area. Most likely, the anticipated drop zone for the boosters lay just east of Route 206, an area even more thinly populated than Lumberton.[36]

With the advent of the Hercules and their nuclear capabilities, the Army stepped up security[37] in three particular ways:

- A second fence was installed around the launch area, with an inner, guarded gate, part of which is still visible in the photograph to the left.
- This area, known as the exclusion zone, featured detection equipment, and armed guards patrolled it by day. At night, specially trained dogs patrolled the zone.
- The military introduced enhanced procedures to prevent any single soldier from either tampering with equipment or attempting to fire the missiles. A two-man system required that every action at the launch area involve two soldiers watching each other, with access to nuclear enablement codes by means of locked safes with armed officers holding two keys.

In 1963, as part of a national program to relieve the regular Army for other duties, the New Jersey National Guard gained control and assumed responsibility for the base. While details are scarce, the general pattern that ensued involved a smaller core of troops housed on the base, with guardsmen rotating in periodically. Off-duty troops typically remained on-call and had to return to the base within a set time period. The Guard carefully coordinated heightened readiness levels among the area bases, so that full protection remained always available, with greater capability available to come online as needed.[38]

Safety was always a concern on these bases, as the troops faced constant danger. In the Ajax years, fuel for the main engine on the missiles consisted of a combination of very dangerous special jet fuel and toxic igniting agents. Troops fueling the missiles did so in restricted

Original inner gate at Lumberton Launch area, November 5, 2021. Photograph by author.

The Ajax versions of the Nike missiles used volatile liquid propellants that were hazardous to the troops. Refueling is occurring in this scene at another New Jersey base; the troops had to wear rubber garb, and earthen mounds surrounded the area to deflect explosions, as was the case at Lumberton. The Hercules missiles that replaced them used solid fuel for both booster and cruise propulsion, making them safer to handle as well as more powerful.[57]

areas protected by earthen berms and wearing protective suits. In July 1960, Sergeant First Class William Hunter was hospitalized at Fort Dix after he was affected by "red nitric acid fumes" that spilled out during a refueling operation. The same month, another soldier, 19-year-old Specialist 4 Thomas Kluck, was killed when his arm got caught as the elevator lifted a missile from a magazine up to the surface.[39]

Another soldier was accidentally shot.[40] To be sure, other hazards existed that required repeated training: high powered radar beams, electric wiring, shifting of heavy equipment, and the presence of numerous chemicals used in cleaning and maintaining the equipment. A common practice of the day, even in the civilian sector, would today be regarded as a hazmat situation, when the personnel dumped volatile or dangerous fluids down sump drains, and allowed them to eventually seep into the soil.[41]

Post-closure soil investigations failed to reveal any nuclear contamination at the base.[42]

Base Closing

As a result of President Nixon and Soviet Premier Leonid Brezhnev signing the 1972 SALT 1 treaty, the military determined it would close the Nike bases. As a practical matter, the ability of Soviet missiles to be launched offshore exceeded the ability of the Nikes to cope. By 1974, the bases closed, and the 150 men then stationed at Lumberton underwent reassignment.[43]

Launch area barracks and administrative buildings 1974, just before base closing.[58]

Lumberton Township submitted a bid to acquire the property. Thus, the township acquired the launch area for $60,000, and received the radar property at no additional cost as it was planned to be used for educational purposes.[44]

In vacating the property, the army removed all missiles, radar, and military equipment, leaving the buildings and empty radar towers intact. Power to the buildings was left connected, and the elevators in the empty underground magazines remained operational.[45]

The Radar Site

The Army sold off a small part of the radar area, located at the intersection of Eayrestown Road and Municipal Drive, when advanced radar techniques no longer required the two towers located on it.[46] Today, those platforms remain there, and a landscape company occupies the property.

Starting in 1977, a nonprofit school for educationally challenged children occupied the main portion of the radar area, north of Newbolds Corner Road, for several decades. It was affiliated initially with the Learning Disabilities Society of New Jersey. Later, Ranch Hope, a Christian organization for troubled youth based in Alloway, New Jersey, operated the facility as the Ranch Hope Midway School, utilizing four of the old buildings. For several years in the early 1990s, its principal had formerly served as a radar operator on the same property in 1956 and 1957.[47]

After several decades of operation, the school closed. With the property abandoned and dilapidated, several proposals to use it for public institutions met with strong local opposition. In 2015, local photographer Richard Lewis took a number of striking photographs of the area during demolition of the buildings and radar platforms. Interior photographs of the former military buildings showed an advanced state of disrepair.[48]

By 2017, a housing development had replaced the facility.

The Launch Area

In 1975, the Township took the initial step to vacate its overcrowded Town Hall on Main Street and

Room at closed Midway School in the former radar section building.[59] Photograph courtesy of Richard Lewis.

Last Line of Defense

Demolition of radar site 2015. Photograph courtesy of Richard Lewis.

move the municipal offices and police department to the Launch site's former barracks and administrative building fronting Newbolds Corner Road. The Public Works Department occupied the expansive rear area where the missile magazines and related buildings stood, providing the department with expanded room.

Of the underground missile magazine storage areas, the township used one to store excess municipal items; a second held school system storage; and the police department employed the third for housing found and confiscated items. The ground area around the magazines, primarily used to house public works trucks and equipment, also provided ample space to store miscellaneous things associated with normal public works property maintenance.[49]

By 2000, Lumberton's population had swelled with suburban growth, and the old base buildings proved inadequate and difficult to maintain. Lumberton constructed a new town hall across Newbolds Corner Road, renaming the roadway Municipal Drive. Township officials relocated the municipal offices and the police department to that location. The former municipal offices underwent demolition for construction of a modern Fire and Emergency services building in 2018.[50]

Doris witnessed all that, but years later, as Lumberton Township leaders endeavored to make good use of the site, she had two encounters with the old Launch area. In the fall of 1985, as Hurricane Gloria worked its way up the east coast, she recalls being hustled underground into one of the missile magazines as local officials sought to protect local lives against the ravages of the massive hurricane. "It was damp and scary down there."[51]

Five years later, now serving as the town's recycling director, she devised the idea of using the area as a center for surrounding towns to bring their plastics for processing. One local account opined that the trucks might dump their loose plastic collections down into one of the abandoned magazines, where it would be baled, and then carried up on the missile elevator to be hauled off for processing.[52]

While such a concept would have been an innovative step, local considerations involving other jurisdictions prevented it from happening, although even today recycling bins stand nearby for resident use.

Walking through the expansive ground area, large concrete slabs remain with blast deflectors and metal bases for the missile moving rails, as do sturdy air handlers, fire hose stands, and heavy steel doors leading underground to the magazines. (See pages 25–26.)

On a visit in 2021, going down the stairs into one missile bay, you entered a different world. The

Radar support structures remained in place until final demolition for housing. Some later passers-by mistakenly thought they were missile launchers. Photograph courtesy of Richard Lewis.

Magazine Alpha, the first of the underground missile magazines, in which defense weapons of unimaginable power had once been tended by young Americans during the Cold War. Most evident on the site are the large doors that would have dropped aside to allow the elevators to carry the missiles up for launching. Photograph by author, October 5, 2021.

Last Line of Defense

(Top four images) Montage of photographs of the launch area. (Bottom) The Launch elevator from down below.

(Left) Door and elevator control buttons. (Right) Hydraulic system for elevator. All photographs by the author.

magazine's ceiling is at least six feet below ground level, with a good ten feet of headroom, and horizontally roughly 50 x 60 feet.[53] Except for the sunlight extending down the stairwell and a thin crack in the overhead doors where the weatherstripping has aged, it is completely dark, and completely silent. Power no longer flows to the lights. Yet, as seen with the aid of flashlights, what has endured is impressive. The missiles are gone, but the signs and painted walls have held up over the decades. The massive elevator rests in its pit, and the large hydraulic system that propelled it stands nearby, as do the electrical control boxes. The buttons to open and close the large door and operate the elevator are in good condition. A few odd items long ago stored and forgotten are strewn about, but the area is mainly clear.

The massive, reinforced concrete ceiling remains intact. Emergency access ladders, reaching up to hardened steel doors, remain. A side hall leading to a blast-proof door, behind which the soldiers would stay during the missile blasts, contains some standing water, so, we did not venture inside.

Back on the surface, several buildings remain, including one where heavy generators once operated, and another where an overhead hoist allowed missile parts to be assembled. Elsewhere, newer public works buildings provide room to store and maintain equipment ranging from heavy snowplows to lawn mowers.

Thus, the service at the former Lumberton Nike Missile base continues in a new way. The vastness of the open launch area, formerly dedicated to the underground magazines, suggests some possible future use. It is still partially bounded by open fields, like it was in those simpler times when young children could play nearby, while not realizing the threats of a hostile world.

The service of those young soldiers who protected Lumberton and the Philadelphia area with tools of

Last Line of Defense

Doris Priest returns to the base, September 22, 2023. Photograph by the author.

incredible destruction in their care, however, cannot be forgotten. During the two decades of the Nike Missile program, not one was ever fired in anger, but they stood ready.

Now, nearly two years after Doris's initial recollections, we visited the Launch Area, and she stood above Magazine Alpha. There was so much that she had not been able to see years ago because of the fences and guards.

But memories flooded back: seeing the raised missiles in the distance behind the fences, the trucks on the road carrying soldiers and supplies, the night down below where residents sheltered from the storm, the kind local people who offered holiday meals to the soldiers far from home. And in the background, blue recycling bins now used by Lumberton residents.

Most telling, with a brief shudder, she relived that moment decades earlier, when her youthful innocence had been jarred by the click of a round being chambered in an Army rifle.

About the Author

Jim Alexander holds degrees from Middlebury College and the University of Pennsylvania. While initially focusing on state and local government management, he has always enjoyed writing on anything he encountered. Much of his work has focused on history, including the Tocks Island Dam project. He has a special interest in railroad history, including New Jersey's pioneering inventor John Stevens, and more recently the Mt. Holly, Lumberton and Medford Railroad.

Former Launch Area – now Public Works Yard and Fire Department.[60]

KEY:
PW Gate	Gate to current Public Works Yard / Launch area
Assy	Building in which missiles were assembled
Gen	Building (now expanded) that housed generators
G	Former Guardhouse, entry to Exclusion Zone
A, B, C, D	Former Hercules Missile Magazines
X	Abandoned Ajax Missile Magazines
F	Location of Ajax Fueling area, berm removed
DK	Former location of dog kennel

New Firehouse: Former location of barracks and administrative buildings, water well, sewer facilities. (Later occupied by Police and Town offices, currently Fire and EMS headquarters).

Endnotes

1. Copyrighted photo by Richard Lewis, used with permission. His additional photos may be viewed on his website at https://richardlewisphotography.com/galleries/cold-war-nike-missile-sites/nike-missile-battery-ph2325/.
2. Series of discussions and full interview with Doris Priest (née Barton) between October 21, 2021, and February 25, 2022, and on September 22, 2023.
3. Discussions with the late Joan Benedict, who grew up while residing near the base. October 21, 2021, and December 11, 2021. Group discussion at meeting of Lumberton Historical Society with local residents to discuss memories of the base, October 21, 2021; participants included Doris Priest (former township official), Elaine Jardine (whose father was local Civil Defense Director), John Jardine (Association President), Ruth Lewis (retired Lumberton Tax Collector and LHS historian) and others. Review of available materials at Lumberton Historical Society, October 16, 2021.
4. Edward Westerman, *Flak: German Anti-Aircraft Defenses, 1914–1945* (Lawrence, KS: University Press of Kansas, 2001). Cited at en.wikipedia.org/wiki/Surface-to-air_missile.
5. Mark. L. Morgan and Mark A. Berhow, *Rings of Supersonic Steel*, third edition (Bodega Bay, CA: Hole in the Head Press. 2010). Also see John C. Lonnquest and David F. Winkler, *To Defend and Deter, The Legacy of the United States Cold War Missile Program* (Bodega Bay, CA: Hole in the Head Press, 2014), originally published by the U. S. Army Construction Engineering Research Laboratories, Champaign, IL.
6. http://www.themilitarystandard.com/missile/nike/overview.php. Site has extensive information on various aspects of Nike systems.
7. "Conelrad Exercise Is on the Air Here," *New York Times*, November 17, 1954, 64. Retrieved from https://timesmachine.nytimes.com/timesmachine/1954/11/17/issue.html.
8. Morgan and Berhow, *Rings of Supersonic Steel*, 23 and following.

9. *Historic Properties Report, Tarheel Army Missile Plant, North Carolina*, prepared by Building Technology Incorporated, Silver Spring, Maryland for the Historic American Building Survey/Historic American Engineering Record, National Park Service, U.S. Department of the Interior. July 1984. Accessed at https://en.wikipedia.org/wiki/Western_Electric_Company-Tarheel_Army_Missile_Plant. Also see John C. Lonnquest and David F. Winkler, op. cit., 91.
10. Gene Beyer, "Guided Missile Plans to Cover Area Defenses," *Chester Times* (Chester, PA), March 27 1954, 1.
11. Tom Tigar, phone interview December 1, 2021. Stationed at Pedriktown in late 1950s, his responsibility entailed contacting the Philadelphia area bases daily to ascertain status. He knew the Lumberton base commander at the time, Captain Fletcher Everett Newland.
12. http://ed-thelen.org/ifc.html and http://ed-thelen.org/launcher_area.html. The website ed-thelen.org contains a massive volume of official and anecdotal information on Nike bases and provides a broad understanding of how most sites worked.
13. B. N. McMaster, et al., *Historic Overview of the Nike Missile System* (Aberdeen Proving Ground: U. S. Army Toxic and Hazardous Materials Agency Assessments Division, December 1984). Accessed at https://scvhistory.com/scvhistory/nike_overview.pdf.
14. Morgan and Berhow, *Rings of Supersonic Steel*, 15. Used by permission of publisher and Ormsby and Thickstun Interpretive Design.
15. Interview with Stephen J. Moorer, former Lumberton Township Public Works Director. November 12, 2021.
16. Paul Loane, "S. Jersey 'Defenses' Are Down," *Courier-Post*, February 17, 1974, 1, 5.
17. http://www.themilitarystandard.com/missile/nike/sitedesc.php.
18. http://ed-thelen.org/missiles.html#wh-h-nuc.
19. "Press Tours Nike Site at Lumberton," *Courier-Post*, May 15, 1956, 4.
20. See note 3.
21. Email from Donald E. Bender to author, February 14, 2022. More details on the Lumberton base may be found in his "Lumberton's Cold War Legacy: Nike Missile Battery PH-23-25," as printed in the Fall 1999 *Burlington County Historical Society Newsletter*. Bender has visited the Lumberton site several times, provided helpful insight to the author, and has written about the missile system generally. Portions of his former website are reproduced on ed-thelen.com, in particular see http://ed-thelen.org/Bender/BenderIntro150.pdf. Current website is https://coldwarpreservation.com/.
22. "Beauty and the 'Beasts,'" *Courier-Post*, May 10, 1960, 5. An earlier open house is documented at "Press Tours Nike Base at Lumberton," *Courier-Post*, May 15, 1956, 4.
23. "Open House Listed for Missile Site," *Courier-Post*, May 19, 1961, 9.
24. Lonnquest and Winkler, *To Defend and Deter*, 58 and following.
25. See "Mt. Holly Court Fines Nike Base GI's," *Courier-Post*, May 17, 1961, 32; and "Indictments Handed Up in Burl'gton Co.," *Courier-Post*, November 2, 1961, 5.
26. "GI Slashed Waitress in Mt. Holly," *Courier-Post*, May 27, 1959, 1.
27. Per Steven J. Moorer, construction plans had been on hand when the township took over the base but were later discarded by somebody to make room for other items.
28. Ed-thelen: http://ed-thelen.org/ppl-n.html.
29. "Lumberton Unit Gets Hercules Missiles," *Courier-Post*, August 13, 1958, 6.
30. http://www.themilitarystandard.com/missile/nike/overview.php.
31. Courtesy of *Together We Served* at https://www.togetherweserved.com/.
32. Courtesy of the Air Defense Artillery Association. Further information about the mascot is available on the Nike Historical Society's website at https://nikemissile.org/Theoozlefinch.shtml.
33. "Nike-Hercules Ready," *Courier-News* (Bridgewater, NJ). October 10, 1958, 23.
34. Individual missiles were manually pushed along on rails to a designated launching position. Telephone interview with Richard Buell, a former National Guardsman assigned to the base part time, February 2, 2022. Order of launch depended on which missiles were above ground, and which had which traditional or nuclear explosives.
35. http://www.themilitarystandard.com/missile/nike/missilefire.php.
36. Drop zones were never made public, but general documentation indicates they were in the direction of initial firing, calculated according to anticipated weather and standard factors, and typically expected to fall within a circle whose closest edge was one mile from launch. See http://ed-thelen.org/overvu.html and http://ed-thelen.org/missiles.html.
37. "Nike Security," https://nikemissile.org/Security/security_was_extremely_tight_on.shtml and "Sentry Dogs," https://nikemissile.org/sentry_dogs.shtml.
38. "Last Line of Defense, Nike Missile Sites in Illinois," https://www.allworldwars.com/Last-Line-of-Defense-Nike-Missile-Sites-in-Illinois.html, provides examples of National Guard site takeover. The Guard assumed control of the Lumberton base in October 1963 per Morgan and Berhow, *Rings of Supersonic Steel*, 166. Email, December 14, 2021, with NJ National Guard Museum did not disclose any available staffing records.
39. "Oil City Soldier Crushed to Death on Nike Elevator," *Kittanning Simpson Leader Times*, July 26, 1960, 2.
40. "GI Shot in Chest," *Courier-Post*, March 30, 1957, 1.
41. B. N. McMaster et al., *Historic Overview of the Nike Missile System*, in extended reviews of many sites, describes various methods of mostly surface disposal.

42 B. N. McMaster et al., *Historic Overview of the Nike Missile System*, Section 7.7. On sites, no maintenance of nuclear warheads (which were sealed and shielded) was performed. Testing materials were required to be returned in lead containers for disposal. Also see United States Court of Appeals for Veterans Claims, No. 18-6827, Thomas C. Graham, Appellant, v. Robert L. Wilkie, Secretary of Veterans affairs, Appellee at https://efiling.uscourts.cavc.gov/cmecf/servlet/TransportRoom?servlet=ShowDoc/01206800690#:~:text=In%20the%20early%201960s%2C%20the,greater%20than%205%20millisievert%20per. That case focused on unique exposure to ionizing radiation, some related to work on radar equipment, and to Graham's claim of having carried certain materials in his pocket, none of which appears to address generalized exposure. Other site reviews, such as at the Kingston, WA, Nike Site 92 by health authorities in 2005 did not disclose residual threats. https://www.atsdr.cdc.gov/hac/pha/kingstonnikesite021705-wa/kingstonnikesite021705-wa.pdf.

43 Loane, "S. Jersey 'Defenses' Are Down."

44 James Lawson, "Lumberton to pay $60,000 for Nike base," *Courier-Post*, December 17, 1975, 28.

45 Steven Moorer interview.

46 "Surplus 'Gift' from Uncle Sam," *Courier-Post*, October 2, 1962, 1; and "Government Sale" notice, *Courier-Post*, May 27, 1963, 40.

47 *New Jersey Ass'n for Children with Learning Disabilities v. Burlington County Ass'n for Children with Learning Disabilities*, Superior Court of New Jersey, Chancery Division. Decided October 25, 1978, 163 N.J. Super. 199. And Lacy McCrary, "Missile sites now playing fields," *The Philadelphia Inquirer*, August 18, 1991, Section B, 1, 4.

48 Richard Lewis Photography, series of photographs taken in 2015 as the radar section was being demolished, photographs are marked with his name and used with permission. See https://richardlewisphotography.com/galleries/cold-war-nike-missile-sites/nike-missile-battery-ph2325/.

49 Discussions with Steven Moorer (previous Public Works Director and Tom Shover (Public Works General Foreman) at launch area, November 18, 2021.

50 George Woolston, "Lumberton Fire Co. to auction off old Main Street firehouse," *Burlington County Times*, January 13, 2020.

51 Doris Priest interview.

52 Marego Athans, "Led by Lumberton, five towns to begin recycling of plastic," *The Philadelphia Inquirer*, November 25, 1990, 14-BR; also see Frank Brown, "Launching the war on plastics; plan would use old missile silos," *The Philadelphia Inquirer*, August 26, 1990, 3-BR.

53 Magazine dimensions vary depending on whether original construction for Ajax, or later modifications for Hercules. Visit conditions did not permit exact measurement. See Morgan and Berhow, *Rings of Supersonic Steel*, 26, for typical dimensions.

54 Historic Aerials by Netronline at historicaerials.com/. Used with permission.

55 Mark. L. Morgan and Mark A. Berhow, *Rings of Supersonic Steel*, 165. Used with permission. A general description of bases in New Jersey, with an emphasis on the northern part of the state and including numerous photographs, may be found at Mary T. Rasa, *U. S. Army Nike: In Defense of the Nation*, accessed at https://www.academia.edu/28537915/New_Jerseys_Nike_Missiles.

56 https://www.nps.gov/gate/planyourvisit/sandyhookniketours.htm. Public domain photo authorized by National Park Service.

57 Photo courtesy of Joseph Bilby, Historian, Collections Management, New Jersey National Guard Museum.

58 Photograph from uncited newspaper, at https://www.flickr.com/photos/42444189@N04/albums/72157624526917061, as part of extensive photographic collection of the base taken by "John" (JSF0864) in August 2010, showing deteriorated condition of many buildings and facilities. Used with permission.

59 Used with permission of photographer Richard Lewis. See Note 48 for additional information.

60 Google Earth, December 12, 2021, showing launch area, with notations by author. Used pursuant to Google Earth Guidelines at https://about.google/brand-resource-center/products-and-services/geo-guidelines/.

Mullica Valley Ports and Landings:
Past and Planned

Kenneth W. Able and Horace A. Somes Jr.

In the past, the Mullica Valley ports and landings were central to coastal commerce. Their growth resulted from their support of various industries,[1] developed during colonial times in the province of West New Jersey and during the Revolutionary War period when used for trade and by privateers.[2] The genesis for these ports began more than 25,000 years ago when this drowned river valley was carved out of southern New Jersey sands and subsequently modified by the effects of glaciers.[3] In the process, and as sea level rose, the broad Great Bay and the Mullica River formed, the deepest of the rivers in New Jersey. Upriver, opposite

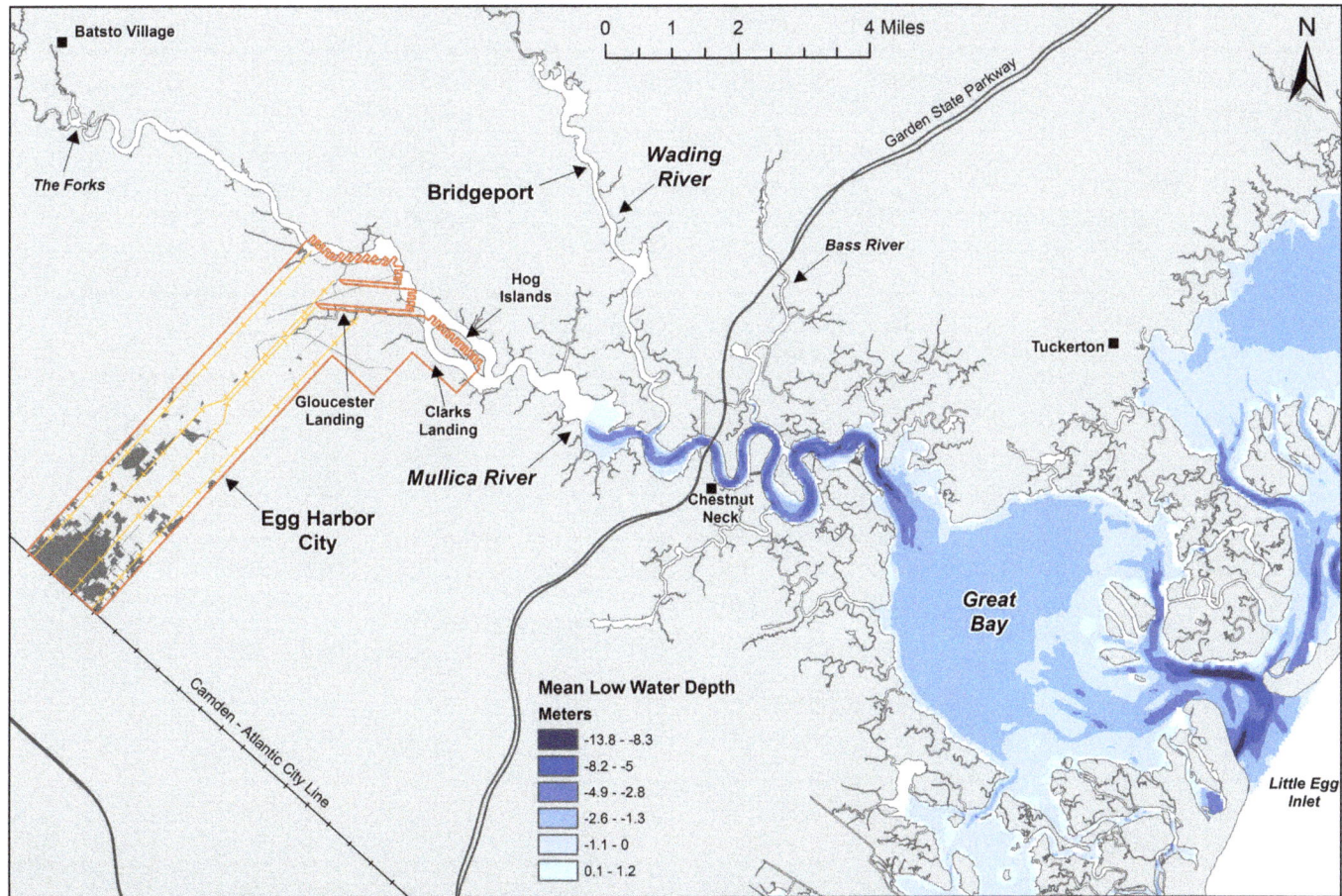

Figure 1. Historical ports and landings both past and planned, in the waters of Mullica Valley, from Little Egg Inlet to Batsto Village. Water depth shown in shades of blue where available. Details of Egg Harbor City shows perimeter in red, railroads in yellow.

Clarks Landing, the prehistoric southern extension of today's Great Swamp was submerged to form Log Bay, with adjacent tidal marshes that include the twin Hog Islands. As sea level continues to rise, "ghost forests" are forming throughout the Valley as the Atlantic white-cedar swamps succumb to inundation and salty waters.[4]

As a result, the Mullica Valley has several characteristics that make it ideal for shipping and the location of ports (Figure 1). First, the Atlantic Ocean inlets to Great Bay and the Mullica River are natural, and as a result, variable, filled with sandbars and shallows.[5] That made it difficult for the British to easily access the upstream ports and ironworks during the Revolutionary War without the knowledge possessed by pilots and local residents. Further, coastal inlet dynamics have resulted in changing openings to the ocean from Old Inlet (Beach Haven Inlet) to New Inlet (Little Egg Inlet) over the time period under study.[6]

Second, this deep drowned river valley provided access to the interior of the Pinelands and closer access, by land, to the Delaware River and the important economic center of Philadelphia. Both of these characteristics assisted the work of area smugglers and privateers,[7] as well as the industrial exploitation of the natural resources within the Pine Barrens that continued into the nineteenth century. This was evident in the importance of The Forks,[8] nearby Pleasant Mills,[9] and other riverbanks along the Mullica River including downriver Mordecai or Crowleys Landing,[10] the infamous privateers' den at Chestnut Neck, Clarks Landing, Upper (today's Green) Bank, Lower Bank, and the major tributaries of the Wading and Bass Rivers. This importance was historically magnified by the British attack on Chestnut Neck in 1778 to eliminate "the nest of rebel pirates,"[11] and the unsuccessful attempt to attack and destroy the Batsto Iron Furnace, a critical source of essential munitions for the Continental Army.

Third, the deep waters of the Mullica and Wading Rivers made the development of these ports easier once shipping made it through the inlet. Imports and exports could then go through Little Egg Harbor to the adjacent Tuckerton port—from which people and goods would travel overland via lengthy stage roads across the Pine Barrens; or could continue to be shipped much farther by water through Great Bay and up the Mullica River—then termed the Little Egg Harbor River.

Another characteristic of the Mullica Valley that was consistent with the commerce in the system was its numerous shipyards,[12] including those that harvested the wood needed from the Valley's extensive forests, including the valuable Atlantic white cedar in the Great Swamp east of Lower Bank and other portions of the watershed.[13] The numerous sawmills producing lumber obtained their critical waterpower through being advantageously located on the many river tributaries, dammed to create millponds for processing both wood and grains, as well as to drive the bellows for the iron furnaces. The finished wood could be transported out of the Pinelands on small vessels and scows to the downriver shipyards on the navigable shipping channels, or ultimately shipped out of the region to Mid-Atlantic coastal ports and beyond. The natural-resource products carried on watercraft for export included charcoal converted in local "coalings" from the upland pine and oak trees. The bog-iron furnaces required this essential fuel, along with tons of local oyster and clam shells delivered by water serving as the flux in the smelting process to separate impurities from the iron ore.

Primary among the shipyards that supported the water-born commerce was the Van Sant "homestead" at Port Republic on Nacote Creek, where production of vessels could range from oceangoing ships to bargelike riverway scows for lighter cargoes into less navigable interior waterways. Other shipyards and building sites in this river included those in The Forks at the junction with the Batsto River, and those in the Green Bank--Lower Bank area. Other shipyards included those at New Gretna on the Bass River and Leeks Landings at what would become Bridgeport on the Wading River.

These sites were augmented by numerous landings, primarily up in the valley stretching from Chestnut

Figure 2. Illustration of the wooden bridge over the Wading River (Bridgeport) from approximately 1900. From the collection of Dorothy McAnney/Somes.

Mullica Valley Ports and Landings

Neck to Clarks Landing, Gloucester Landing, Mordecai Landing, and up to The Forks;[14] and numerous smaller ones scattered into the Pinelands above Bridgeport on the Wading River. The commerce in the watershed experienced further enhancement in 1817 with completion of the first bridge in the Mullica Valley across the Wading River (Fig. 2). This established a bridge port on the river that penetrates deep into the Pine Barrens, and, as a result of its connection with the Mullica River, provided for water-born commerce throughout the valley. Together, both rivers had access through Old Inlet (Beach Haven) and New Inlet (Little Egg) to the broader coastal commerce along the east coast of the United States, including elsewhere in New Jersey, down to Virginia, and up to New York City,[15] and as far as the West Indies.[16]

In addition, the bridge at Bridgeport supported commerce from both the water (upstream and downstream) and by land, such as the wagon and coach lines that existed at the time, traveling on the "stage roads" from Tuckerton to Coopers Ferry (present day Camden) and thus to Philadelphia. As a result, the port of Bridgeport (Figure 3) developed, in part, because the bridge deck's low elevation made it usable for docking vessels and offloading cargo.[17] The bridge stood at a critical location because the river above the bridge was too shallow and winding for large vessels, prompting the use of shallow draft, bargelike scows that moved numerous products downstream (e.g., salt hay, charcoal, wood, iron) to the bridge for transshipment elsewhere. Numerous landings upstream from the bridge supported this commerce, including: Goldeckers, Anderson, Half Moon, Smiths (or Milley Place), Charcoal (or ThreePole), Scotts, and finally Hay Landing adjoining the Tuckerton Stage Road river crossing at Bodine.

In addition to local forest products, exports included paper products manufactured from salt hay at Harrisville, located on the East Branch of the Wading. Iron output from Martha Furnace, upriver on the Oswego River or East Branch of the Wading River, passed downriver to sailing ships at Bridgeport. Often forged elsewhere, these metal products consisted of cast-iron pipe, metal rims for wagon and cannon wheels, and metal hoops for wooden barrels—the equivalent of today's cardboard boxes for shipping.[18]

The Plans for the Port of Egg Harbor City

Incorporated in 1854, the Gloucester Farm and Town Association formed to create the planned development of Egg Harbor City (Figure 4) and its surrounds, including the Gloucester Furnace and Landing, as a German settlement.[19]

The city's original plan stretched from the Camden and Atlantic railroad, connecting Atlantic City and Philadelphia, and the port on the nearby Mullica River (Figure 5). On paper, it seemed reasonable that the port

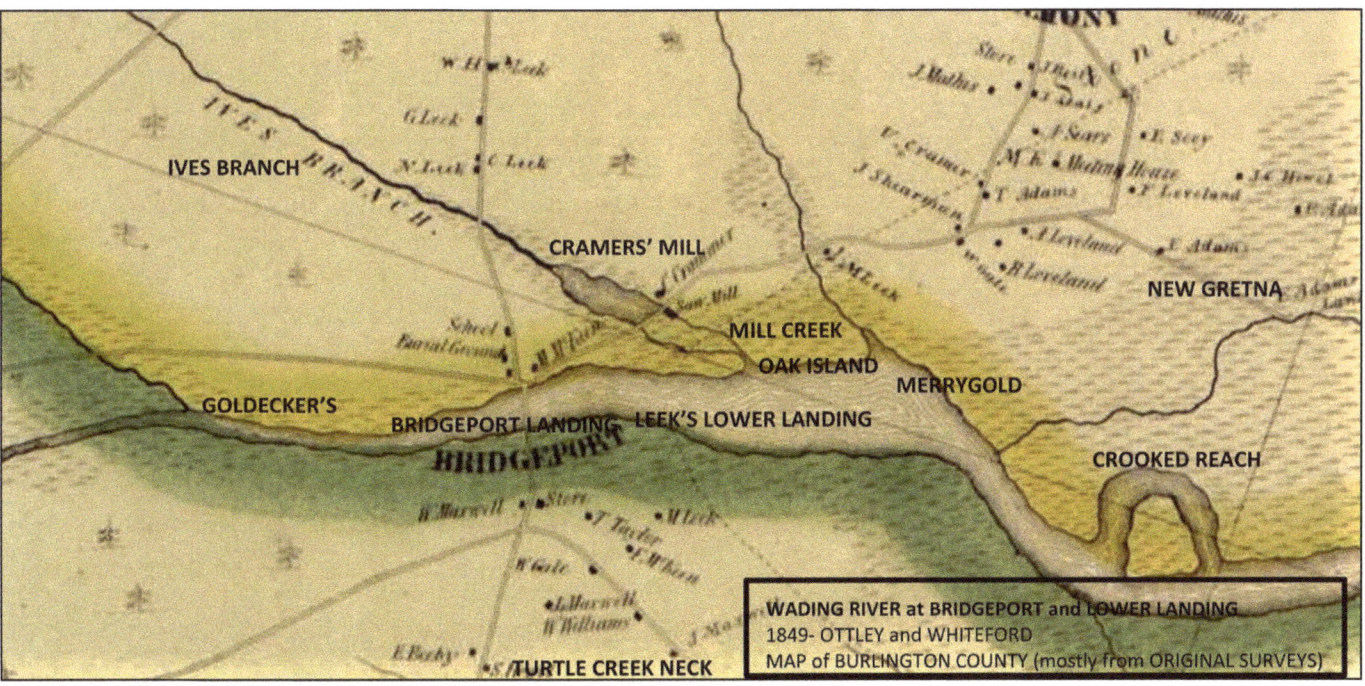

Figure 3. Location of Bridgeport at Leek's Upper Landing and downriver Leek's Lower Landing in the Wading River (see Fig. 1 for location) from 1849 *Map of Burlington County* by Ottley and Whiteford.

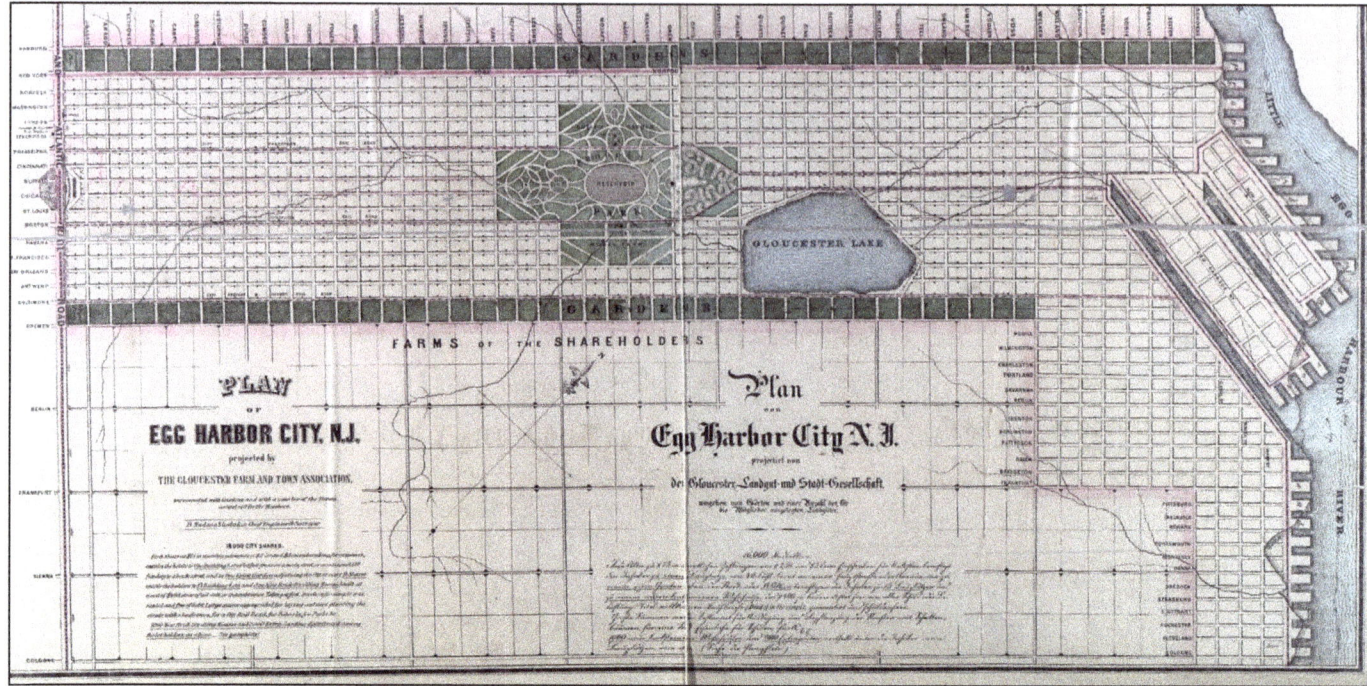

Figure 4. The proposed port of Egg Harbor City based on the "Bullinger Map" that was prepared between 1864 and 1866 and made available by the Egg Harbor City Historical Society. Note the extensive planned streets extending to the Mullica River along with the planned docks and ship channels at the water's edge.

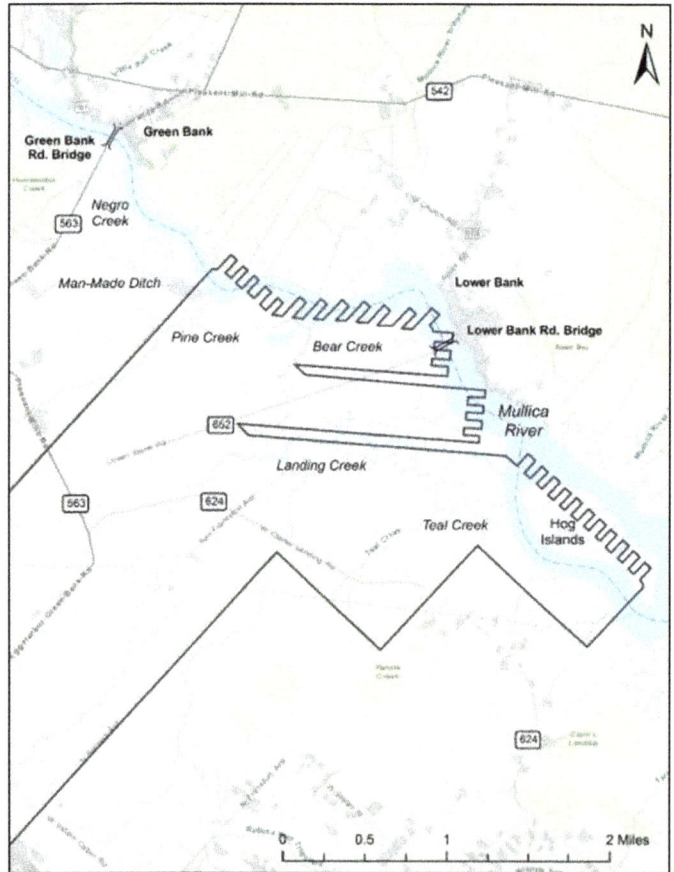

Figure 5. An outline of the proposed port of Egg Harbor City with important localities mentioned in the text, as they exist today.

would be the crown jewel in the watershed with extensive docking facilities above the Hog Islands and into the freshwaters of the Mullica River (Figure 1). The optimism relative to a port on the river was reflected in the local newspaper, the *Egg Harbor Pilot*,[20] and the name "harbor" in the city's name.[21]

THE PLANS FOR HERMAN CITY AT GREEN BANK

Upriver of Lower Bank a broad swampland existed along the shoreline at Cakes Spruto—a small tributary millstream that once divided Washington Township to form the short-lived Randolph Township (1870–1893).[22] Beginning at "Upper" or Green Bank, the northern shoreline provided riverside high banks where ships could land. This geography extended west to Crowleys Landing at today's State Park, beyond which the north shore again became swampland that continued to The Forks, at the confluence of the Batsto River, where another landing was favorably situated a mile from both Batsto Furnace and Pleasant Mills. The local industries included glassworks that used the "sugar sand" from the Pine Barrens in wood- or charcoal-fueled furnaces, harvested from the local forests.

On the west side of the Bull Creek tributary, a small community developed named, at its outset, "Town of Hermann," nucleated around a glassworks with its river wharf, hotel, boarding house for workers, and village

Mullica Valley Ports and Landings

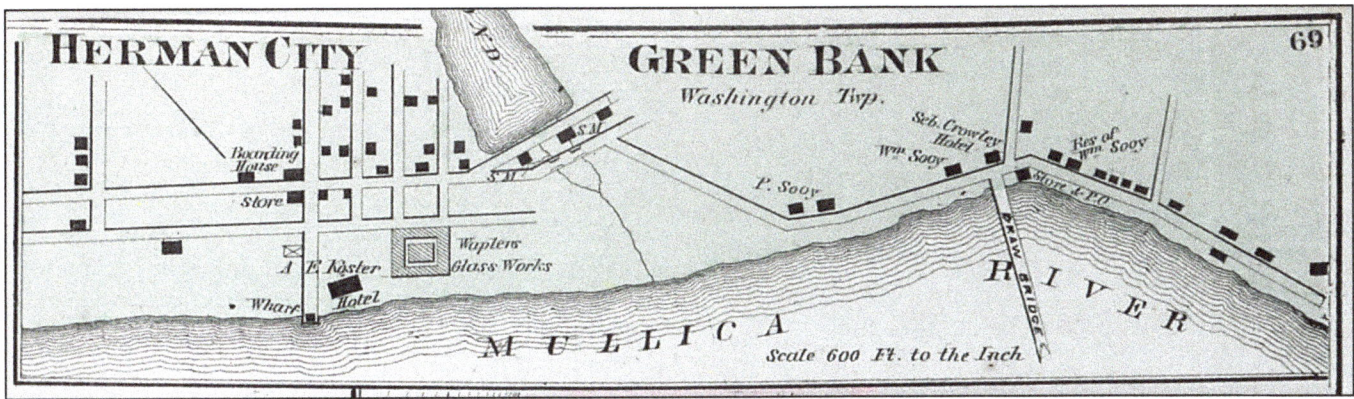

Figure 6. Map of Herman City and its wharf, glassworks, hotel, and boarding house. Note the two sawmills powered by the adjacent Bull Creek—today's Belhaven Lake. The Koster hotel and residence was the last abandoned structure that was destroyed by fire in 1979. J. D. Scott, *Combination Atlas Map of Burlington County, New Jersey* (Philadelphia, PA: J. D. Scott, 1876), 69.

store (Figure 6). The planned grid pattern for streets appears much like the prospectus for Egg Harbor City. The glass business continued here, and at nearby Batsto, until the center of this industry moved from the region.

The Present

Chestnut Neck ceased to be a privateering port at the end of the Revolutionary War. Today, recreational boating occurs along the Mullica River within sight of the battlefield and the Garden State Parkway. The small village remains historically noteworthy for the monument to the battle during the American Revolution, when a British force only partly succeeded in its attack and penetration of the Mullica Valley. More significantly, this privateering center contributed to the American success in the war.[23] Herman disappeared after a fire in 1979. The only remnant is an apparent slipway (Figure 7).

Today, little remains of Bridgeport as a shipping center. It might have been transformed if either of two proposals for extending the Tuckerton Railroad had come to fruition, with river crossings either downriver at Merrygold from New Gretna to Lower Bank or upstream at Bodine.

There is a new Wading River bridge that joins the rural community in Bass River with its twin to the west on Turtle Creek Neck,[24] but the rest of the wharfs and landings are remnants. This includes a large accumulation of ballast rocks downstream from the bridge[25] and some wharf remains that are visible on blow out tides (Figure 8). Other physical evidence includes a large wooden cleat recovered from the mud site (Figure 9). Little else remains of this forgotten port, whose varied

Figure 7. Location of the former wharf at Herman City. Note the apparent slipway for ships at the water's edge in the foreground. The abandoned wrecks of three sailing ships that plied the Mullica and Wading Rivers remain in the offshore river bottom: Two Marys, Argo, and Mary Francis (personal communication from Donald McDougall, 2021).

Figure 8. Historic evidence of Leeks Lower Landing at Bridgeport in the Wading River including wharf construction and ballast piles now visible only at low, blow-out tides.

Figure 9. Large wooden cleat (approximately 12 x 8 inches) for mooring recovered by Frank R. Somes from the riverside mudbank at Leeks Lower Landing.

and far-reaching business has been documented and preserved in a number of nineteenth-century accounting "daybooks" of the local Cramers and McKeens, which are now archived in Special Collections at Stockton University's Bjork Library.[26]

Despite the low-cost advantages of water transportation in developing the port at Egg Harbor City, this never became a harbor. Thus, despite the early development of wharves and docks at Gloucester Landing (Figure 10), and the remnants of the bridge from there over the creek and toward Lower Bank,[27] today, large timbers from the wharves are only visible on very low tides along with bog-iron slag. The city never expanded enough to reach from the railroad to the river and the waterway lacked enough depth throughout to be navigable by large vessels. Furthermore, the railroad soon dominated much of the commercial and passenger traffic to and from Egg Harbor City.[28] A "what-if" scenario for many of these ports would have been the nineteenth-century proposal to build a rail line for connecting the Central New Jersey Railroad across the central Pinelands, via the Tuckerton Railroad, to the Gloucester Landing's extension from Egg Harbor City and the Camden & Atlantic Railroad—which remains the only active route, now connecting Atlantic City to Philadelphia.

When these plans failed, the potential negative impacts of piers in urban waterfronts[29] were negated, and much of the natural beauty and ecosystem contributions of this portion of the Mullica Valley was preserved (e.g., marsh production, freshwater-saltwater interface for fish and crab nurseries, and habitat quality). Instead, the region and watershed are protected from development by the Pinelands National Reserve, Wharton State Forest, Bass River State Forest, Forsythe National Wildlife Refuge, and the State Wildlife Management Areas at Port Republic, Swan Bay, and Wading River. Together, these and the low human population density make this watershed and the area of the proposed, but never developed, port one of the cleanest natural ecosystems on the east coast of the United States. As a result, the area is covered by extensive salt and freshwater marshes and associated creeks (Figure 11) which together serve as important spawning and nursery areas for fishes,[30] crabs, turtles, and a variety of mammals, waterfowl, and other birds such as eagles and ospreys.[31] This becomes all the more important because the freshwater-saltwater interface location is critical to economically important species such as adult striped bass,[32] adult and juvenile alewife,[33] and all life history stages of white perch.[34] At the same time, these unique characteristics allow for teachable moments for the watersheds' many visitors through the Jacques Cousteau National Estuarine Research Reserve.

About the Authors

Ken Able is a Distinguished Emeritus Professor in the Rutgers University Department of Marine and Coastal Sciences and former director of the Marine Field Station in Tuckerton. His interests include the faunal habitats and ecology and human history of the Mullica Valley.

Horace Somes of Turtle Creek Neck in Wading River has ancestry through the McAnney family for several generations to Batsto and Harrisville. His inter-

Figure 10. A portion of the former wharf at Gloucester Landing on Landing Creek (see Fig. 1) at a very low tide in March 2021. Note the bog iron slag, probably from nearby Gloucester Furnace, that was used as fill. Photo by Steve Jasiecki.

Figure 11. Recent aerial view from a helicopter of an area along the Mullica River at the bridge to Lower Bank, October 2016. The portion on the right, southern side of the river would have been buried under the proposed port (see Figures 4 and 5). The area is covered by extensive intertidal marshes that are divided by Landing Creek with Teal Creek further in the distance in front of the extensive maritime forest in the upper part of the image. Note present-day boatworks for recreational craft at the left, northern end of bridge, opposite to Gloucester Landing in Landing Creek (see Fig. 1).

ests include natural and human history of the Mullica Valley. After various employments in environmental consulting and with the New Jersey Department of Environmental Protection, he retired from a career with the State Forest Fire Service.

Acknowledgements

A number of individuals from the Rutgers University Marine Field Station assisted in preparation of the text and images. The Egg Harbor City Historical Society provided access to the Bullenger Map and other pertinent information. Other sources include those by Peter Stemmer from the Bass River History Committee and Donald McDougall. Rob Auermuller provided a drone image of remains at Herman City.

Endnotes

1. Kenneth W. Able and Gabe Coia, "The Recovery of New Jersey's Mullica Valley," *Underwater Naturalist* 32, no. 2 (2017): 36–43.
2. Arthur Pierce, *Smuggler's Woods: Jaunts and Journeys in Colonial and Revolutionary New Jersey* (New Brunswick, NJ: Rutgers University Press, 1960).
3. David P. Harper, *Roadside Geology of New Jersey* (Mountain Press Publishing Company, 2013).
4. Kenneth W. Able, J. Walker, and B. P. Horton, "Ghost Forests in the Mullica Valley: Indicators of Sea-Level Rise," *SoJourn* 2, no. 2 (2018): 87–96.
5. Kenneth W. Able, *Station 119: From Lifesaving to Marine Research* (West Creek, NJ: Down The Shore Publishing Corporation, 2015).
6. P. L. Plusquellac, "Coastal Morphology and Changes of an Area Between Brigantine and Beach Haven Heights, New Jersey," (M.S. thesis. University of Illinois, 1966).
7. Pierce, *Smuggler's Woods*, 1960.
8. Barbara Solem-Stull, *The Forks: A Brief History of the Area* (Medford, NJ: Plexus Publishing Inc., 2002).

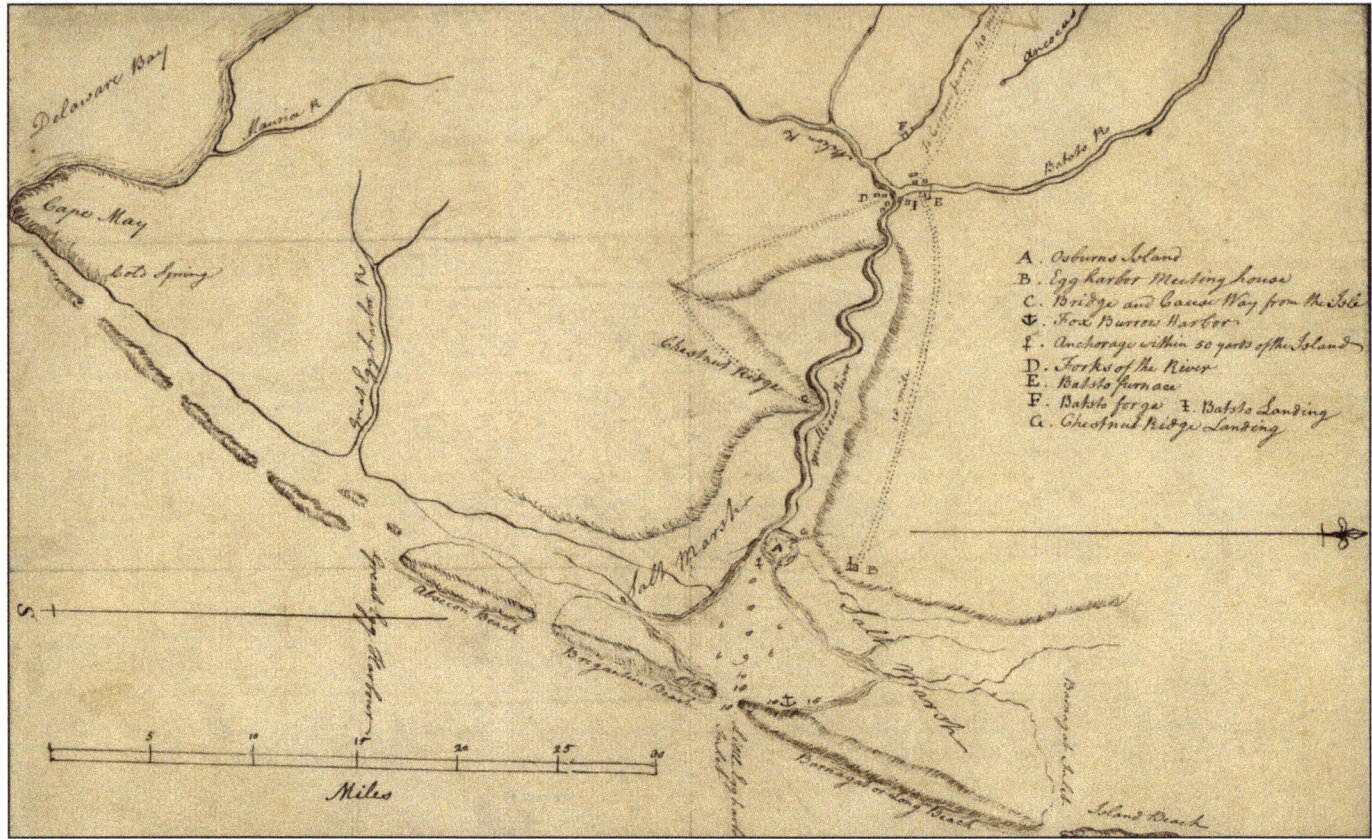

Figure 12. Little Egg Harbor Area. Detail of Map of the coast of New Jersey from Barnegat Inlet to Cape May. 1770s. Courtesy of Library of Congress Geography and Map Division.

9   Pierce, *Smuggler's Woods*, 1960.
10 Gabe Coia, "Mordecais Moorings," *NJPineBarrens.com* (2010) https://www.njpinebarrens.com/mordecais-moorings/.
11 Pierce, *Smuggler's Woods*, 1960.
12 S. W. R. Ewing, "The Van Sant Family Shipyards," *Atlantic County Historical Society Yearbook with Historical and Genealogical Journal* 8, no. 2 (1977). J. N. Van Sant, *Van Sant Shipyards, 1760–1970* (Peoria, Arizona: Grechen Aleta Van Sant Heyer, 2000).
13 Henry C. Beck, *Jersey Genesis: The Story of the Mullica River* (New Brunswick, NJ: Rutgers University Press, 1963). John E. Pearce, *Heart of the Pines: Ghostly Voices of the Pine Barrens* (Hammonton, NJ: Batsto Citizens Committee, Inc., 2000).
14 Arthur Pierce, *Iron in the Pines: The Story of New Jersey's Ghost Towns and Bog Iron* (New Brunswick, NJ: Rutgers University Press, 1990).
15 J. B. Kirk, *Golden Light: The 1878 Diary of Captain Thomas Rose Lake* (Harvey Cedars, NJ: Down the Shore Publishing, 2003).
16 D. G. Shomette, *Privateers of the Revolution: War on the Jersey Coast, 1775–1783* (Atglen, PA: Schiffer Publishing Ltd, 2016).
17 Pearce, *Heart of the Pines*, 2000. Horace A. Somes, "Geography of Maritime Commerce up the Wading River," *Tuckerton Historical Society Newsletter* (2021).
18 Henry H. Bisbee, *Martha: The Complete Furnace Diary and Journal* (Self-published, 1976).
19 D. Cunz, "Egg Harbor City: New Germany in New Jersey," *Report of The Society for the History of the Germans in Maryland* 29 (1956): 9–30. A. Doell, "A Short History of Egg Harbor City, Egg Harbor," *Egg Harbor Centennial* (Egg Harbor City, 9–29. Beck, *Jersey Genesis*, 1963. Henry C. Beck, *Forgotten Towns of Southern New Jersey* (New Brunswick, NJ: Rutgers University Press, 1983). A. Baden, G. Fenstermacher, and R. E. Gronlund, "An Early Planned Community: Egg Harbor City," *The Atlantic County Historical Society Yearbook with Historical and Genealogical Journal* 12, no 4 (1995).
20 Cunz, "Egg Harbor City," 9–30.
21 Cunz, "Egg Harbor City," 9–30.
22 Pearce, *Heart of the Pines*, 2000.
23 Franklin W. Kemp, *A Nest of Rebel Pirates* (Atlantic City, NJ: Batsto Citizens Committee, 1966). Shomette, *Privateers of the Revolution*, 2016.
24 Kenneth W. Able, *Beneath the Surface: Understanding Nature in the Mullica Valley Estuary* (Rutgers University Press, 2020). See Fig. 2.10.
25 Able, *Beneath the Surface*, 2020.
26 Pete H. Stemmer, "The Isaac Cramer Account Book: Transcription," *History Committee of the Bass River*

Community Library (Stemmer, undated private publication).
27 Beck, *Jersey Genesis*, 1963. A steamer named Eureka operated for a least two years between New York City and Egg Harbor City in the early 1860s.
28 Beck, *Jersey Genesis*, 1963.
29 T. M. Grothues, J. L. Rackovan, and K. W. Able, "Modification of Nektonic Fish Distribution by Piers and Pile Fields in an Urban Estuary," *Journal of Experimental Marine Biology and Ecology* 485 (2016): 47–56. Kenneth W. Able and J. T. Duffy-Anderson, "Impacts of Piers on Juvenile Fishes in the Lower Hudson River," *The Hudson River Estuary* (New York: Cambridge University Press, 2006). J. T. Duffy-Anderson, K. W. Able, "Effects of Municipal Piers on the Growth of Juvenile Fishes in the Hudson River Estuary: a Study Across a Pier Edge, *Marine Biology* 133 (1999): 409–18.
30 Kenneth W. Able and M. P. Fahay, *Ecology of Estuarine Fishes: Temperate Waters of the Western North Atlantic* (Baltimore, MD: Johns Hopkins University Press, 2010).
31 Able, *Beneath the Surface*, 2020.
32 C. Ng, Kenneth W. Able and T. M. Grothues, "Habitat Use, Site Fidelity and Movement of Adult Striped Bass in a Southern New Jersey Estuary Based on Mobile Acoustic Telemetry," *Transactions of the American Fisheries Society* 136 (2007):1344–55. Kenneth W. Able and T. M. Grothues, "Diversity of Estuarine Movements of Striped Bass (*Morone saxatilis*): a Synoptic Examination of an Estuarine System in Southern New Jersey," *Fishery Bulletin* 105 (2007): 426–35.
33 Kenneth W. Able, T. M. Grothues, M. J. Shaw, S. M. VanMorter, M. C. Sullivan, and D. D. Ambrose, "Alewife (*Alosa pseudoharengus*) Spawning and Nursery Areas in a Sentinel Estuary: Spatial and Temporal Patterns," *Environmental Biology of Fishes* 103, no. 11 (2020):1419–36; DOI 10.1007/s10641-020-01032-0.
34 Able and Fahay, *Ecology of Estuarine Fishes*, 2010.

Beneath the Surface by Kenneth W. Able

The Mullica Valley estuary and its watershed, formed over the last 10,000 years, are among the cleanest estuaries along the east coast of the United States. This 365,000-acre ecosystem benefits from a combination of protected watershed, low human population density, and general lack of extensive development. In *Beneath the Surface*, marine scientist Kenneth Able helps the reader penetrate the surface and gain insights into the kinds of habitats, the animals, and plants that live there. Readers will gain a better understanding of the importance of these shallow waters; how the amount of salt in the water determines where animals and plants are found in estuaries; the day-night, seasonal, and annual variation in their occurrence; and how change is occurring as the result of climate variation. Throughout the book are insightful sidebars telling intimate stories of where various animals came from and where they are going as they travel through the estuary on their way to and from other portions of the east coast. *Beneath the Surface* emphasizes the kinds and importance of the animals and plants that live beneath the surface of this unique ecosystem. *Published by Rutgers University Press.*

www.rutgersuniversitypress.org.

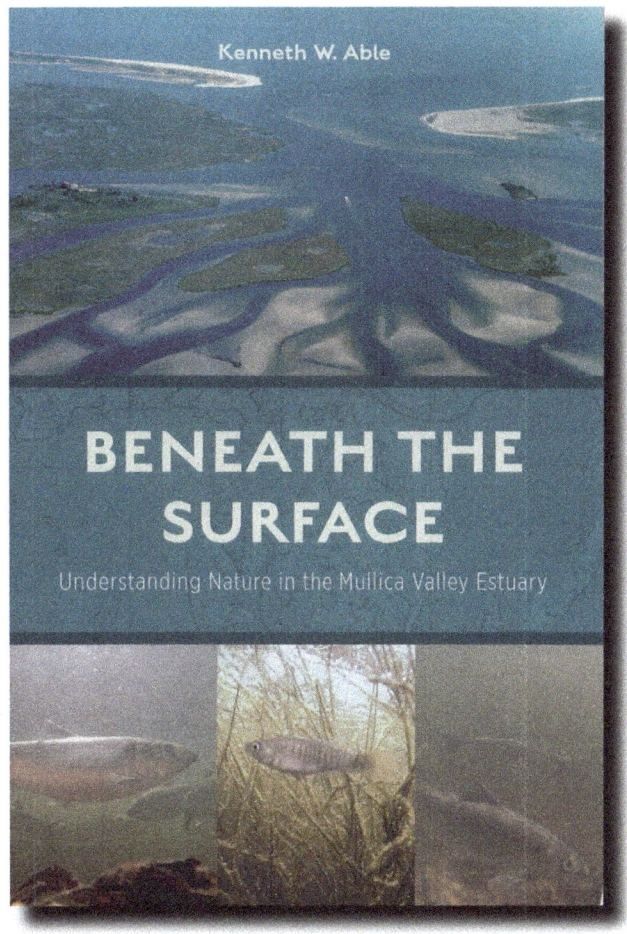

The Little Indian Day Camp:
"A Woodland Experience"

Stephen C. Fiedler

This is a historical look at the Little Indian Day Camp, now a memory fading into the mist of summer mornings past. It might have been only eight or ten, maybe twelve miles by bus or car from Atlantic City, which could be seen in the distance across the meadows and bay. Situated on ten acres of land on a slope overlooking the southeast end of Lily Lake, a historic lake in the Oceanville section of Galloway Township between Absecon and Smithville, the camp property today provides access to the entrance of the present-day Edwin B. Forsythe National Wildlife Refuge. To the kids from "The Island," that first trip to the day camp must have seemed like a forever journey.

The Little Indian Day Camp, with its Native American imagery and lore, would certainly be considered politically incorrect today. It was a widespread theme throughout the camp exemplified through the advertisement language and imagery, printed materials, grouping the campers into "tribes," totem poles, and decorations. "From Little Indians, Great Chiefs Do Grow!" was a favorite marketing phrase, as well as credo.

A "Woodland Experience" for "urban kids" was a dream of the camp's beloved owner and director, Dr. Richard Cohen. It was my privilege and pleasure to finally meet, interview, and become an acquaintance of Richard's for a few years until his death in 2020 at the age of 93. Until his last days, he was a warm, engaging, funny, and intellectually curious man with an incredible memory.

Richard Cohen was the son of a service station owner and a homemaker. He was born in Philadelphia in 1927, but the family grew up together in Atlantic City. He was self-admittedly a shy but friendly boy who was the studious kind, always appreciating a couple of friends who protected him from bullies in the Ducktown section of Atlantic City. Self-confidence came slowly, and he never forgot the value of friendship and camaraderie.

After graduating from Atlantic City High School, Richard joined the Navy, serving as a medical unit assistant in Maryland. After World War II, he studied at Western Maryland College for his bachelor's degree, the University of Alabama for his master's degree, and later, Temple University in Philadelphia, from which he received his doctorate in Psychology. He became an educator in the Margate school system, teaching seventh grade reading and literature. He married Bernice "Bunny" Heiffetz in 1951, and enjoyed traveling and camping with Bunny and their son, Sandy, and daughter, Faith.

Through the early 1950s, Richard pondered and explored the perfect spot for a camp for large numbers of children to enjoy. Thinking of an "away destination," he made trips with friends and realtors through the Poconos and down into the Bucks County area. What Richard found in his travels was the 1950s version of "sticker shock." It seemed the parcels of sufficient size and interest were priced far above what a school-teacher's salary and borrowing power could afford. He very much liked a piece of land that had historical features from Colonial times, or as he called it, "the George Washington place"—with a whopping $200,000 price tag. He knew he had to modify his ambitions and decided to get the help of a real estate agent.

Richard began exploring some sites closer to home, now concentrating solely on the idea of a day camp. After looking at the Abbott House by Nacote Creek in

Oceanville Mill, c. 1906. Sometime between 1812 and 1828, Daniel S. Shourds (b. 1777) constructed a dam on Tanners Brook and established a gristmill, powered by today's Lily Lake. By 1850, Daniel and his son, Daniel, continued to work at the mill. When the mill ceased operations is unknown, but it is clearly abandoned and decaying in this view. Courtesy of the Paul W. Schopp collection.

Pleasure boats at Lily Lake, Oceanville, N.J. Photography by Max H. Kirscht. Courtesy of the Paul W. Schopp collection.

Port Republic, and finding that the residents were not enamored with Richard's plans, he heard from his friend Dr. Matthew Weiner. Also interested in the idea of a day camp, Dr. Weiner learned that their mutual friend, Dr. Samuel Shuster, was looking to sell his cottage that was located "somewhere along the Mullica River." It turned out that the cottage was on Lily Lake, a man-made body of water formed in 1740 out of Tanners Brook. The lake was formed primarily to provide water pressure to run various mills that existed over the years: structures like Shourds' Mill and Doughty's Mill.

A day camp at Lily Lake would not be the first time the lake was a source of enjoyment for children. In 1921, Charles Kessler, an Atlantic City entrepreneur, built an amusement park on the lake with two merry-go-rounds, a roller rink, bathhouses for the beach at the edge of the lake, docks with rowboats, canoes, and a barge to host floating parties. The park was a popular location for school field days and became a destination for picnics for folks of all ages. A high-ceilinged

The Little Indian Day Camp

The pavilion at Charles Kessler's amusement park built on the lake in 1921. The park was a popular destination for school trips and picnics for local community members.

The pavilion, renamed Dox Folly after its purchase by Drs. Davidson, Mason, and Uzzell, in later years.

pavilion was built on pilings over the lake, which housed a restaurant (renowned for its $1.00 chicken dinners!), a bar, and a dance hall. In 1924, the lake and amusement park were sold to Sam Schellenburg, who continued the park's operation until 1931, when the Great Depression left its mark on the park and made it more difficult to afford maintenance. Three local doctors purchased the lake, park, and pavilion renaming the latter Dox Folly. The doctors included Dr. Harold Davidson, Dr. James Mason III, and Dr. Edward Uzzell. They hosted regular meetings of the Atlantic County Medical Society, the Atlantic County Dental Society, other civic groups, fraternal societies, and Boy Scout groups. In the summer they sponsored a Fourth of July celebration with fireworks, and in the winter it was a popular spot for ice skating. This operation continued past the Depression and World War II until 1951 when it ceased to be maintained. The doctors had built homes along the lake. One of them, the home of Dr. Uzzell, was the cottage bought by Dr. Sam Shuster and then eventually by Dr. Matt Weiner; it became the first building of the day camp.

By the time the Little Indian Day Camp came to Lily Lake, what was left of the park was in total ruin.

The pavilion collapsed under snow load on the roof in 1967, and the remains were intentionally burned down in 1968 by the Oceanville Fire Department. The remnants of the pilings from this large, old pavilion can still be seen not far from the site of the camp.

After Dr. Matt Weiner purchased the cottage and its ten-acre tract in 1955, the idea of the day camp started to take shape. Matt started the Little Indian Day Camp in 1956 with a modest number of children, mostly from Margate. Apparently, the building was also used for a time as a Unitarian Congregation meeting place during the winters. Richard Cohen became quite impressed by the location and situation, eventually offering to buy into the operation when he could afford to make the investment. Matt offered Richard co-ownership of the camp for $15,000. Richard used savings and borrowed money to make this contract official in December 1958. The two co-owners made plans for the camp for the summer season in 1959. In February of 1959, however, Dr. Weiner had a serious heart attack. Doctors helped him to survive, but they recommended that he stick to his medical practice only. After just becoming a half owner of the camp, Richard was faced with the decision of buying out Dr. Weiner's share to become sole owner. As difficult as it was to come up with another $15,000, he took the leap and found himself fully immersed in the reality of owning and operating a summer day camp for the "woodland experience" at long last.

Richard admitted to me that he was never good with financial planning. He used this opportunity, and many others in the future, to seek advice from his friend

Campers holding the camp motto: From Little Indians Great Chiefs Do Grow. Children who attended the camp, now grown, donated most of the photographs that illustrate this article. Some of the attendees are identified, but most are not. If you have additional images or can identify people in these photographs, please reach out to the author.

The Little Indian Day Camp

The first building for the Little Indian Day Camp. This home, built for Dr. Uzzell, was the cottage bought by Dr. Sam Shuster and then by Dr. Matt Weiner. When Richard Cohen purchased the property, it became the camp headquarters and sometime rec center.

Morris Batzer, an Atlantic City insurance broker, financier, and well-known civic leader. Mr. Batzer, he said, gave him advice and confidence to go after his dream. Fortunately, Dr. Weiner recovered enough to advise Richard by the summer of 1959. The camp was still housed in the tiny cottage with a relatively small group of between 40–60 campers aged five to twelve. That was soon about to change in a big way.

Richard became a man with many hats. He had by now become a doctor of psychology, and was much in demand, but also had the reputation as a tireless public servant and as such, had many friends and allies become a part of his new summer camp venture. Even though there were several summer camps to choose from, such as Camp by the Sea in Margate, many Margate families wanted to follow his leadership, signing up their children to Richard's day camp for about $20–$25 per week, a common price around that time. Even though he was now Dr. Richard Cohen, he was always more comfortable just being addressed as Richard around town or "Uncle Richie" at the camp by campers, counselors, staff, and even parents.

Richard wanted the camp kids to look sharp and to be identifiable as group members on outing trips. He worked with local clothing merchant Murray Raphael, of "Gordon's Alley" fame, to supply uniforms: shorts, T-shirts, bucket hats, jackets—all with the logo of the Little Indian Day Camp imprinted.

As the camp started to grow, Richard insisted on hiring staff who were teachers or college students on summer break, or recent college graduates. He sought out other professionals to fulfill other roles such as cooks, medical aides, and administration. One early and long-time camp staff member was Jack Bretcher, a Brigantine teacher who helped not only as a counselor, but as a builder of structures and features, helping Richard's ideas to become reality. Richard often reiterated to me that he was not a handyman, and that staff members like Jack were great not only with the kids, but with building and setting things up. Richard recounted that Jack was quite physically fit and would sometimes use a rowboat or small motorboat to reach the camp from his home in Brigantine.

Richard's wife, "Aunt" Bunny, was another tremendous worker and cheerful advocate of the camp. In addition to raising their two children, she taught art and other classes in the camp, filled in everywhere as needed, helped with administration, took many photographs, and inspired the children and other counselors.

One of the early campers, a camper from before Richard Cohen purchased even part of the camp, was Susie Feldman of Margate. She later became a counselor, like many of the original Margate kids who attended the camp in the 1950s. Susie had many fond memories of the camp, providing many photographs and interviews, by herself and with other camper friends. She identified many campers from the photographs and was able to speak about what became of some of the other campers. It was apparent from talking with Susie, as well as Richard Cohen, that she was a huge help to him during the camp years and beyond. She felt that he helped to inspire her with all she learned at camp and through his mentorship.

Two of the early maintenance kids were Ron Ross Cohen and Gary Cleveland, two kids from the Midwest. How did they wind up in South Jersey? Ron Ross Cohen's parents met Richard and Bunny Cohen (no relation) while on vacation in Florida and got to talking about their children. It seems it was decided that Ron and his buddy Gary might benefit from Dr. Cohen's leadership, mentorship, and work ethic for a summer away from home. These two buddies had a great time and did their jobs well. Both decided that

Front Row (Left to Right): Scottie?, Richard Cohen, Bunny Cohen, Jim McGettigan, ?, ?, Mrs. Yvonne Booker. Back Row (Left to Right): Don Dion, Ricky Shuster, Terry Steed, Jack Bretcher.

The Little Indian Day Camp

South Jersey was the place for them and have since lived here. Ron Ross Cohen is a renowned sculpture artist with a studio in the Noyes Museum Arts Garage in Atlantic City. Gary Cleveland has been a local painting contractor and handyman over the years.

One of the staff members who worked with Richard for a long period during his directorship was Mrs. Yvonne Booker. She was head of the kitchen for all the kid's lunches and special events, and they ate very well! During the school year, Mrs. Booker was the head of the cafeteria kitchen operations at the New Jersey Avenue School in Atlantic City. Never one for taking much of a break, she loved her work and the camp kids. For a few years, her daughter Charlene was a camper who excelled at sports and as a performer in the camp shows. She later went on to compete in local beauty pageants.

Richard always insisted that every camper who attended must learn how to swim. To him this was paramount, as he was always dismayed by the frequent and devastating news of drownings along the shore communities. He carried this message wherever he went, even beyond the camp. He was a scoutmaster in Margate as well and made arrangements for swimming lessons through the Jewish Community Center. All counselors at the Little Indian Day Camp had to be proficient swimmers and were required to have their Red Cross certification in the teaching of swimming and administering rescue and first aid.

To provide a workable teaching area for swimming and boating, Richard and Jack created a dock arrangement that squared off a generous-sized area in the cove of Lily Lake. Richard hired a contractor to bring in

Dr. Cohen giving personalized swimming lessons. He insisted that every child must learn how to swim.

equipment to dredge out the area of underwater stumps, roots, and muck. In its place, he had soft, white sand trucked in and spread through the area to define the space and make walking in the shallows much easier for teaching and learning. The white sand is still discernible on the lake bottom near the shoreline of the old camp, over sixty years later.

The dock was also handy for mooring the many canoes, rowboats, sailboats, and motorboats over the years as the camp developed. For a time, there was instruction on water skiing for some of the older campers, although the lake was rather shallow, and the motor often struck bottom or became entangled with vegetation. Richard always wanted to sail around the lake in something larger than a single person, "sunfish" style boat, so he purchased an eighteen-foot sailboat. Unfortunately, Richard did not take into account the fixed skeg on the underside of the boat, which prevents the sail's power from tipping the boat over, making the range of his new boat extremely limited on the lake. For a while, it became a decorative feature and provided an opportunity to learn about rigging.

Sailboat to nowhere. (Left to Right) Frank Pearl, Sam Picagar, Jon Slotoroff, David Golden, and (standing) Richard Cohen.

Other outdoor activities grew as the camp developed such as playground equipment usage, baseball, softball, trampoline, archery, ham radio, basketball, boxing, hiking, boating, on-site miniature golf, field trips, and much more as opportunities arose. Indoors, in that original, tiny cottage cabin were arts, crafts, storytelling, music, and theater. Many performances were presented in those cramped quarters before parents and friends.

As the numbers of campers grew, Richard had some additional structures built, in semblance of the log cabin style. He also purchased old motel cottages along US Rt. 30 (the White Horse Pike) and Rt. 9 (New York Road.) These tiny buildings used to be everywhere as "efficiency" accommodations along the corridors before the Garden State Parkway and the Atlantic City Expressway were built. Richard used them for bunk houses. Some of the staff and counselors stayed overnight in the bunk houses during the camp season. On most days, the campers needed them for changes of uniforms, swimming gear, and costumes. Also, some overnight stays were planned along with night hikes through the wood trails, and perhaps down to the wildlife refuge to see the lights of Atlantic City, Brigantine, and Long Beach Island. Bonfires, storytelling, games, and nature walks made up the nighttime experience.

Thanks to a chance discovery of a long lost Super 8 movie roll, a camp outing recorded on film in 1959 has been saved. A large group of campers, probably between 100–200 kids, can be seen cheering and applauding at the unique "Ski Follies of 1959" just off the White Horse Pike. This short-lived attraction took place on a modified meadow water impoundment located right behind the old Absecon Drive-In Theater, whose screen still stands today in ruins. The impoundment was created around a small creek, and when the tide brought in water to fill it like a bathtub, a "sluice gate" was shut to keep the water in. There was parking for 800 cars available at the Drive-In, and then a walkway across the levee led to bleachers and a concession stand for the show.

The kids are seen at a daytime show featuring synchronized and trick water skiing, a boat and skiers flying through the air off a ramp, and "Kite Man" aka "The Flying Bat": a skier towed behind a speedboat who soared high in the air under a huge kite. Problems with keeping enough water in the impoundment and the incessant insects on the meadows during shows eventually caused the feature to close down after just a handful of day and evening sessions. Fortunately, the Little Indian Day Camp kids got a chance to witness this sensational show.

The Little Indian Day Camp

Baseball at the Little Indian Day Camp in the late 1950s.

Campers who attended the first phase of the camp 1959–1965, were generally from Margate. From 1966–1978, campers came mainly from Atlantic City.

Camp counselors. (Left to Right) Linda Garfield, Frank Pearl, Vicky Chasens, Barry Schwartz, and Marilyn Klass.

Dox Folly, visible in the background, was burned down by the Oceanville Fire Department in 1968.

Hammell's Stables c. 1960. (Left to Right) Michelle Zetooney on white horse, instructor BeBe Bayer, Lee Pattison, Howie Panitch on dark horse.

49

The Little Indian Day Camp

(Previous page) Rowing on the lake and counselors relaxing after a long day.

(This page, clockwise from top left) Matt Weiner, Linda Lewis (with hammer) and Barbara Satter. Linda is nailing the bottom on her bookend project. It is upside down so it has her initials "LL," not number "77"!

Girl on trampoline.

Nurse Betty Devos and camper Sandy Cohen.

Boat over launch ramp and water skiers at the Ski Follies in 1959. Notice the structure for the Absecon drive-in theater screen in the background of the boat image; the screen still exists today.

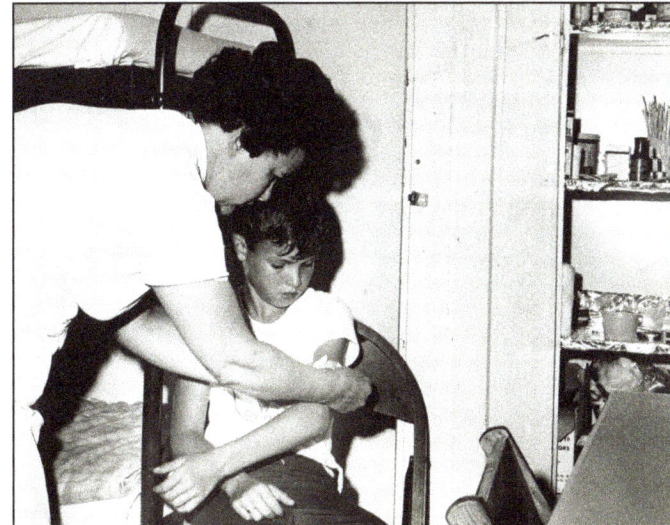

During many years of the camp, Richard would invite world-class participants of the then-famous "Around the Island Swim" to come to the camp. One year, 1961, was well-documented when swimmer Benson Huggard came to visit. Mr. Huggard worked with the kids on their swimming efforts, and then would put on a bit of a show right there in Lily Lake. He swam back and forth across and lengthwise to show good form. Then he raced canoing counselors, to the delight of the campers cheering him on. He beat them all! On race day around Atlantic City, Richard rented a motorboat from Capt. Applegate's Bait and Tackle Shop and took a select number of campers with him. They followed Benson Huggard out into the ocean to cheer for him and carry some of his supplies. Unfortunately, Mr. Huggard was dashed against the jetty rocks at the Longport turn and had to leave the race with an injury. He did his best and greatly inspired the campers.

The Little Indian Day Camp was very fortunate to have the summertime services of the wonderful music and theater counselor, "Uncle Jim" McGettigan. During the school year, he was Dr. Jim McGettigan, a special education teacher at the Woodbine State School. At the camp, he would put together ensembles of kids to do their version of well-known Broadway plays and other solo or group performances. They made theater props and costumes and worked hard on their skills that many may not have even known they had. McGettigan was adept at bringing out special talents and achievements from the kids. They put on many plays at the camp, at the Granville Avenue School auditorium, and elsewhere. Most of the shows were fundraising events that were very well attended. There are many photographs and articles showing Dr. Richard Cohen presenting checks from show proceeds to the Atlantic County Mental Health Association and other charitable organizations. Sadly, Dr. Jim McGettigan was killed in the crash of a small airplane at the age of 70.

A camp performance at the Granville Avenue School auditorium. The admission money to these programs was donated to local charities.

The Little Indian Day Camp

The story of the Little Indian Day Camp and former Margate resident Ivan Merilson is one of tragedy and triumph. At the age of seventeen, the talented local sports player had a tragic accident that resulted in the loss of one of his arms. Dr. Cohen counseled, mentored, and eventually hired Ivan to work with him at the camp. Ivan actually helped to build the recreation/dining hall at the camp. With one arm he troweled and smoothed the concrete pad that formed the floor. Perhaps as a tribute to Ivan, the only visible feature of the camp that remains to this day is that concrete pad, now being used as a recreation surface by the most recent owners.

An important decision was made by Richard Cohen that differentiated the "first half" of the camp's history from the "second half." Nationally, in 1964, President Lyndon Johnson declared a "War on Poverty." This led to the "Economic Opportunity Act" and funds became available for many underprivileged areas. Atlantic City received funding under Title I of "The Elementary-Secondary School Act of 1965." This funding would be spread out and offered up to the eleven schools that existed and qualified at that time. Richard spoke with Atlantic City School Superintendent Jack Eisenstein and their Business Agent/Secretary John Ordile about extending the "Woodland Experience" to Atlantic City youth. As a result, the camp was offered $80,000 per year, starting in 1966, if the camp experience would include a remedial education component. Dr. Cohen accepted the challenge with the firm continuation of his rule that every student/camper must learn how to swim.

Significant new facilities and upgrades were now needed. It was decided that 800 children were to be served over a ten-week period. There were to be two five-week sessions of 400 campers each; 200 in the morning and another 200 in the afternoon. Everyone was to be served lunch, whether they were a morning or afternoon camper. This new camping project was dubbed "Project Grow."

A 40' by 80' building was constructed as a new recreation/dining hall. Richard admitted that there was no architect hired for this building, he drew some lines on an index card and the builder interpreted his requests through the construction project. The main building contractor was Vincent Ponzio, from the old Ducktown

The recreation/dining hall, built c. 1966. There was no architect hired for this building. Richard Cohen drew some lines on an index card and the building contractor Vincent Ponzio, from the Ducktown section of Atlantic City, interpreted his requests throughout the construction project.

Little Indian Day Camp attendees at a class outing to Adventure Village in Egg Harbor Township in 1966.

neighborhood where Richard grew up. Along with that project, the whole complex needed upgraded septic system capacity, a new well, and extensive electrical work. The cafeteria staff leader Yvonne Booker was given more assistants and was consulted on her needs in the new kitchen to meet the demand of so many new campers.

A school bus deal was forged with George Hoenes of the Hoenes School Bus Company, to provide the large and timely transfer of all these kids, Monday through Friday at midday. Richard said that the Hoenes firm always performed their services professionally and that "they ran like clockwork!" The Hoenes company still provides reliable school bus services all around the area, based in the Germania section of Galloway Township.

To accomplish the remedial education requirement, Richard brought in three mobile classroom trailers. Within these trailers, teachers were hired to work with the student campers. Also, he purchased a new type of device that he simply called "teaching machines" from a company called "The Learning Foundation" from Athens, Georgia. This technology involved the use of tape recorders and television screens. Through a process of display, listening, answering questions, and hearing your own voice and pronunciation, the machines provided real time feedback for language and math skills. Workbooks filled out by the campers were analyzed by The Learning Foundation and recommendations were sent back to the teachers through Dr. Cohen. This allowed a few teachers to keep more kids engaged at one time, while still providing personalized interactions. These sessions took about an hour of each day's camp time. The kids took to these hybrid sessions in a positive way and it was estimated that rather than losing edu-

The Little Indian Day Camp

cational ground during a summer slump, the kids averaged a raise in accomplishment through testing by 1 to 1½ grade levels. This teaching method was cited as a national educational model for a summer camp hybrid program during this time period of the mid-sixties.

Richard later reflected that he observed improved concentration and curiosity when kids were able to repeat, advance, or seek help regarding lessons on their own terms. The fun camp setting made for a good environment for learning. Richard was always an advocate, as a teacher and psychologist, for a good balance of recreation and outdoor time in any student's learning day.

When "Project Grow" got going at the camp in 1966, there was some local push back to the increased bus traffic and to the rapid expansion and multi-use of the camp. Dr. Cohen was called into City Hall to answer these concerns. Fortunately, some other locals and even the manager of the neighboring Brigantine Wildlife Refuge spoke out in support of the constructive, bustling activities that were taking place there. The overreacting residents backed down when their concerns were addressed directly.

Common again among comments from former Atlantic City campers of the "second half," like the "first half" kids, was their reaction when they would be taken out on a hike onto the high meadow and levee road of the Wildlife Refuge. Many had never been out of the city before, and here they were looking at the skyline of their hometown and many other areas in a whole new way.

A great supporter of all things Little Indian Day Camp, particularly in the 1960s and 1970s, was Sam Greenberg, a former-star basketball player and later an award-winning coach. Mr. Greenberg helped to set up countless unique opportunities for field trips, athletic competitions, and entertainment events. Another camp field trip was partially documented on some Super 8 movie film that was found damaged along with the "Ski Follies" film. This silent film, estimated to be from 1966, was of an outing to the legendary local attraction, "Adventure Village" in Egg Harbor Township. "Slippery Sam," "the Mayor," the tremendous live shows, the "Nickelodeon Movie Theater," rides, and concessions are all gone now, but were absolutely enjoyed by the kids. Trips were made to Historic Batsto Village, to competitions in track and field events at Bader Field in Atlantic City, down river canoe trips, swimming meets at the Jewish Community Center in Margate, roller skating at Young's Skating Center in Mays Landing, to a wax museum, visiting other camps, bowling alley competitions in Absecon and West Atlantic City, and much more. Most were wholly or partially arranged by Sam Greenberg.

Sam was further known for his great generosity of time and money for the kids. He didn't want any kid to feel inferior simply because they were poor. When a kid would show up with worn-out street shoes or flappy sneakers, he would quietly make sure that the kid would get a new pair to go with the camp-supplied shorts and T-shirts. There were also thousands of tribe portraits and individual photos for the kids taken; the film was supplied and developed at no charge to the camp. Other

Swimming area at the Little Indian Day Camp.

supplies appeared mysteriously without invoices being submitted: trophies, certificates, and plaques. Sam believed deeply in the camp, and this kind of "Santa Claus" activity gave him great satisfaction and made many impoverished kids feel more comfortable and welcome as part of the Camp.

Richard and Bunny Cohen were still the camp owners during the "second half" of the camp's history, with the help of some very fine Head Counselors. One was Frank Ervin, a sixth-grade teacher at the New Jersey Avenue School in Atlantic City. He was truly Dr. Cohen's right-hand man and Project Grow Camp's Director during the "second half." Frank was one of a group of Atlantic City teachers who answered the call for summer supervisory jobs. Other early Atlantic City teachers who came over as counselors were Paul Godwin, Bill Steele, Warner Jones, Lou Graham, and Eddie Fleming, among others.

Interestingly, "Uncle Frank" Ervin had a night job at the famous Club Harlem in Atlantic City. He often talked with visiting performers about the kids and the camp. Notably, in 1971, James Brown came to the Club Harlem while touring to promote his new hit record, "Hot Pants." When Frank asked Mr. Brown if he would like to visit the camp, he did not hesitate to say yes. Frank offered to bring him to the camp, but Mr. Brown insisted he would find his own way there since Frank would have his hands full with the kids. After all, Frank and the staff were going to keep all 400 kids from the morning and afternoon sessions together at midday for James Brown's visit. Mr. Brown had his limo driver stop just short of the camp, over the hill from where the staff was keeping all of the kids organized and somewhat orderly, sitting on folding chairs waiting. As Frank described it, James Brown walked over the crown of that hill on Lily Lake Road, into view, and with a couple of his signature moves and famous shouts he unleashed the pure joy of the kids. He sang to and with them, and they sang karaoke to his songs through the camp loudspeaker. He showed them how to do some of his famous dance moves, with kids wiggling and giggling all over the place. Mr. Brown managed to sneak in a pep talk about staying in school and distributed free 45 rpm records of his new hit song. It was a day these

Class in portable trailer, August 8, 1974.

The Little Indian Day Camp

Mike Weiner (left) and Richard Cohen with the kids at lunch.

kids would never forget, especially as James Brown became more and more of a globally famous performer. Frank Ervin was the catalyst for this, a visit that is documented in still photos.

A couple of weeks later, another opportunity came around. Sammy Davis Jr. was at the Club Harlem and Frank approached him as well about the Camp. Mr. Davis also did not hesitate in agreeing to come to visit the kids and staff. He also entertained, spoke to the kids about his journey in life, and about the importance of staying in school. He was invited down to the lake to see the kids swimming and learning how to swim. Frank Ervin said it was crazy as so many kids excitedly shouted, "Mr. Sammy!" "Mr. Davis!" "Look at me!" "Watch me swim!" Well, Mr. Sammy Davis Jr. was overcome with the scene; he actually peeled off his shoes and shirt to leap into the lake with the kids. Frank said it was a crazy scene and they all couldn't wait to swim a bit along with "Mr. Sammy." After his visit, the kids made thank you cards and notes for Mr. Davis. When presented with these, the famously emotional performer was apparently moved to tears!

The following year, Frank was able to set up yet another visit, this time by the very popular soul singer Sam Cooke. Frank said that he tried to get the parents of the campers to attend as well. Unfortunately, Frank got a lot of "Why didn't you tell us?" phone calls after the event, to his bewildered dismay. It seems that the method of giving kids a note to take home to their parents didn't work very well then, as it doesn't work very well today!

A lead counselor with Frank was "Uncle Gene" Hudgins, a teacher at Pleasantville High School. Mr. Hudgins was also an excellent basketball player and played for a time with the Harlem Globetrotters. He helped to raise the profile of local basketball at the camp and in the area in general. The team that the Globetrotters traveled and performed with, the hapless Washington Generals, were run by their legendary star player, "Red" Klotz. Gene got "Reds" interested in the camp, as well as local radio personality and basketball supporter, "Pinky" Kravitz. Through their efforts, they brought many basketball celebrities to the camp to sign autographs, shoot hoops and give some advice to kids to learn to swim and do well in school. Some members of the Globetrotters, the Washington Generals, the Philadelphia 76ers, and other teams participated, including Wilt "the Stilt" Chamberlain, then with the 76ers, and Freddie "Curly" Neal, basketball superstar and bald-headed funnyman with the Harlem Globetrotters.

Richard Cohen's psychology practice brought him to local prominence during the camp and long after. He was once hired by Atlantic County to counsel troubled youth at the old juvenile detention home in Egg Harbor City, prior to the Harborfields facility. The previous home was on the site of the present Egg Harbor City Hall, where a portion of the famous "healing waters" facility of Dr. Charles Smith once stood. For a time, Dr. Cohen shuttled between that facility and the camp as needed. He became on-call for local hospitals, police departments, law firms, corporations, family counseling offices, and of course his own private clientele practice. He began to teach at regional colleges and served on hospital and charitable boards. For quite a while until the end of the camp, he established a "branch" office at the camp to cut down on his crazy amount of travel.

More and more, Richard had to delegate tasks to his professional camp colleagues. A local teacher at Pleasantville High School, Chuck Worthington, helped to run the camp in the mid 1970s. Mr. Worthington later went on to become the Atlantic County Chief Executive. Eventually, the "War on Poverty's" Economic Opportunity Act monies ran out, and thus the very

James Brown visited the camp in August 1971. This singer is singing with Mr. Brown over the camp loudspeaker.

The Little Indian Day Camp

Frank Ervin, James Brown, Dr. Cohen.

Frank Ervin worked nights at the Club Harlem in Atlantic City, where he met artists like James Brown, Sammy Davis Jr., and Sam Cooke and invited them to the camp.

Camp in the 1960s. There were obvious opportunities on the archery range for things to go wrong. Strict rules came from the state leading to changes.

successful Camp connection with Atlantic City was immediately cut back. The camp continued to operate, but with the appropriate charges to attend. Attendance dropped and Atlantic City considered buying the camp to extend its effective programs. The school system tried to raise $125,000, which Richard would have accepted, but they could not arrange that kind of funding.

Dr. Cohen had many services still operating that were geared toward helping troubled youth and those with cognitive and physical disabilities. Atlantic County paid to provide a "Kids in Need" summer day camp program. "Aaron's Rod" was a program to help those who had gone astray to lead better lives. He established the Ortho Psychological Institute there in 1975 to use some of the meditation, yoga, music, head/neck massage, and gentle conversational therapy techniques that were a hybrid approach to emotional and behavioral wellness.

In an effort to keep things going on a larger scale, Richard joined forces with the owners/operators of the Camp Mohawk of Pleasantville in 1976. That camp was run by Pleasantville High School teachers/coaches Joe Clements and Ken Leary. By this time, the fees for attending the Camp were $300 for the whole season and $150 for a half season.

Finally, economic pressures and time constraints led Dr. Richard Cohen to make a very difficult and rather painful choice. Accounts vary about what happened toward the end of the Little Indian Day Camp, but I take my cue directly from Richard's words to me. He said that one day in April 1978 he was sitting alone in his camp office when he heard cars pull up outside. He stepped outside to find a man getting out of a car, looking and pointing all around with a couple of "blonde ladies" and another man. Another car followed behind and out stepped two more men with briefcases. The man in the lead was none other than Fred Noyes, of Smithville Inn and the Historic Towne of Smithville fame. "I want to buy this place" said Mr. Noyes. "How much do you want for it?"

Evidently, he had been checking out this property for some time. Richard explained to him that he still had an offer outstanding with Atlantic City for $125,000, although he knew nothing was formally binding, and that a deal was looking very unlikely

August 8, 1974. Another fun day at camp. A counselor tells stories, sings songs with the kids, and works on crafts by the Lily Lake shore.

there. Fred Noyes said, "I'll double that, I'll give you $250,000."

Dr. Cohen was kind of taken aback and simply joked to everyone, saying, "Where do I sign?" After consulting with Bunny and his staff, he agreed, and the next day the two men met with the necessary people to write up the deal.

The Noyes Museum was built directly on the site of that tiny cottage where the Little Indian Day Camp was born in 1956. This new, large, and innovative building was designed by Paul Cope and built to embrace the slope down to Lily Lake. It fully opened in 1983, and featured an extensive collection of art, duck decoys, unique carvings, sculptures and more. After the death of Fred Noyes, the museum was run by the Board of Directors of The Mr. and Mrs. Fred Winslow Noyes Foundation.

Persistent HVAC and structural problems plagued the building and it was closed in January of 2016. Ownership of the building and artwork were transferred to Stockton University in August of 2016. Eventually, the remaining assets of the Foundation, listed as $2.2 million dollars, were donated to Stockton University which created the Noyes Foundation Fund to support and build on the original mission. The Museum contents were relocated to new facilities such as Atlantic City's Noyes Arts Garage, Claridge Hotel, and the AtlantiCare Medical Complex; as well as Stockton's Kramer Hall in Hammonton and Shore Medical Center in Somers Point. The original building has since been sold by Stockton in 2021, refurbished, and reopened as the Lifepoint Church.

The concrete slab of the recreation/dining hall is all that remains today of the Little Indian Day Camp, a playing surface on a slight rise across the road from the Church. But the Recreation Hall itself lives on! After the camp closed and the site was being demolished, a deal was made to cut the building apart and haul it away on flatbed trucks and trailers. It was modified for length and placed on a new foundation. It has since stood for over 40 years as the Log Cabin Recreation Hall at the Gabriel Field Sports Complex on Duerer Street and Zurich Avenue in Galloway Township. This second life of the Little Indian Day Camp recreation building has hosted countless meetings, weddings, receptions, shows, indoor sports, and other events of all types. On one of our talk and drive trips out into the countryside, I pulled up to the Hall and told Richard that his work is still serving youth today. He nodded slowly, smiled and said, "You know what? That makes me very happy."

To paddle a kayak on Lily Lake today is a treat. To float quietly into the little southeast corner cove of the lake is to be in the place where thousands of kids learned to swim; where "Captain Cohen" stood on the deck of his "sailboat to nowhere"; where the strong, handsome "around the island" swimmers wowed; where world-class stars and dignitaries splashed and cheered the kids on; where young people fell in love; and where, if you dip your paddle into the lake bottom, you can still bring up some of the white sand that was spread there. Lean back and look up into the tree boughs and you will hear the laughter on the breeze of kids having a wonderful "Woodland Experience" so many years ago. . . .

ACKNOWLEDGMENTS

I would like to thank the many people who have helped uncover this history. Thanks to interviewees: Nancy Blumberg, Gary Cleveland, Dr. Richard Cohen, Ron Ross Cohen, Frank Ervin, Susie Feldman, Ivan Merilson, Linda Lewis Moors, Jackie Lewis Polimeni, Annette Scott. Thanks to those who submitted photographs, Super 8 films, news clippings and camp paraphernalia: Nancy Blumberg, Dr. Richard Cohen, Ron Ross Cohen, Susie Feldman, Annette Scott. Thanks to those who helped with photo restoration and reproduction: Stephen Fiedler, Tom Kinsella, Mary Reitmeyer, John Seyler. Thanks to those who helped with site exploration: Mark Ferguson, Barbara Fiedler, Stephen Fiedler. Additional research and museum Camp display were provided by the Board members of the Galloway Township Historical Society. The Museum is located at the front of the Galloway Municipal Complex grounds: 300 Jimmie Leeds Road, Galloway, NJ 08205.

ABOUT THE AUTHOR

Stephen Fiedler is a retired custom kitchen and bath contractor who lives in Galloway Township. He is the Secretary of the Galloway Township Historical Society, where he became interested in researching the history of the Little Indian Day Camp. Stephen would like to keep the conversation going, as there are still many unanswered questions. If you or someone you know may have attended the camp, please contact Stephen Fiedler at scfiedler@gmail.com.

(Left) The Little Indian Day Camp Rec/Dining Hall in its new life at Gabriel Memorial Field at 265 S. Zurich Ave in Galloway Township, NJ. (Right) Steve Fiedler with Dr. Richard Cohen in 2018.

The Cuts in the Mullica River:
From Oyster Plantations to Thoroughfares for Navigation

Kenneth W. Able

History of Oyster Plantations and the Cuts

The oyster industry has been a critical component of the fisheries of New Jersey since the late 1800s[1] including in the Mullica River–Great Bay estuary in southern New Jersey.[2] Central to the success of the oyster populations and the fisheries that depend on them is the ability to create conditions for settlement of the larvae from the water column to the bottom[3] in New Jersey estuaries.[4] At this time the late-stage larvae are looking for a hard substrate, or cultch, to settle on. Once they have settled or attached they are referred to as seed oysters or spat. In an attempt to create optimal conditions for the development of seed oysters, cuts were created in the marshes of the Mullica River from lease sites adjacent to the oyster beds. This occurred in large part because of the decline in seed oysters, and thus harvestable oysters, in many locations in New Jersey from the late 1880s into the early 1900s.[5] This is especially apparent in numerous local newspaper articles from Great Bay and the Mullica River at the time.[6]

History of the Cuts

The accounts of the construction of the cuts in the Mullica River, all between the Garden State Parkway and downstream to Great Bay (Figure 1), occurred early in the 1900s based on notes of Rutgers University scientist, Julius Nelson, who "saw dredge at work at Chestnut Point" on July 11, 1902, presumably making the cuts near the town of Chestnut Neck (Figure 1).[7] Subsequently, in 1906, this same scientist observed other cuts at Swimming Over Point (Figure 1) where E. T. and Watson C. Sooy, of the Sooy Oyster Company, had "vast oyster plantations" built on riparian grants in the wetlands.[8] Part of the overall justification for these cuts was for "improvements" related to riparian grants to the Sooys[9] in an attempt to create oyster-growing grounds from the marshland portion of these riparian grants.[10] At this site and further up the river, the Sooys excavated ditches "twenty feet wide, a thousand feet long and six feet deep" that connected different sections of the river. Elsewhere the ditches were reported to be thirty feet wide and three feet deep at low water and varied in length from 100 yards to one-half mile.[11] These provided strong tidal currents for the setting and culture of oyster seed or spat that settled on the oyster shell deposited within the ditches. A later report indicated that a good set of oyster spat was detected at Swimming Over Point and in other of these ditches or cuts made by the Sooys.[12]

Status Today

While there are numerous modifications to the salt marshes in the Mullica River–Great Bay estuary, and ditches of numerous types are common,[13] the cuts in the Mullica River for oyster plantations are by far the largest. The setting for these cuts is similar as they occur over a relatively short distance, approximately two miles in an area previously referred to as the Gravelings (Figure 1). This area, in the meanders of the Mullica, encompasses the current distribution of natural oysters.[14] The cuts connect the naturally deeper portion (25–50 feet) of the estuary. All of the cuts are also embedded in the intertidal *Spartina* marshes, or meadows, that characterize the shoreline of the downstream portion of the Mullica where salinity, as measured with a long-term data logger near the Garden

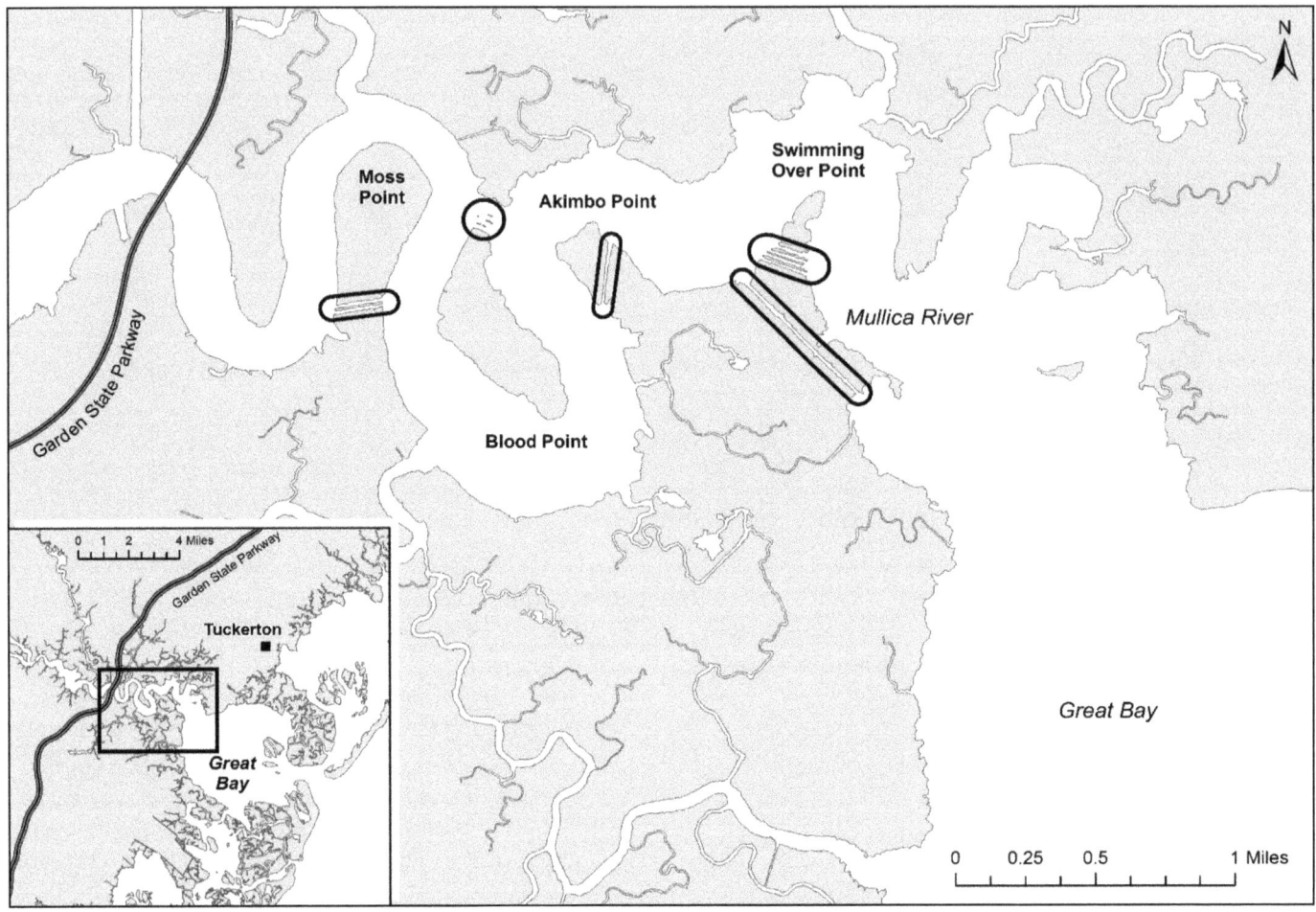

Figure 1. Study area (general location in southern New Jersey—see inset) in the Mullica River just upstream of Great Bay and downstream of the Garden State Parkway bridge with location of individual man-made cuts originally constructed as oyster plantations for the harvesting of seed oysters.

State Parkway, ranges from 18–29.[15] These marshes, and the cuts in them, are all exposed to the twice a day flood and ebb tidal currents and thus the planktonic oyster larvae and their food in the natural oyster beds. The same food source is available to ribbed mussels and the oysters that set on them along the vegetated edge of the cuts. In some places, as in the short cuts at Swimming Over Point, the oysters can be abundant on the marsh surface as well.

The cuts have changed since the early 1900s when they were used for culturing oyster spat. In the approximately 100 years since that time, the cuts or ditches have maintained their locations (Figure 1) based on aerial photographs during 2015–2017. The furthest upstream, at the base of Moss Point, just downstream from the Garden State Parkway, is about 850 feet in length (Figure 2). The next set of four individual cuts are at the base of Blood Point and typically referred to as Blood Ditch and these are about 350 feet long (Figure 3). The cut at Akimbo Point is over 1200 feet in length (Figure 4). The lowest site in the river, just before entering Great Bay, is at Swimming Over Point where the number and types of cuts are quite diverse (Figure 5). These consist of four cuts through the marshes between the river and the bay of approximately 85 feet. Another long cut at this location is evident just to the south which connects the river to Great Bay at Goose Cove and is about 2950 feet long.

The cuts currently vary in depth, based on observations with a depth finder on a moderately low tide in the center of each cut in April 2021. The shallowest, at 4–7 feet, were in the long ditch at Swimming Over Point and at Akimbo Point, 5–7 feet. The short ditches at Swimming Over Point varied in depth with those closest to the main marsh the shallowest, at 5–7 feet, and the deepest, at 12–20 feet. Those in between had intermediate depths, at 8–12 and 9–13 feet. The cuts at Moss Point had overlapping depths of 9–13 feet. The deepest and most variable cuts were at Blood Ditch (Figure 6). The three cuts closest to Blood Point were

The Cuts in the Mullica River

Figure 2. Aerial image of former oyster culture cuts through extensive salt marshes in the Mullica River at Moss Point near Chestnut Neck where the river is bordered by maritime forest with the Garden State Parkway in the center of the upper part of the image.

Figure 3. Aerial image of multiple oyster culture cuts through extensive marshes at Blood Ditch near Blood Point in the Mullica River. Note the vessel, near the channel marker, that is navigating through these cuts.

(Below) **Figure 4.** Aerial image of single, long oyster culture cut through Akimbo Point (lower left) in the Mullica River. Note that the upstream cuts at Blood Ditch and Moss Point are visible with the Garden State Parkway in the background.

Figure 5. Aerial image of four oyster culture cuts through extensive salt marshes at Swimming Over Point with the Mullica River in the lower part of the image and Great Bay in the upper left. Another, the longest cut, stretches from the river to Goose Cove in upper Great Bay. The shorter cuts are navigable as indicated by the wake of a boat that just passed through one of these cuts.

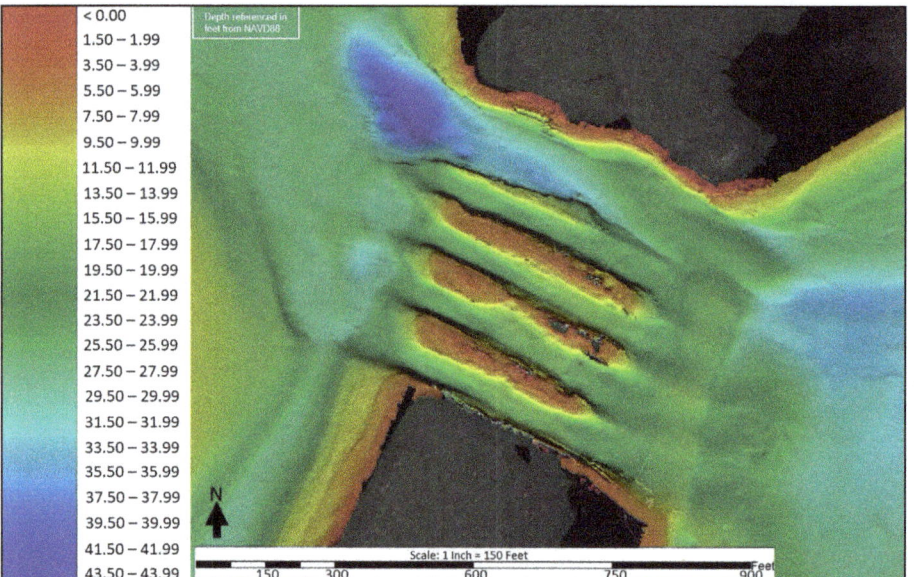

Figure 6. Multibeam images of the five cuts at Blood Ditch (Figure 3) with depth indicated by different colors. Prepared by Peyton Benson, Stockton University Marine Technology Society.

similar, at 16–21 feet, but the furthest was much deeper and the most variable ranging from 18–44 feet. This is obvious from multibeam imaging from June 2017 with a deep hole at the upstream end that eventually becomes shallower over the short distance of the ditch until, at the downstream end, all of the ditches are similar in depth (Figure 6).

The width of the ditches has probably changed as well given the presence of ice-rafted pieces of the marsh edge or peat reefs[16] on the marsh surface at some of the ditches. Also, all of the ditches have submerged peat reefs that were detected with side-scan sonar in June 2017. Both kinds of peat reefs were more abundant at the downstream-most cuts. All, or most, of these cuts have apparently changed since they were created in the early 1900s.

Since that time, the depths and widths of the cuts have increased, perhaps due to erosion enhanced by strong tidal currents, patterns of sea level rise in the estuary,[17] and boating activity, because many of them are frequently used as shortcuts through the meanders of the river and all of them are navigable at high tide. The cuts at Blood Ditch even have a channel marker to advertise this. Thus, these 100+ year old features have become an accepted part of the lower Mullica River landscape.

The Cuts in the Mullica River

Acknowledgments

Several individuals assisted in bringing this study together. Judy Redlawsk provided her expertise and helicopter for the aerial images. Jennifer Walker also assisted with some of the images. Ryan Larum prepared the figure of the study area and analysis of some of the images. Peyton Benson, of the Stockton University Marine Technology Society, and Steve Evert provided the multibeam images of Blood Ditch. Christina Welsh and Roland Hagan helped interpret the sidescan sonar images. Pete Stemmer and John Yates assisted with background information.

About the Author

Ken Able is a Distinguished Professor Emeritus in the Department of Marine and Coastal Sciences and is located at the Rutgers University Marine Field Station in Great Bay. His interests include the natural and human history of estuaries.

Endnotes

1. T. C. Nelson, "The Conservation of New Jersey's Oyster Industry," *Report of the Board of Shell Fisheries* (Trenton, New Jersey, 1920), 8–15; C. R. Woodward and I. N. Waller, *New Jersey's Agricultural Experiment Station 1880–1930* (New Brunswick, New Jersey, New Jersey Agricultural Experiment Station, 1932); S. E. Ford, "History and Present Status of Molluscan Shellfisheries from Barnegat Bay to Delaware Bay," *NOAA Technical Report NMFS* 127 (1997): 119–40.
2. B. J. McCay, *Oyster Wars and the Public Trust: Property, Law, and Ecology in New Jersey History* (Tucson: University of Arizona Press, 1998); M. R. Carriker, *Taming of The Oyster: A History of Evolving Shellfisheries and the National Shellfisheries Association* (Hanover, PA: The Sheridan Press, 2004); Kenneth W. Able, *Station 119: From Lifesaving to Marine Research* (West Creek, NJ: Down The Shore Publishing; West Creek Publishing, 2015).
3. V. S. Kennedy, R. I. E. Newell and A. F. Eble, *The Eastern Oyster: Crassostrea virginica* (College Park, MD: Maryland Sea Grant, 1996).
4. T. C. Nelson, "Aids to Successful Oyster Culture. I. Procuring the Seed," *N. J. Agr. Exp. Sta. Bulletin* 351 (1921): 1–59; M. R. Carriker, "Ecological Observations of the Distribution of Oyster Larvae in New Jersey Estuaries," *Ecological Monographs* 21, no. 1 (1951): 19–38.
5. Ford, "History and Present Status of Mulluscan Shellfisheries," 119–40.
6. S. Dodson, "Chapter 19. Shellfish: Oysters and Clams," *Tuckerton: A Newspaper History, 1852–1917* (Tuckerton, NJ: Tuckerton Historical Society 2018), 491–595.
7. New Jersey State Agricultural Experiment Station, *Report of the Biologist for 1905. II. Studies in Oyster Propagation* (Trenton, NJ: John L. Murphy Publishing Co., 1906), 400–425; New Jersey State Agricultural Experiment Station, *Report of Biologist for 1902* (Trenton, NJ: John L. Murphy Publishing Co., 1903).
8. New Jersey State Agricultural Experiment Station, *Report of Biologist for 1906* (Trenton, NJ: John L. Murphy Publishing Co., 1907).
9. McCay, *Oyster Wars and the Public Trust*.
10. Ford, "History and Present Status of Mulluscan Shellfisheries," 119–40.
11. NJDOH, *First Annual Report of Department of Health: Bureau of Food and Drugs* (Trenton, NJ: State Gazette Publishing, 1918), 57–91.
12. New Jersey State Agricultural Experiment Station, *Report of Biologist for 1922* (Trenton, NJ: John L. Murphy Publishing Co., 1923).
13. Kenneth W. Able, "History and Ecology of Salt Marsh Ditches in the Mullica Valley," *SoJourn* 5, no. 1 (Summer 2020): 7–17.
14. Kenneth W. Able, *Beneath the Surface: Understanding Nature in the Mullica Valley Estuary* (Rutgers University Press, 2020).
15. Able, *Beneath the Surface*.
16. Kenneth W. Able, C. J. Welsh and R. Larum, "Salt Marsh Peat Dispersal: Habitat for Fishes, Decapod Crustaceans, and Bivalves," *Peat* (Rijeka, Croatia: Intech Ltd., 2018): 9–28.
17. Able, *Beneath the Surface*.

Early morning view of Bass River fire tower near Greenbush and Bucto. Courtesy of Robert Auermuller.

The Bucto Wildfire:
1930—New Gretna to Little Egg Harbor

Horace A. Somes Jr.

On the east side of the Bass River in New Gretna, Burlington County, close by a large area of river docking, marina, and boat works, lies a short cul-de-sac with several homes. It is scarcely noticeable from State Route 9. In the past, a small settlement called Bucto existed along this road, as well as more homes and farms to the northeast at neighboring Greenbush.

A 1925 aerial view shows farms along the local roads extending northward from the State highway east of New Gretna, as well as the pineland and swamp expanse that extended further north. In 1906, this expanse had become Bass River State Forest, the first Forest Reserve established in the New Jersey State Park system. At that time, the original State Reserve facility was an office on Greenbush Road in the old homestead of the former French farm. The location provided a work yard that was the base of operations for the State's projects on the Reserve. The adjacent old fields were developing into squared plantations where tree plantings were in progress to demonstrate techniques for forestry. Further within the Forest, parallel patterns of clearings within the pine and oak woods indicated management activities and logging. The future camp of the Civilian Conservation Corps (C.C.C.) was yet to be established on Greenbush Road during the later Great Depression of the 1930s. No dam had been constructed on the River's East Branch to create Lake Absegami at the future core of the Park's recreational area on Stage Road. Adjacent cabins and camping for outdoor recreation were not yet established.

Another purpose of the Reserve was to demonstrate that wildfire protection was necessary for forest management and productivity, as well as community and property protection. A wooden lookout tower had been constructed on the old farmland behind the office

Bucto-Greenbush state road area of Bass River, 1925. Courtesy of Peter H. Stemmer.

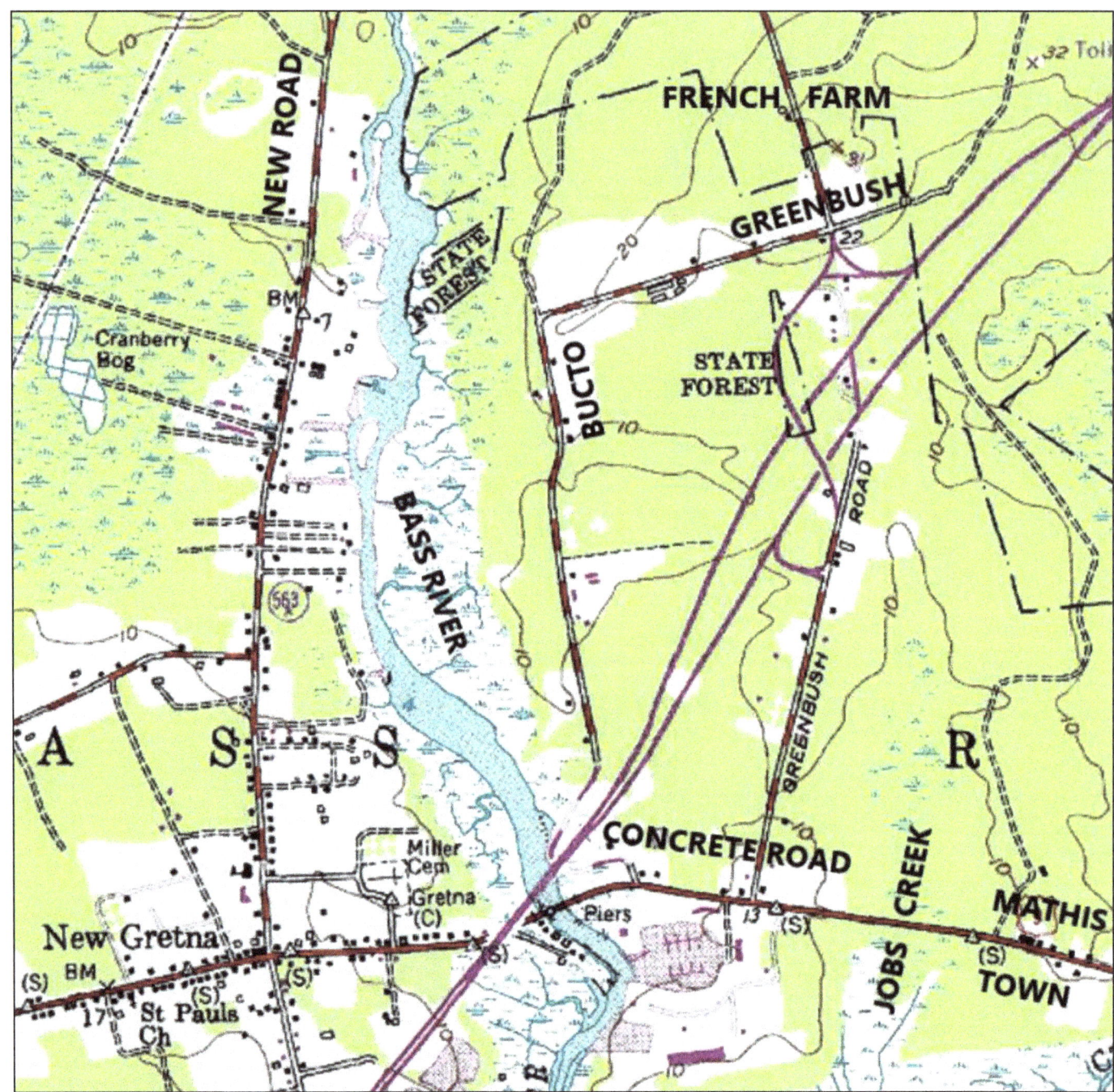
New Gretna/Bass River today with older place names. From NJGeoWeb: USGS Topographic 1:24,000.

on Greenbush Road, and later would be upgraded from the original construction to today's metal structure. This allowed not only for the discovery of smoke rising from a fire, but also cross-readings with adjacent lookouts to determine the location. Later radio communications would allow for prompt dispatch and coordination of firefighters, with essential observations of fire behavior and spread. Work on the Reserve included development of the old woods roads into viable roadways for local traffic that would also provide firefighter access and control lines. The thinning of trees and removal of brush as safety strips along road shoulders enhanced the narrow roads as fuel breaks for wildfire containment and the tactic of backfiring. Former farm fields, old burned-over areas, and stands that had been logged were planted with seedlings raised at the tree nursery established in neighboring Washington Township along Lovers Lane at Green Bank State Park.

The Bucto Wildfire

Forest Fires

The 1899 annual report of the State Geologist included Gifford Pinchot's "A Study of Forest Fires and Wood Production in Southern New Jersey." Pinchot, who would later lead the US Forest Service, noted the "Moral Effects of Fires on Population."

> It is obvious that where the forest is constantly exposed to fire and there is no adequate protection, its value must be greatly depreciated. The result is that the timber is often cut before its maturity. Landowners believe that with proper protection against fire the value of forest property will be greatly enhanced. The fires have been so abundant that the people have come to look upon them as inevitable, and there is a deplorable lack of real interest among landowners in regard to any attempt to introduce State protection. Large tracts of land are owned by non-resident capitalists, and timber-stealing is very common, especially after fires. When the timber is killed many persons consider it better to use the dead trees for cordwood than to allow them to rot on the ground, and they cut such timber on tracts of land to which they have no right. There is no doubt that forest fires encourage a spirit of lawlessness and a disregard of property rights.

Seven years would pass before recognition of the on-going wildfire problem, along with the impact of hundreds of years of vast industrial cutting of the region's timber, would give rise to changes recommended by the State Geologist, whose annual reports provided yearly recordings of destructive fires.

The Forest Park Reservation Commission, established in 1906 with Bass River as the first of the future Parks, oversaw the development of a system of local Township Firewardens who were to address the hazards of fire. Firefighting resources and capabilities were rudimentary at the time. The Commission initiated Public education programs and instituted permitting requirements for open burning and land clearing.

In 1927, the organization of the State Forest Fire Service included construction of an improved system of fire towers and the appointment of additional Township and Special District Firewardens who were to recruit local helpers to respond to forest fires. The workforce would include foremen and employees of the railroads from the different systems that passed through the Pine Barrens and its flammable forest cover.

All of this would come together in 1930. Wildfires ignited during the recognized spring wildfire season when weather and forest conditions could result in destructive conflagrations across the Pine Barrens. When it was dry and windy over the region, an ignition might occur intentionally, carelessly, or accidentally—and spread throughout the Pineland expanse, threatening small communities and scattered homesteads. It was known that the predominant forests of resinous Pitch Pine, *Pinus rigida*, were particularly flammable, with the dense undergrowth of shrubs. However, grassy fuels on fields and marshes also could burn, and were often in proximity to villages, homes, and farms. Springtime was particularly critical because last year's plant growth had died during the fall, been dormant through the winter, and now had little fuel-moisture content or shade as

Bass River Forest Reserve, 1907.

warmer drier weather arrived with the winds of passing weather fronts.

The volume of combustible materials could produce intense fire behavior in both live foliage of evergreen trees, and the understory brush, grasses, and dead accumulations of leaves and twigs. The rate of spread translated into a hundred feet per minute and hundreds of acres per hour. Windblown embers called "firebrands" could create new ignitions a quarter mile or more ahead of the main body of the fire. This would spread fire across roadways that might otherwise serve as firebreaks, and also through wetlands and across streams and small rivers.

Geography, terrain, and wind direction dictate how and where wildfires spread. Upland forests of pine provide fuel. Ineffective fuel breaks, whether natural waterways, man-made lakes, or constructed roadways, contributed to the danger. Too often, extensive unbroken areas of hazardous fuel cover allowed fire to spread unchecked around or across fuel breaks.

Influenced by prevailing seasonal winds and daily weather, forest fires spread across the landscape following natural corridors that impact their rate and direction of travel. This is comparable to the area within a floodplain along a river or coastal tidelands. Coastal storms with driving easterly winds push tidewaters inland and up the floodplain of river valleys. The spring fire season, when ground cover is made up of accumulated dead plant materials, is accompanied by frontal passages that bring strong westerly wind and low humidity. This tends to push firefronts in an easterly direction towards the coast. A significant seasonal exception in South Jersey occurs during the summer, when coastal meteorological conditions of sea-breeze and shifting wind directions can result in varying and erratic fire spread and behavior.

At Bass River in 1930, a conjunction of events would occur involving wildfires, their prevention, suppression by firefighters, and protection of properties. James MacDonald was the appointed Firewarden for Section 12 that included both the State Forest and nearby communities. There was a local organization of District Firewardens with helpers, whose capabilities had improved since the horse-and-wagon transportation of the nineteenth century. Firefighting equipment remained rudimentary, and fire engines were nonexistent for the forest and local communities.

It was late spring and dry across the region. Plants were just starting to leaf-out with fresh green foliage. Ground cover leaf litter, brush, and grasses remained unshielded from daytime sunshine and winds. Coincidentally, a large fire had started far to the west of Bass River and was spreading from Batsto across the Wharton Tract, which had not yet become the largest State Forest.

French Farm Ranger Station, Bass River Forest, c. 1927. Courtesy of the archives of the Forest Resource Education Center (F.R.E.C.).

The Bucto Wildfire

Flames crowning into the Pine Canopy. Photograph of the Warren Grove Wildfire, at Route 532, April 20, 1994.

Firewarden's Narrative

A Report of the Bucto-Harrisville Fires, May 2–13, 1930
Written by J. C. MacDonald

Cause

This fire was caused by Mr. Lang of Bucto Road.[1] He was burning rubbish with a permit and allowed the fire to escape into the woodland next to his house.

History of Work on Fire

The fire escaped on May 2, at 11:30 a.m. Standard Time, and was discovered about 11:45.

A crew was put on the fire in a few minutes. The wind was blowing from the South west and carried the fire toward Greenbush road. The crew were placed on the Greenbush Road, and the fire was held in the block between the two roads. It burned an area of approximately 30 acres.

The next day (May 3) the fire broke out and we were obliged to fire in[2] along the Greenbush Road. At approximately 1:00 p.m. the fire crossed the Greenbush Road and caught in a sawdust heap about 200 feet east of the Greenbush Road.

We trenched around the sawdust heap and held the fire there until the next day at 1:00 p.m. The fire then broke out approximately 100 feet east of the sawdust heap.[3]

---

1 Bucto Road then extended northward from an intersection with State Route 4 (now Route 9) east of the Bass River bridge. Although now a short cul-de-sac, it originally paralleled the east side of the river, northward and into the State Forest.

2 To "fire in" is to set a backfire intentionally, creating a burned area that would deprive an approaching wildfire of fuel and arrest its progress.

3 The Pinelands then contained numerous sawmills that converted timber into cedar, pine, and oak lumber. The mills accumulated large quantities of sawdust and log slabs that were fire-prone when dry. Accidental fires could burn intensely and be difficult to extinguish, and might burn the mill down.

We saw as soon as it started, but, before we could run the 100 feet the fire was beyond our control.

We immediately went to the State Highway Bridge at Job's Creek and tried to fire up along the west edge of the stream. The fire was upon us before we could get an effective backfire started.

We found we could not control the head fire, which jumped the concrete road and burned to the bay shore, so we fired in the sidelines of the fire to protect the houses along the concrete road.[1] We succeeded in saving all of the houses but one. This house was surrounded by grass and weeds, and was directly in the path of the head fire.

As soon as possible we started to backfire in the burning areas. We back fired along an old road from Headley's Farm to the Millie Place, from the Millie Place along the Millie Road[2] to the Greenbush Road, and South at the edge of the woods along the Greenbush Road to the point where the fire started. We completed this work at 5 a.m.

At dawn (Monday) the wind started to blow very hard from the South. The fire which had gone to the Bay Shore on the previous day had been smouldering [sic] all night, and the wind change[3] made a head fire out of the East side of the fire. The head fire was sweeping rapidly toward the concrete road at Wadeson Service Station at Mathistown.[4] We backfired along the South side of the concrete road and held the head fire here. We also saved all buildings in the path of the fire.

The fire along the Millie Road was burning but it was inside of the fired line and appeared to be safe, but to make sure we went to the tower and looked across the burned area.

About half-mile East of our fire another fire was burning. This fire positively did not escape from our fire area because we had patrols on the burning area, and they reported no out breaks of fire.

We suspect that someone set this fire as a backfire because they thought we had not been able to hold the fire on our lines.[5]

The fire was burning rapidly and burning over the Millie Road before we could get enough men in there to backfire the Millie Place and Stage roads. We could not hold the head fire at all, but did hold the side fire by backfiring an old road which crosses compartment 1K.[6]

At night after the fire had burned almost to the Munion Field[7] we went along the edges and put out the fire. We put out the west edge of the fire and Section Warden Jerre [sic] Bozarth put out the east edge of the fire.

On Tuesday morning we found that the fire had broken out in a few scattered spots. These were quickly put out and the area was left with patrolmen. This area was patroled [sic] constantly until all danger was past.

Batsto Fire

As soon as we put out the Bucto fire and left it with the patrolmen we immediately went to Harrisville,[8] as the Batsto fire[9] was beyond control and was coming into our section.

We arrived at Harrisville just as the fire jumped the Wading River. We started to backfire an old road from

---

1 Before paving with modern asphalt, the pavement on the State highway Route 4 (today's Route 9) was of concrete panels, with a distinctive pattern of expansion strips that gave old traffic a distinct "bumpety-bump" traverse and sound.

2 Millie Road is now a cul-de-sac west of Munion Field Road, a short distance from the Stage Road intersection.

3 The strengthening and shifting winds may have been related to a changing weather pattern. Such may result in increasing fire intensity and changes in the direction of spread.

4 Mathistown was a small hamlet on Route 4 midway between Jobs Creek and Munion Field Road.

5 Backfiring was an established tactic for fire containment and property protection. The early State Forest Fire Law provided a specific exemption for a property owner to set a backfire to protect his own property, provided that the backfire was contained on the property and did not escape the owner's control.

6 The Forest Reserve included a number of units for forest management that ranged from several acres to several hundred in size. These were designated for planting of tree seedlings and management of the cedar stands.

7 Munion Field is at the intersection of several historic stage and woods roads between Bass River, Stafford Forge, and Warren Grove: Munion Field Road that originated on Route 4 at Mathistown (now bisected into two sections by the Garden State Parkway); Oswego Road that originated at Martha far to the west on the Oswego River; Andrews Road that originated far to the northwest at Penn Forest; Stafford Forge Road to the east; and Log Swamp Road that continued northeastward to Governors Branch.

8 The historic industrial town was centered around the Harrisville/McCartyville Paper Mill. This "forgotten town" was destroyed by a forest fire in the early 1900s.

9 The Batsto conflagration had been spreading eastward across the Wharton Tract from Atlantic County.

The Bucto Wildfire

Harrisville to the shore of the river. We completed the backfire just as the head fire hit it. The line held and the fire did not jump it. The fire then went back across a bend of the Wading River and jumped the river again lower down. We then backfired along the main road to Harrisville[1] and held the fire in. We completed this firing at 8:00 p.m.

We then went to Harrisville and beat out the fire which had crossed the Wading River above us.[2] Men had extinguished much of this fire in the afternoon, and we completed the work that night in a few hours.

On Wednesday morning we returned to Harrisville at dawn. The fire was out or well under control. We left patrolmen above Harrisville, and went below to Harrisville where we fired in on the previous day. Some of the firing had been done after dew had fallen and was not very successful. We refired the unburned portions of the area and made the line safe.

At noon we went to inspect the New Gretna fire area, and to get lunches for the men.

At one o-clock we returned. As we went up the Harrisville Road,[3] we saw smoke near Bridgeport.[4] The fire appeared to be on the other side of the river, and as the River was 700 feet wide[5] at this point we could see very little danger of the fires crossing the river.

We left sandwiches with the men and returned immediately to inspect the fire. When we returned the fire was sweeping across the Harrisville road. (Local people claim that the fire did not jump the River but was set on this side.)[6]

We drove thru the headfire, but Rueben McAnney[7] and his crews could not follow us. After we went thru the fire, we met Warden Updike.[8] We gave him instructions to attempt to fire in the South side of the fire along the Leektown-Bridgeport Road.[9] He tried to do this but he had only three men and could not hold the fire.

We next went to Nichols Bog on Ives Branch. We had no helpers and could not backfire. The bogs were full of water so we tore out the floodgate and flooded Ives Branch below the bogs.[10] The fire went through the swamp in the tops of the cedars and cut off our escape to the South.

We immediately went to Leektown by way of the Stage Road.

When we arrived in Leektown the head fire was in the village, and had already destroyed two houses on the west edge of town.

The rest of the houses, with the exception of Smith Cramer's, were saved by throwing water on the roofs and sides.

Mr. Cramers [sic] barn was surrounded by brush and had hay stacks piled against it. It was impossible to save the barn, and the burning barn fired the house.

---

1 Today's Bodine Field Road accesses the State camping area and Beaver Branch (formerly Hay) Landing for outdoor recreation on Wharton State Forest. The historic boat landing, near the head-of-tide on the Wading River, was used by cargo scows from downriver Bridgeport and its shipping. The heavy traffic by scows imported salt hay for the manufacture of paper, and exported paper, charcoal, lumber, and pig iron from the Pinelands industries.

2 Rivers and streams in the Pine Barrens are typically narrow and may be bordered by upland forests that are hazardous fuels for wildfires. Windblown firebrands may easily spread spotfires across the waterways and adjacent swamps.

3 Harrisville Road was probably the old stage road from Bass River to Bodine on the Wading River, although the alignment has shifted over the decades. County Route 679 now follows a large portion of the route.

4 The community name of Bridgeport dates back to the early 1800s when a drawbridge was constructed across the river, and the low height of the road deck allowed sailing vessels to dock and unload at what had been Leeks Upper Landing for coastal commerce.

5 The Wading River passed through the Broad Place between Bridgeport and the narrowing waterway as the channel enters the Pine Barrens at Charcoal Landing.

6 A local lore is that a backfire was improperly set and not controlled by a local cranberry grower to protect property in anticipation of the wildfire jumping the river—which it did further upriver.

7 Rueben was the great-uncle of the author, in his mother McAnney's family.

8 Henry Updike was the Firewarden for District 1, lived in New Gretna, and had an early telephone listing of 38R13. His heirs continue to live in Wading River.

9 Today's County Route 653 connects Leektown to Wading River at the Route 542 highway bridge.

10 Floodgates for water control were positioned on causeways that divided individual bogs. The cranberry vines are flooded during the winter. After the danger of frost, which will damage emerging flower buds on the vines, has passed, the water is drained. Although in wetlands, the mat of cranberry vines dries out after drainage in the summer and is at risk from wildfires as the crop of berries develop for harvest in the fall.

We immediately tried to beat out the fire when it hit Merrygold swamp,¹ but the swamp was too dry and the fire burned thru it.²

We went to the Allen Road but the fire was there too quickly to allow us to do much. We backfired in the rear of all houses between Red Tavern³ and the New Road in New Gretna. We saved all houses.

The back fire could not stop the head fire which was racing toward us with a gale of wind behind it.⁴

The fire burned across the West and East branches of Bass River, and continued to burn in a North East direction until the head of the fire hit the area burned by the Bucto Fire.

During the afternoon we beat out the South line of the fire from Bass River to Greenbush Road, fired in compartment 10, and beat out the fire across 1D, 1H, 1E and 1F to the Stage Road.

At night we fired in along the Stage Road as far East as the Bucto Fire Area.

At the same time we back fired the New Road from New Gretna to Bridgeport. This work tied in the entire South edge of the fire.

The next day we tried to tie in the North edge of the fire. Much backfiring⁵ was done along the Allen, Coal, Martha and Oswego Roads. Some backfiring was done along the Bass River back of the French Farm. This was done to keep the fire from creeping out of the cedar swamp and getting into the plantations at French Farm.

The fire in the cedar swamp would apparently go out at night but would blaze up at daylight.⁶ The winds were constantly shifting and it was impossible to tell where the fire would be swept to next.

We decided that we would at least keep the fire from going to Sym Place and Warren Grove so on Sunday morning we took a crew of men to Old Martha and backfired the Oswego Road⁷ & as far east as the Coal Road.⁸ This work took one day and one night to complete but, it kept the fire in our Section.

With the fire tied in in [sic] this manner, we kept patrols on it until several rainy days had passed. Small fires broke out every day until the rains, but the fires were all kept in by the patrolmen.

On May 13 we considered the fire safe but we watched it carefully until all danger was past.

Aftermath

No map has been located for the perimeter of the Bucto Fire, although The Eastern Extent of the Batsto/Harrisville Fire is indicated on the "Wharton Quadrangle Fire History 1924–63" of the State Forestry Services.

The Firewarden's report would summarize the aftermath:

- Burnt, 12,396 acres of forest and 2,464 acres of grass that would include tide marsh
- Suppression cost of $4,083.90—without time or mileage for Section Wardens
- Great damage to the forest and research plots, conservatively estimated as $18,613 with areas: Cedar = 243 acres; Planted upland = 318; Upland not planted = 4,171.89 acres
- Fire statistics for 1930 between March 5 to October 10:
    - Open burning of piles of brush and limbs 1

---

1 Large cedar swamp and associated wetlands extending north from Merrygold Creek and into Bass River State Forest. Historically spelled as "Marigold." The small subdivision of Merrygold Estates is now located adjacent to County Route 679.

2 The southward spread of the fire towards New Gretna was contained at the Mink Path roadway.

3 Red Tavern was the former hotel and post office at the intersection of Stage Road and Allen Road. Then mapped as the old town of Bass River at the forks of the Bass River, it contained an iron forge for pig iron manufactured at nearby furnaces, and a sawmill to produce lumber. It would later become the small community of Allentown north of the Stage Road with homes and a cranberry bog on the West Branch.

4 Large intense wildfires typically generate their own local "fire wind" of in-drafts of air and out-drafts of super-heated smoke from the flames.

5 Backfiring would involve the burnout of all fuel areas within the control lines and roads around the head, flanks, and rear of the wildfire.

6 Wetlands of White Cedar contain a ground cover of shrubs and moss that can dry out during summer heat and droughts, and become flammable with underground turfing that can persist for weeks without visible surface flames. This can consume several feet of the organic turf, lower the ground surface, and destroy the underground root system without the tree foliage having been burned or scorched.

7 Oswego Road burned over by 1994 Warren Grove-Bass River Fire between Allen Road and Coal Road.

8 Coal Road extended north from the Stage Road east of the Bass River near today's Pilgrim Lake, across the East Plains and to Warren Grove. The name doubtlessly evolved from the historic Pinelands industry of charcoal production.

The Bucto Wildfire

Approximate origin and spread paths of Bucto Fire and "Harrisville" section of the Batsto Fire.

- fire = 40 acres
- Discarded materials or carelessness by smoker 1 = 4,988 acres
- Cause of fire undetermined 6 = 12,412 ¾ acres
- Total = 17,439 ¾ acres
- 108 fire permits issued by local firewardens

The operational area then covered by Section B-12 of the Forest Fire Service was north of the Mullica River, and extended from Green Bank and Jenkins eastward to Barnegat Bay and Little Egg Harbor. The northern part of the region is described in MacDonald's report as uninhabited and consisted "largely of high arid plains which support a growth of scrub oak and pine about 4 feet high. There are few roads or cedar swamps to act as fire breaks." The southern half was described as coastal and the center of the population was in Green Bank, Lower Bank, Leektown, New Gretna, and West Creek. "This half of the Section is well broken up with roads, many of which are too narrow to be of much value as fire breaks. There are also quite a few cedar swamps which run in a North and South direction across the Lower part of the Section. At some times these cedar swamps will act as fire barriers, but when they are dry, or the head fire is large, they have very little value as fire breaks."

In addition to the pinelands, the fire hazard also included the "fields surrounding the towns, houses and farms in this Section [which] are usually supporting a heavy mat of dry grass. This grass and the presence of people makes a very serious fire hazard."

"The salt marshes that form the East boundary of the section present a great hazard because the local people see no harm in burning them and set many fire [sic] in them every spring." Tidal marshes, when the water was low and the grasses dormant, were flammable to burn with fast spreading fire—similar to the upland grass fields. It was an established practice to burn off the short meadow grass and reeds to enhance the summer growth of the native Salt Hay, *Spartina patens*, for harvesting and pasturage. Historically in the nineteenth century, the hay also provided the raw material for paper manufacture at the upstream mills of Harrisville and Pleasant Mills.

The Tuckerton Railroad traversed the eastern coastal area between West Creek and Tuckerton, and then extended inland through the pinelands from Manahawkin to Whiting where it connected with the Jersey Central Railroad that was routed through the western core of the Pine Barrens. The railway was "classed as a hazard because it cannot be operated without danger of fires during any dry time." Although the Tuckerton spur was east of the Bass River area, it and the other rail lines were a major source of wildfires that could sweep through fire corridors of the Wharton and Bass River areas.

The ignition hazards and wildfires in the Bass River area would have been far different if any of the several considerations for extension of the Tuckerton Railroad had occurred in either the late nineteenth or early twentieth centuries. The most significant would have been the traverse though the core of the Wharton Tract to connect with the Central Railroad at Atsion. This also would have created wildfire risks along the natural fire corridor that followed the same east-west alignment, and coincided with the most hazardous weather of the spring fire season with high westerly winds and low humidity.

The firefighting resources listed in MacDonald's report indicated an organization of 7 Districts, each with a warden, deputy and helpers. The population was relatively low and sparse, and local fire companies did not exist at that time. Additional help might be hired from local farms and towns as well as the timber industry that continued to harvest wood for both lumber and charcoal. Outside of the immediate area, section foremen and railway crews were a workforce to respond to rail side fires and maintain the right-of-way. After local C.C.C. camps were established later in the 1930s at Green Bank, Penn, and Lebanon, in addition to the Bass River S-55, their personnel and equipment also became available. However, it was the Forest Fire Service in coordination with the early Park Service, that provided the basic organization and mechanism to respond to wildfires under the State Forest Fire Law.

A system of utility lines for electricity and telephones, expanding in the 1920s and into the 1940s in the rural pineland and coastal communities, succeeded the older telegraph lines along the railways between different towns and switching towers. The 1930 summary of wardens identified Henry Updike of New Gretna with number #38R13, which apparently indicated thirteen rings on a party line that was shared with others in the community. Updike's other endeavors from this home on North Maple Avenue included the buying of furs from local trappers, skinning, and sales to fur brokers. Levi Downs Sr., of Wading River, could be contacted through the telephone operator for the party line to a phone #75D.

Equipment relied upon hand tools that might be readily available from local work and farming: shovels, brooms, buckets, axes, brush hooks, rich tools (heavy-duty "fire rake" with cutting teeth on the head), garden rakes, and turf hoe. Improvised "tools" included tree branches, shrub brush, and wet burlap sacks. These could be used to "brush out" by beating down very low flames and spot fires. Firing devices were described as Hauck torches and firing irons. Backpack tanks with spray nozzles were and still are manufactured as D. B. Smith "Indian" Tanks that could hold 5 gallons of water. Originally of light sheet-metal construction, more-modern tanks are of fiberglass or plastic; and now include "bladder bags" of lightweight fabric or rubberized material. Transportation of firefighters and equipment originally relied upon horses and wagons, but at Bass River the pick-up truck from the State Park was also available.

The names of "Bucto" and "Greenbush" are now relegated to street signs—and not to place names. However, the small subdivision of Offshore Manor on the old "concrete road" is east of the Munion Field Road where the Bucto fire was contained. Forestry plantations from the C.C.C. plantings continue to grow

C.C.C. firefighters with "Indian Tanks." Courtesy of the archives of the Forest Resource Education Center (F.R.E.C.).

along the paved but narrow street, which now provides driveways to scattered houses. To the north and east of the intersection with Stage Road, extensive wooded subdivisions extend into Little Egg Harbor Township. Coincidentally, the northern part of Munion Field Road was backfired as the control line for the Ballangers Wildfire of 2021 that originated at Offshore Manor, and spread northward to threaten the Wildland-Urban Interface along Stage Road—where a protective control line was backfired in the rear of the homes without the loss of property.

About the Author

Horace A. Somes Jr., a lifelong resident of the coastal New Jersey Pinelands, spent his career working for the New Jersey Forest Fire Service and as an environmental consultant and in various NJDEP positions. Though retired, he is currently a member of the Tuckerton Historical Society and operates the family Wading River Christmas Tree Farm. He also continues his activity in various local organizations for fire protection and emergency services.

The 2021 Ballangers Wildfire between Munion Field Road in Bass River, Otis Bog Road in Little Egg Harbor, and Stage Road. Courtesy of the New Jersey Forest Fire Service.

Maurice River Memories

Joseph S. Reeves

The Garden of Eden

My dad always arose early in cold weather to get a fire going in the big iron range and take the chill out of the kitchen for the rest of us. Today wasn't real cold but when he shook me awake he'd already been up for some time. We kept as quiet as possible, because it was very early on Saturday morning and there were five others still sleeping. My older sister, Irene, wouldn't be going to her job in Millville today and there wasn't any school in Port Norris for Louise or me. Our living room was being used as a bedroom for my grandparents David and May McClain, who were old and in failing health. Mom worked a lot nowadays to take care of them and us too and still manage the house. I know she'd been up a during the night for my grandad, who was going on eighty-three.

With three final stories, we complete our republication of Joseph S. Reeves Jr.'s Maurice River Memories: Cumberland County, New Jersey 1937–1947 *(1993), begun in* SoJourn *5.1 (Summer 2020). Reeves' stories, chronicling his adolescence in the Mauricetown area, are at once time capsules and love letters to life on the Maurice River in the first half of the twentieth century. The river supplied the fish, game, and employment that enabled the extended Reeves family to live a good life, hard-working but happy. With the passage of time and the intrusion of the outside world, particularly America's participation in World War II, life on the river would change. Reeves has depicted a time now gone, but one worth knowing. These stories have been republished with the kind permission of the Mauricetown Historical Society, the copyright holder, for which we are very grateful. The accompanying illustrations are from the original printing.*

I made a trip to the outhouse in the corner of our backyard. The air felt cool for mid May, probably around forty degrees. In the early morning twilight all but the brightest stars had winked out. The planet Venus glowed brightly low in the east and Jupiter was descending in the west. Back inside I drew a basin of water from the well with the iron pump and washed up. The cold water on my face felt good and woke me up fast. We ate hot oatmeal with milk; I topped it off with a thick slice of Mom's homemade bread and jam, washed down with a glass of tomato juice.

After slipping on our hip boots and our well-worn jackets and caps, we checked the backyard ice chest. Last night's cool temperatures had prevented much melting and a good layer of chipped ice covered the half dozen roe shad left unsold from yesterday. We made sure the ice was well insulated with more newspapers, the lid was tight, and a tarp was draped over the chest. We tried hard to keep cash outlays for ice to a minimum. Mom would probably sell these fish to people stopping by while we were out on the river this morning. Anyone interested wouldn't miss the painted wood sign with the word "SHAD" nailed to the maple tree out front.

In the dim light we saw the little brown wren flying to her birdhouse mounted on a tall post near the corner of the garden. We were sure she had a brood inside, because she was making many trips carrying bugs and anything else she could find. The little wren nested here every year. This was 1943, four years after I had made the birdhouse, so I wasn't actually sure it was the same wren every year.

Dad started gathering up a linen gill net which had been spread on horizontal poles to dry overnight. As he stacked the net on a piece of canvas, Dad paused at the cork floats, which were attached every six feet with two and a half foot long cords. He took an extra half hitch around each float, thus shortening the cords to one and one half feet. We were going to drift the net upriver today, where the depth was not as great. The eighteen inches of float cord plus the fifteen-foot depth of the net would cause the lead line to average a distance of almost seventeen feet below the surface. I folded the four corners of the canvas over the net and carried it in one hand like a sack. A dry shad net, floats and all, weighed only about fifteen or twenty pounds. Dad got a pair of oars which were leaning up against the house. He took a third oar along, because heavy wear at the places where they bear on the steel oarlocks indicated one could break.

We were anxious to get on the river, so we didn't tarry to check my backyard vegetable garden, which looked green and neat in the growing light. Our cats were curious and followed us to the river, hoping we would clean a fish. They watched forlornly when we pushed off from the wharf and rowed out into midstream toward the bridge. I rowed through the main draw under the bridge, waving at the bridge tender, Dewey Stites, who waved back while leaning against the railing above us. The fast current in mid river aided our progress. It was a nice morning on the river with the wind calm and the surface glassy smooth.

A short way above the bridge, Dad motioned me over to a spot about twenty yards off the east bank. I rowed slowly cross-river while he laid the net off. The sun was coming up behind the tree line beyond Woody Boggs marsh a half mile to the east. The flood tide swept us rapidly upstream and, for a few minutes, we raced the orange ball through the distant trees. The flat cork floats laid on the glassy surface like pancakes, but one at the far end started bobbing like crazy before Dad was through laying off. It was a strike, but it would have to wait until the entire net was in the water. I spun the boat quickly when Dad flung the end buoy away, and rowed back to the far end. We boated a five pound roe and our day was off to a good start.

We drifted through Upper Mauricetown Reach with no more luck, then I towed the net around the bend into Bricksboro Reach. The tide was moving fast, so I had to row hard, but I was nearly seventeen and could handle it. Dad gave me advice on how far away from the banks to drift the net. We drifted by the bungalows which sat near the shoreline at Bricksboro. Bricksboro is the first high ground (land elevation above peak high tide) on the east side upriver from Dorchester. On the west bank Mauricetown sits on the first high ground upriver from the Delaware Bay. The marshes take over again above Mauricetown and Bricksboro. The tree line marking high ground sits back one quarter to one half mile or so on either side. The river's Flood Plain is even wider in the lower reaches, especially on the west side downriver from Mauricetown.

The sun climbed higher as we drifted up Bricksboro Reach, taking two shad there. Swinging the long gradual bend around Old Ferry, we tried not to tow the drift net any more than necessary, because fish did not gill well when the net was taut. We did take a strain on the net occasionally to keep the fast-moving current from drifting it aground on the river bends. We caught another roe shad in the upper part of Steep Run Reach and Dad swapped places with me for the pull around the bend into Port Creek Reach, where the river nearly doubles back on itself.

Dad rowed hard to keep the net in mid channel while the strong current tried to ground it on the north bank. He slowed his pace, then relaxed when we drifted past the mouth of the Manumuskin River, one of the Maurice's main tributaries, which flows down past Port Elizabeth. A small flock of diving ducks was feeding near the estuary. They were repeatedly diving and surfacing—then, as diving ducks do, the entire flock took flight and headed upriver not more than two feet above the surface.

A keen observer would have detected changes in the river by now. It was slightly narrower than farther down stream, the reaches were shorter, and the treeline beyond the marshes came closer. Drifting up past Port Creek, we saw a doe and fawn drinking at water's edge about fifty yards up the waterway. We remained perfectly still but they saw us and darted into the brush. Deer were rarely seen downriver, because the treeline was so far back they had no cover. Here there was a big stand of evergreens about one hundred yards away, so they had ventured out. We then had two strikes in succession and both turned out to be buck shad. There were always more bucks upriver. They didn't sell for as much as roe, but wouldn't be wasted, so we kept them.

Swinging around the gradual bend into Steve Clark's, we noticed a lot of fish jumping. Dad said they were herring. An osprey patrolling overhead wasn't going to miss this opportunity. The bird (my dad called it a fish hawk) swooped down across the river from us and took a fish, then flew off toward Buckshutem. We knew we wouldn't catch herring, which were smaller than shad. They easily swam through our 5 and 3/4-inch mesh. Even small shad, including many bucks, could slip through. The river bank on the south side of Steve Clark's was so deteriorated the flooded marsh beyond looked as though it was part of the river. A few small clumps of mud poked above the surface, marking where the dike used to be. A pair of colorful wood ducks flew along the western shoreline and descended into a stand of dead trees at the edge of the marsh there.

My dad had drifted on the river since he was a boy and knew most of the hazards. He would occasionally tow the net, positioning it closer or further from one bank or the other as we drifted upstream. The river's depth was decreasing as we progressed, although this was somewhat offset by the incoming tide. The net's lead line pulled up a foot or two when being towed. That's why he towed it where he knew a hazard to exist. He towed the net for a bit mid way through Lore's Hill Reach, even while fish were striking, to clear a bad spot. We took two roe and a buck in Lore's Hill. The current started to slow somewhat as we rounded the bend into Bailey Reach with only a half hour or so of flood tide remaining.

The sun climbed higher now, so we opened our jackets and enjoyed its warmth. The shad hit one after another in Bailey's. We had many strikes and wound up taking six roe and a buck there. Our net was close to the west bank when suddenly the last four or five floats on that end all went under. I held my breath for about five seconds until the bottom fast released and everything popped up to the surface. Dad grinned and shook his head once or twice. The river here appeared almost too narrow for our 210-foot-long drift net. Looking cross-river the opposite end seemed to be dragging the shore line: however, when we rowed across the amount of clearance appeared adequate; but then the end we had just left appeared too close to its bank.

Upriver drift definitely slowed when we moved up Spring Garden Reach. On the eastern bank high ground came right up to the river and a forest of oak, gum, and maple covered the land. We drifted slowly through one of the most beautiful places on the Maurice and caught the peak of the flood tide in Acorn Gut. The water here was much darker than downstream, probably because of the tannic acid from the forests along the river and its tributaries. A mallard duck with eight ducklings came out of Menantico Creek and paddled through short rushes in the calm waters along the shore line. The fish were not jumping as much as they had been but one broke the surface now and then.

Our boat floated motionless on the calm water, surrounded by the beauty of nature. The spring foliage covering the banks was lush and green. Bird song and the occasional splash of a jumping fish were the only sounds. I thought about the Indians and how they must have loved it here before the white man came. If I were an Indian and were choosing a place to live, it would be the Maurice River and on the Maurice it would be here in the reaches we called Acorn Gut and Spring Garden. We drank from the river, scooping up the cool water in cupped hands. The water was fresh, not a bit salty as it could be at the flood tide's peak in the lower reaches nearer the Delaware Bay. After about twenty minutes, we noticed a slight drift downriver. We were starting to retrace the seven miles or so back to Mauricetown.

We took two more roe shad drifting down Spring Garden. While dad was untangling the second I watched a flying crow trying to get away from a sparrow which kept diving on it from above. I never could get over how a tiny sparrow could hold sway over the much larger bird. A light morning breeze sprang up out of the northeast. Temperatures had warmed up to about sixty-five degrees and the warm rays of the sun in the clear blue sky felt good. We had just taken a shad in mid river drifting through Bailey reach when the cork floats on the end of the net near the west bank went under. Then the floats on that whole half started going under! We were fast! While dad rowed quickly to the end buoy, I looked back to see the whole net starting to go under with the far end swinging in line with the current. I grabbed the end buoy as Dad rowed close to it and braced it under the stern seat. Dad rowed directly upstream into the current. Only the last two floats on the far end were visible now and the whole net had swung down river, held fast by whatever caught it on the river bottom. All the stories Dad had told me about being fast raced through my mind. However, almost as soon as we took up the slack in the buoy line and towed on the net, all the floats popped to the surface. Dad relaxed on the oars and we were drifting again. Whatever had snagged the net released when Dad pulled it toward the direction from which it caught. He gave me another one of those grins and shook his head again. I could see a little twinkle in his eye.

Now our net wasn't properly aligned cross-river and would have to be towed. Dad switched seats with me again and towed the net from the downriver end, then came back to the west end and towed it round the bend into Lore's Hill Reach. When we cleared the bend and settled on a straight drift, I eased the boat over so Dad could take a look for damage. He pulled the lead line to the surface and worked along it to a spot where a few loops were torn away—minor damage only, about four feet from the end. We had almost missed the fast. Dad dropped the net back in the water and gave me another one of those grins.

We drifted through Steve Clark's, Port Creek and Steep Run, taking a half dozen more roe shad. The ebb tide gained speed and the water level along the banks dropped more than a foot from its high water mark. Swinging the gradual bend from Old Ferry into Upper Bricksboro Reach, we saw a boat using an outboard motor coming upriver along the north shoreline. When it drew closer we recognized Albert and Morty. They were towing Morty's boat. They idled their motor, waved, and pointed upriver. Dad held up both hands outstretched twice, then one hand once, giving them our fish count. They nodded, throttled up to speed and continued on their way. Sounds from the little outboard faded when they rounded the bend into Steep Run Reach.

Dad towed the net around the bend into Upper Mauricetown Reach while I watched a snapping turtle making its way across the river. Most would have thought it was a little stick floating because all you saw was the tip of its nose and a bit of its eyes above the surface. Halfway down reach we took strikes from rock. They hit much harder than shad. Two or three corks would go under suddenly. If the floats popped back up and lay still, there was no use checking because the rock had torn through. At other times the fish became entangled and couldn't escape. We took four rock in about five minutes while more of them tore through the fine thread net. One was a large ten pounder. The others were about six pounds each.

The sun was past its zenith when we closed on the Mauricetown bridge with the tide drifting us downriver fast. Dad got on the oars while I took up the net. I finished taking it in as the current swept us into the main draw under the trestle bridge. Dad angled cross river to our wharf, two hundred yards below the bridge.

The tide was partially down so we had to lift our heavy box of fish up on the wharf. We made one trip to the ice chest carrying eight fish each by hooking our fingers through their gills, then came back and lugged the others up in the box. Mom had sold all of yesterday's fish and a guy was waiting to buy one. He wanted it cleaned, which Dad did for him after I fetched a bucket of water. Another man drove up while we were doing this and bought two bucks. The roe sold for 25 cents a pound and the bucks 15 cents. Both bucks together weighed only six and a half pounds.

Mom gave us dinner but we were interrupted twice by people buying fish. Some asked if we had rock, so they went fast, but Dad put one aside. Some folks like rock because they have fewer bones than shad. Many people bought shad just for the roe, which was delicious when fried. After dinner, we spread the net on poles to dry. We noted several holes from the rock and checked the fast damage. Dad planned to repair it later.

Uncle Robert stopped and asked if we needed ice; he was driving to Ogden's ice house in Port Norris. Mom gave him 50 cents for a 100-pound block. He was driving Albert's old beat-up Ford station wagon and would pick up ice for everybody.

I asked Dad if I could use his spare net, an old one left over from last year, and catch the ebb tide. He tested it for strength first, by putting his hand in a few meshes, spreading his fingers and checking to see if the fine linen thread would break. Shad nets normally lasted for one season but with care they could be used a few times for a second year. He okayed it, so I took the net down to the boat. I had drifted by myself only once, the previous week. A light breeze was blowing from the northeast and the tide was well down. I rowed directly across the river from our wharf and, following the example set by my dad, laid the net off while allowing the wind to drift me back to the town side. Then I towed the net a bit to straighten it cross-river so it was in good position by the time I'd drifted past the shipyard. The ebb tide was slowing halfway down reach with no strikes yet. I was careful to keep the net equidistant from both shore lines. Mauricetown Reach was deep compared to the river farther up but, with the tide full out, it was possible to strike a fast.

I caught slack water just off the point where Mauricetown Reach turns northeastward into Noman's Friend. I watched the long row of cork floats strung out across the river while I thought about how lucky we had been not to have seriously damaged our net on the fast in Bailey's. Was it luck? My dad had drifted for shad on the river for more than thirty years. He knew the river between Leesburg and Mud Haul like the back of his hand. The lucky part was that he was spending his life on this beautiful river providing for us in the way he knew best.

Maurice River Memories

I thought I heard voices but could see no one else on the river or on the banks and there couldn't have been anyone within a half mile. People were talking clearly! Then I looked up to see two free balloons about 100 yards apart drifting overhead. They were only a couple hundred feet up and the occupants, suspended in baskets underneath, were talking to each other. The words "U S NAVY" were painted on the big gas bags. They waved and hollered at me and I waved back. The balloons drifted southwesterly toward the bay. I presumed they were from the blimp base at Lakehurst and thought about the crash of the Hindenburg there just a few years ago.

When the tide started the drift net back upriver there was a strike and I took a five-pound roe. I caught another halfway up the reach, then had to take up for the bridge. I took the net up starting from the town side because the wind was still out of the northeast, which kept the boat from drifting over the top of the net as I took it in. I was surprised to see a roe shad tangled in the last few feet of net. It was around four p.m. when I tied up at the wharf and carried the three shad up to the ice chest. Robert had brought the ice for us so I packed them in with the other fish, which Dad had covered with chipped ice insulated with layers of newspaper.

Dad asked me to take the rock he'd put aside to Ed Fisher, who lived a few houses away on the back street. We trapped on his land in the lower meadow, so Dad gave him fish now and then. On the way back I saw Mrs. Trout tending her flowers. She had been my teacher in grades one through four in our town's little two-room schoolhouse and had even taught Uncle Robert when he went to school there. Bertha Hunter, who lived two doors along, asked me about school as she always did. I thought she already knew I'd be graduating from Port Norris High School next month but told her about it anyway.

Dad was repairing the damage to our net, which had dried. When he finished, we spread the net I had just used on the same poles. People kept driving up to buy fish. They all wanted to talk about the war. Nearly everyone had relatives in the service overseas. Most people asked when I'd be going in. I usually replied that the draft would catch me in another year. One guy bought three shad and wanted them cleaned; we took them down to the river, because it was easier there.

The cats followed us, so Dad threw them the heads, which they dragged off into the bushes while growling and snarling at each other.

About six o'clock, Hammond Ferguson, who had graduated from Port Norris High School in my sister Irene's class last year, drove up and took her to a movie in Vineland. Hammond worked at New York Shipbuilding in Camden and would probably be drafted anytime. Just after they left, Uncle Allen McClain and Aunt Dolda drove in from Green Creek in Cape May County. Allen was Mom's oldest brother. They had come to see how Grandpa and Grandma McClain were doing. Allen was a very successful farmer, a self educated man as were all of Mom's three brothers. I enjoyed chatting with him a lot. They visited for a while, then Dolda said they had to go.

Around eight-thirty I heated some water on the iron range, chased everyone out of the kitchen, made up a screen in the corner from two high-backed chairs and towels, and took a sponge bath. After cleaning up after myself, I joined Dad for the nine p.m. war news on the radio. Dad kept dozing off in his rocking chair while H. V. Kaltenborn described the battles going on in Italy and the South Pacific. Mom had been taking care of Grandpa and Grandma all day and was still busy.

Making a late trip to the outhouse I thought the mosquitoes would be numerous, but a light breeze prevailed, so they were not bothersome. The wind had shifted around to the southwest, temperatures were warmer than yesterday, and there was a light halo around a half moon hanging high overhead. Dad always said it would soon rain under these conditions. I noticed the moon shining on the river, now nearly at peak high tide, and decided to walk down to Haley's wharf.

The river was nice in the dim moonlight. I could hear voices above the gentle lapping of tiny waves against the pilings. Albert and Morty were standing on the shipyard pier talking. Every now and then I could make out a word, enough to know they were discussing where to fish next. The trestle bridge sat waiting to receive traffic, its red and green navigation lights casting reflections on the surface, but no cars were in sight. Then I saw the glow of a cigarette a short distance away and realized it was Robert standing on his dock and looking out over the river.

I wondered why anyone working all day on the river would want to spend time just standing around looking at it.

I walked up to the house, where everyone had turned in for the night. I studied an hour for final exams which were due in two more weeks, then went to bed. I was asleep before my head hit the pillow. . . . .

Fisherman's Luck

I awoke just after daybreak. There was something about this morning which was unusual. I thought for a minute or so before I realized what it was—my dad wasn't up yet. The house was quiet and I didn't hear him moving about. This was different because he was always up before anyone else. Never mind that. I wanted to get going. I donned my work clothes and descended the narrow staircase. The door to Mom and Dad's bedroom was ajar and I could see they were still sound asleep. I slipped on my hip boots and made a trip to the outhouse, seeing what a beautiful morning it was. Actually, we expected this kind of weather in southern Jersey during the first week of May. Not wasting any time, I returned to the house. I worked the handle on the iron pump to draw a basin of water from the well and splashed the cold water on my face. Then I wolfed down a quick breakfast of shredded wheat and milk.

Our shad nets had been drying overnight on horizontal poles in the side yard. I gathered mine onto a tarp, picked up a pair of oars, and headed for the river without delay. The sun wasn't up yet but morning twilight revealed the exposed mudflats along both sides of the river. Low tide would occur in less than an hour. I liked the timing because tidal conditions were right for a drift downriver and return, which meant no hard rowing either way. I saw no one else on the river. This was strange. Here it was at the peak of the shad season and my dad and uncles were not to be seen—very unusual. Maybe it was because no big catches had yet been made although the first shad had been taken more than three weeks ago.

I rowed my bateau a few yards off shore and started laying off immediately. There was no wind at all so I headed for the opposite bank, gave a shove on the oars then dispersed net over the stern until the boat's momentum slowed. I turned around, pushed on the oars again, then repeated the process until the entire 210 foot long net was in the water and positioned cross-river. I had a strike when only half the net was in the water. It was a hard strike, several corks bobbing crazily on the glassy smooth water. As soon as I finished laying off I let go the end buoy and rowed back but another hard strike occurred midway along the net and I checked it first. I took a four-and-a-half-pound roe shad while noting that the floats where the first strike happened were still partially submerged. This showed that the fish was still in the net. It took me a minute or two to get the tangles caused by the first fish out of the very fine threaded fifty/two cord. Then I rowed over and brought up the other shad, another roe slightly larger than the first.

I had drifted well past the shipyard and hadn't had a chance to straighten the net since laying off in calm conditions. It was bunched up in spots and positioned across only half the river. While I was returning to the east end to tow it, another fish struck. The sun came up while I was bringing this fish in and clearing the tangles. I spent a few minutes straightening the net cross-river by towing it, then relaxed on the oars. No sooner had I done so than there were two more strikes, one midway along the net and one on the far end. While I was retrieving fish from these strikes, the net drifted well down reach. I kept looking back upriver for someone else to come out and lay off but no one did. I took more shad just before reaching the bend into Noman's Friend and had to rush to get them in the boat and start the tow around the point. As I drifted around the bend, I took a last look back up toward town before it was lost to view, but still there were no other boats.

The ebb tide was starting to slow, so I could let the net go slack with a minimum amount of towing around the bend. I stayed on the downriver side of the net, because the rising sun was low and very bright and I could watch the floats with it at my back. Shad kept striking during the drift through Noman's Friend and I kept boating them. The ebb tide had slowed nearly to a standstill as the net drifted through the bend into Dorchester Reach. Downriver drift stopped completely when the Dorchester shipyard came into view. One end of the net had lagged due to unequal currents on either side of the river. The net wound up in mid river more or less positioned parallel with the banks. I hadn't put a box to hold fish in the boat. Shad were scattered from bow to stern and I counted fifteen, all good-sized roe. Ordinarily a catch of six or seven roe shad on a single drift was considered good. I had twice that many and was about to drift back for more!

After a few minutes with the net lying off the river bend between Noman's Friend and Dorchester reaches, the flood tide started the net drifting back up river. The end which was farther downriver started drifting up first. Shad started striking again and I was busy all the way up Noman's Friend boating them and keeping the net positioned cross-river. Fish started striking in pairs. Every fish was a good-sized roe. The tow around the bend into Mauricetown Reach was easy again because the tide hadn't gotten up to full force and there was very little wind. After I relaxed on the oars with the net in good shape for the drift up to Mauricetown Reach, I took a look upriver but there was still no sign of anyone. I couldn't remember when I had been the only one out on such a good morning and my dad, who always beat everyone out, was still not to be seen. All the way up the reach I kept taking fish out of the net, with hardly any time to keep the tangles clear or to keep it positioned in mid river.

The tide was moving at good speed when I passed the shipyard and had to take up for the bridge. Fish were still striking while I was taking the net up. I boated three shad along with the net, laying them aside with the net around them, because I was drifting into the bridge fast and couldn't take the time to remove them. I got the net all in as I passed the south end of the bridge pilings, grabbed the oars, swung the boat around and headed back to our wharf against the strong tide. I didn't know for sure how many fish there were in the boat because there were too many to count while rowing. I still saw no one out on the river.

The tide was still low and I couldn't climb over the wharf with both hands carrying fish. I ran the fingers on my left hand through the gills of four shad, climbed the wharf and ran for the house. I dropped the fish in the ice chest out back and went inside. Everything was quiet as I had left it. The clock said 7:30. I got my dad up right away and told him about the catch, then ran back to the river, carrying a box. I untangled the three fish that were taken up with the net, then loaded all the shad in the box. Just then Dad came down and helped me. We took the heavy box of fish up to the ice chest. I had caught thirty-six roe shad on one drift, all good-sized roe. That was more shad than we normally caught all day long.

I got back in my boat and started rowing downriver for another drift. Dad had to go back up to the yard to get his net off the poles and would be right behind me. I angled over to the east side for the row down Mauricetown Reach; the row against the current would be easier over there. About halfway down reach I saw activity underway back up near the wharves. First I saw my dad rowing downriver then saw Uncle Robert in his rowboat, heading my way. Before I got much further, I saw Frenchy Gerbereaux start out. I couldn't figure out why Albert wasn't coming out too.

It took me about forty minutes rowing against a strong flood tide to reach the lower end of Noman's Friend Reach, where I started laying off. A light northerly breeze had sprung up, so I dispersed the net from the north side of the river as the wind drifted me across. When my net was partly in the water I saw Dad rowing along the shoreline more than halfway down reach. Uncle Robert was a short distance behind him and Frenchy was just rounding the point. When I finished getting my net in the water I saw a boat using an outboard motor round the point behind Frenchy and pass him up. It was Uncle Morty. As had happened on my earlier drift, I started getting strikes right away and took the first fish out of the net while my dad was starting to lay off about two hundred yards downriver. The currents in Noman's Friend started playing tricks with the net as they always do when the tide is running strong. In mid reach the net was aligned up and down the river, bunched up in places, and not placed well. Today it didn't matter. Fish kept striking no matter what position the drift net was in. Uncle Robert yelled something at me but I couldn't hear him because Morty was too close with his outboard. I held up a couple of shad that I'd caught on this drift already and went back to tending the net.

The net wasn't in good position at all approaching the bend into Mauricetown Reach, so I started towing it early. The strong tide tended to send the net toward the opposite shore but I had no trouble towing it around the point. Houk was rowing downriver while I was still towing the net, and passed close enough to ask me what was going on. I kept towing my net while yelling to him about all the shad in the river and he wasted no time in continuing on his way. I drifted up Mauricetown Reach, taking shad frequently, took up the net just before the bridge and headed back downriver for another drift. I counted twelve more roe shad as I rowed back. I tried to stay out of the very strong current by keeping as close as possible to the eastern shoreline. Dad and the others were drifting upriver as I rowed back and I could see them taking fish out of their nets frequently.

It took me a full forty-five minutes or so (we didn't own watches so I had to guess the time) to return to the lower end of Noman's Friend and lay off again. The other boats remained at about the same interval as on the previous drift, behind me. The tide was very strong this time so I had to row hard on the tow around the bend into Mauricetown Reach but the fish were striking at least as often as they had on the earlier drifts. I took fifteen more shad. After taking up for the bridge, I rowed over to our wharf to get them on ice. I made two trips with the box holding half the fish each time.

Mom said that Albert wasn't around. We guessed that he had gone upriver while I was on my first drift. We were going to run out of ice, so Mom went across the street to ask Hattie, Morty's wife, to call for the ice man to stop on his route. I headed back down to the boat but just before I pushed off from the wharf Mom came after me. She asked me to come back up and help her with Grandma McClain. I half hitched the boat painter around a piling, then followed Mom, who had already started back up to the house. Grandma McClain's health had been satisfactory until Grandpa McClain died February 1st after a long illness. After that she started acting senile and sometimes what she said wouldn't make any sense. She was walking slowly up the street, not looking capable of going very far. I caught up with her in front of Carolyn and Ida G's. She told me she was going to walk to Leesburg and couldn't stand it here anymore. I knew she was not responsible for what she was saying, and tried to calm her down. I was somewhat surprised when she let me take her arm and lead her back to the house, where Mom managed to make her feel comfortable. After that I headed for the river again.

My dad and Robert had finished their drifts and were rowing back for another. Morty was just taking up his net as I rowed across to the east bank and started downriver. He started his outboard and caught up with me and offered me a tow, which I accepted. I threw him my painter, which he half-hitched around an oar wedged under his boat's stern seat. He hollered at me from his boat but I couldn't hear him over the engine. I think he was asking me how many fish I'd caught. We overtook my dad and Robert. Morty took them in tow too. While he pulled us downriver, everybody tried to yell at each other over the outboard's noise. Robert and Morty were very excited and screamed and laughed at each other over the noise. My dad just grinned a lot and didn't say anything. We were all doing well. There was a big shad run coming upriver today. Morty towed us to the lower end of Noman's Friend and left us along the bank while he went out from shore a bit and started laying off. We would take our turns in the same order that we had been rowing downriver so dad was next, then Robert. While we all waited for Morty to drift upriver a distance, we compared counts. I had a big running start on everybody because of my early drift.

The sun had passed the zenith well before it came to my turn and the tide had slowed a bit. I laid off knowing that I wouldn't have enough upriver drift to make it to the bridge this time. The wind died down and with the sun high in the sky it was warm. I had my shirt off and was getting a very dark tan because of getting the reflection of the sun off the water, as well as its direct rays. I would have burned except that I already had a good tan going from the past couple of weeks on the river. It would have been very funny if anyone could have seen me in a bathing suit. I was dark tan from the waist up and pale as a ghost below that. The fish kept striking as I was drifting up Noman's Friend, then the tide slowed a bit as I was rounding the bend into Mauricetown Reach. I had been so busy for the last several hours that I suddenly realized it was well after noon, and hunger pangs overtook me. On an ordinary slow day I would have taken up my net when the tide stopped upriver drift and gone in to eat. Not today. There was no letup in the shad run. Every few minutes a fish would strike and I boated it. I caught slack water midway up the reach and could see Robert drifting just off the shipyard and my dad nearly at the bridge.

I heard airplane engines and looked up to see a navy F4U Corsair tangling with one of the P47 Thunderbolts from Millville Army Base. They were not more than a couple of thousand feet up and they were really putting on a show. Of course, I was rooting for the navy guy. I had been sworn into the navy's aviation cadet program just over a month before—on March 31st. I removed the little identification card from my wallet and took another look at it. My military service number, 768-42-68, was typed on it. Three months ago I wasn't sure what the future would bring. At that time I expected to be drafted into a branch of the military service when I turned eighteen in June. Then I heard this guy on the radio early in February: "*High school graduates can join the navy's aviation cadet program. Receive eight months of college and fourteen months of flight training and become a naval aviator.*"

Mom accompanied me in February when I took the written test and physical at the Office of Naval Officer Procurement in the Widener Building on Juniper Street in Philadelphia. I had to make more than one trip to get the written and physical exams and the interviews. The officer interviewing me said that only five or ten percent of guys entering the program would eventually get their wings. Mom and Dad didn't want to sign the papers giving me permission to fly but they finally did; they knew I would be drafted anyway. The navy was soon going to let me know when I'd go on active duty. That's why I kept checking the mail right on time every day.

I'd never been up in an airplane. In fact I think about as close as I'd ever been to one was when some guy landed in Al Hilliard's field when I was about nine or ten. I could still remember it well.

I came out of my daydreaming when the tide changed and the net started to drift downriver. I drifted to the lower end of Noman's Friend, then rowed back up to town. I had caught another twenty-two roe shad, so I took them up in two trips to the ice chest. I put away two of Mom's big whole wheat bread sandwiches. Then I chipped some ice onto the fish in the chest from a one-hundred-pound block which had been delivered from Ogden's ice house in Port Norris. Dad came up from the wharf carrying five shad in one hand and four in another. I went back to his boat and helped him bring a couple dozen more up. We both went back down to the river to lay off again.

I made two more drifts to the lower end of Noman's Friend and started a third but took up at the lower end of Mauricetown Reach. The fish stopped striking and we had caught so many we didn't have a place to put them. When I tied up at the wharf and brought the last fish up to be iced down, the count for me was one hundred and eight roe shad. Everyone else had done extremely well but didn't come close because they were late getting started that morning. Albert came in a few minutes later, around five o'clock. He had gone upriver and done very well. In fact he had actually caught one hundred and ten shad. Several of them were bucks. Even so, that was a lot of fish. We found out that he had laid off above the bridge around sunrise—about the same time I was catching slack water at the bend into Dorchester Reach.

Mom had sold a few shad during the day to customers who drove up in cars. Billy Dill, who owned Dill's Fish Market in Bridgeton, drove up in his truck. A truck from Hickman's in Ocean City arrived about the same time. They purchased all the shad from everyone, paying 22 cents a pound for roe and 10 cents for bucks. Shad sold very well during World War II because there was some rationing and meat shortages.

While we were weighing up the fish, Louise came running with the mail from Boyden's post office and handed me a letter from the Navy Department. It ordered me to report for active duty at the navy V-5

1940: LIVE CARP ARE TRANSPORTED BY TANK-TRUCK AFTER WEIGHING

unit at Drew University in Madison, New Jersey, on July 1st. They sent me some vouchers to purchase bus and train tickets. Mom and Dad didn't seem too happy but it was too late to change anyone's mind now. The more I thought about becoming a navy pilot the better I liked the idea anyway.

Mom gave us supper and we ate everything in sight; we were hungry because of all the rowing we had done that day. I should have been tired but wasn't, either because of all the excitement from the big catch or because of having received the orders to active duty. I had an unused "A" ration coupon worth four gallons of gas. About six-thirty I cleaned up, jumped into my '29 Plymouth, and headed for the bowling alley in Millville. I didn't drive the car a lot, because gas was rationed to four gallons a week for anyone without a "job." I drove to the lanes on Buck Street and ran into my friends Joe Shannon and Bill Newhouser there. I told them about my navy orders. They were my age and would soon be drafted, so they were interested.

Joe and Bill had become my friends the previous summer. We all went to work about the same time at Armstrong Glass, in Millville. The three of us couldn't get interested in the factory routine and got into trouble by just goofing off. They tolerated our behavior for a few weeks because of the manpower shortage caused by the war; then the foreman hauled us up before Mr. Dalton, the plant superintendent. Dalton read the riot act to us, including his rather dim forecast for our future. Then he fired us on the spot. It was probably the best luck that happened to me since graduating from high school a few months before. I spent the rest of my 18th year with my dad fishing, trapping, duck hunting, and just being his son. And what a year it turned out to be.

We bowled a couple of games and just for laughs tried to catch the pin boy off guard while he was racking the pins. He had seen wise guys like us before, however, and always managed to escape unharmed. We tipped him and left. I drove to the little submarine sandwich shop on Broad Street at the north end of town near the railroad station. The three of us stood around eating the large subs and talking about what it would be like in the military service. Then Joe walked home and I drove Newhouser down Delsea Drive to his family's gas station at the end of Station Road, dropped him off and came home. Everyone had gone to bed.

Two weeks later, on May 19th, my Grandma McClain died. She hadn't smiled even once since Grandpa had died in February.

The big shad runs gradually tapered off and as usual were gone by the first week of June. Towards the end of the month I parked my '29 Plymouth out front with a "FOR SALE" sign in the windshield. It couldn't be driven: no one else in the family had a license. On July 1st, a week after my 18th birthday, I left Mauricetown and the Maurice River for the navy unit at Drew University.

When my dad and I wrote letters to each other in the years following, the record catch of that May day was often remembered. Dad said that the spring of '44 was the best season ever. He should know because he had been drifting for shad on the Maurice River since 1910, when he was about thirteen years old.

Last Time on the River

The guy I'd heard on the radio in February 1944 was somewhat off on his estimate. "*Eight months of college and fourteen months flight training to become a naval aviator*" turned out to be almost three years. Actually, he couldn't have known then that World War II would end abruptly with the dropping of two atomic bombs on Japan in August 1945. As soon as the war ended there were many opportunities to quit pilot training. Many of my cadet classmates, now free from the threat of the draft, elected to get out. The popular attitude of the country, with the war over, was to forget the military and go back to civilian life. At this point, however, I had definitely decided to finish flight training. Separation from naval pilot training would not be voluntary on my part. The training became more rigid and thorough than it had been during the war, because there was no longer any pressing need to produce aviators rapidly. I finally received my gold wings as a naval aviator in May 1947, much later but much better qualified than I would have been if the original training schedule had been followed.

I spent three more months in advanced training after graduation at Pensacola. My new base was NAS Whiting Field in northwest Florida. There I flew PB4Y2's, the navy's version of the B-24 Liberator. At the end of August 1947, I was granted several days leave before reporting to my first squadron at NAS Patuxent River, Maryland. I decided to spend some time at home. It was the first real leave time I'd had since Christmas of 1945.

By the time I arrived in Mauricetown it was the first week of September and railbird season was underway. My dad had a busy schedule during this period, with several pushing engagements. It wasn't the same as before the war, though. Since Grandad Reeves had passed on in April of 1943 the gunners were scheduling their engagements directly with the pushers. Railbirding had dropped off, because many gunners had either served in the military or had been busy at defense-related jobs. Wartime gasoline rationing had an adverse effect as well. As for the pushers, their standard of living was better than it had been in the '30s. They were not desperate for the supplementary income available from pushing as they had been during the depression. The mood had changed. I remembered former times when my grandad's yard was overflowing with the big chauffeur-driven limousines. The air of excitement which surrounded the big crowd of wealthy gunners and enthusiastic pushers while preparing for their outings was gone.

The town had changed some too. I stopped by the post office to pick up the mail for Mom and saw Boyden Robbins. He wanted to hear all about my training. I remembered from before the war when Boyden told me about being in the army in World War I. Now it was my turn to tell him about the navy. The town's "HONOR ROLL" was still standing across the street from the post office, its white paint beginning to fade a bit. My name was well down the list. The older guys at the top had all left town for the service early in the war. All had been rushed through basic training, allowed to come back home for a short furlough, then sent overseas. Most had returned to civilian life as soon as hostilities ceased.

By now some of the folks in town had given up on my case. I had been home on short leaves several times during my three years of training. They always said, "I thought you were going to be a pilot." Some surmised that a few weeks of training were all that would be necessary. Now that I finally was one, the impatient types were not around. Boyden wasn't one of those. He had monitored my progress and now congratulated me with enthusiasm.

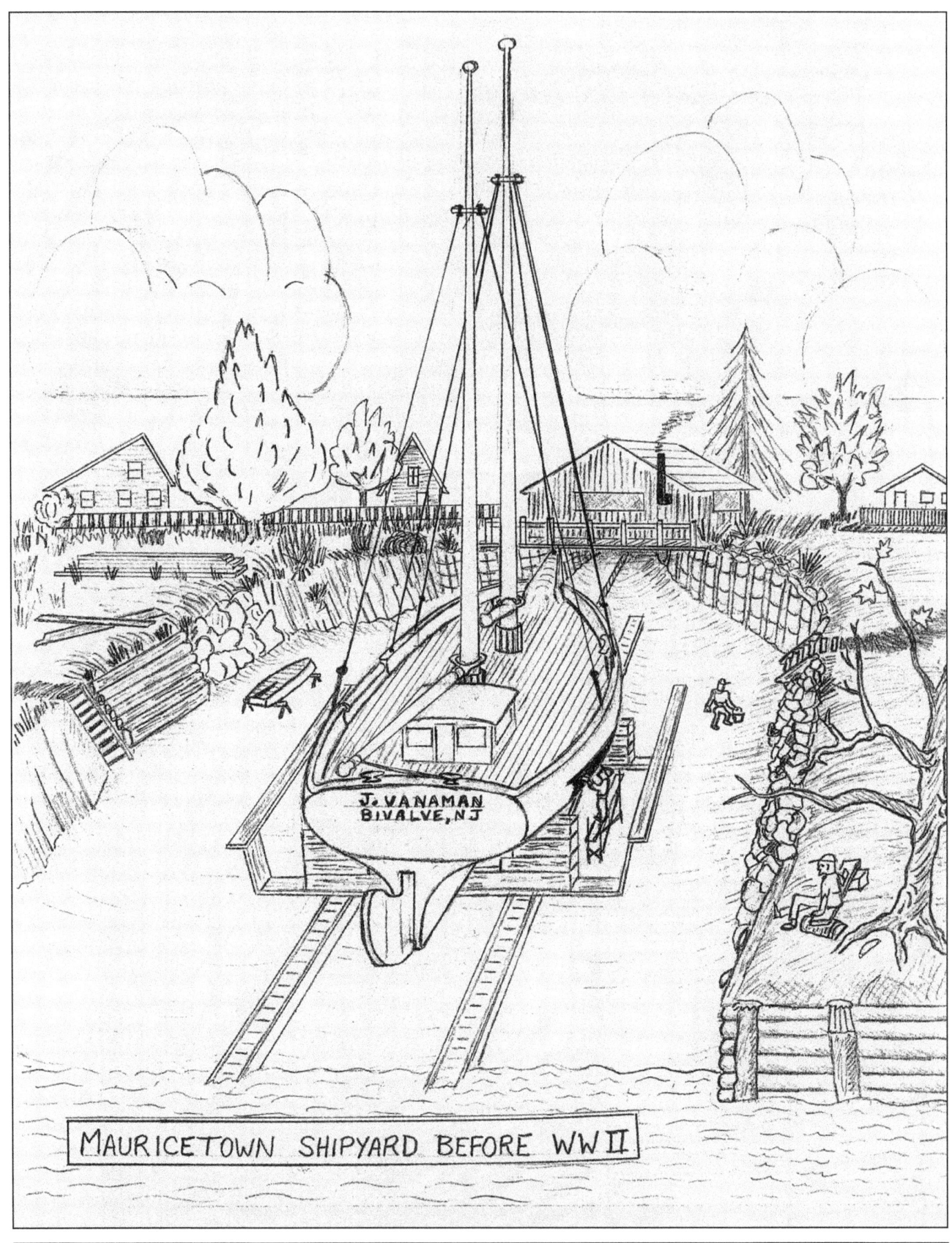

Maurice River Memories

While I was walking home, Jim Steelman called me from his front porch. He was chatting with his dad, Earl Wyatt, and wanted me to settle an argument they were having. I suppose one of them had seen me arrive in town the day before, because right after that their problem came up. Jim said that an army 2nd lieutenant's rank was senior to that of a navy ensign. His case was that army officers wore bigger bars on their collars. Earl Wyatt said the bars made no difference, so the two men were stalemated. I didn't know how to settle the argument without sounding biased, since I was navy. I told them that Earl was correct. There was no difference. Jim Steelman didn't like my verdict and kept up the pressure on Earl. I walked on home and tried not to laugh. The pitched argument faded after I'd gone some distance down the street. If those guys could have known how ensigns regarded rank among themselves they wouldn't have given the subject ten seconds' thought. Maybe I had been away too long already.

My dad offered to push me for a railbird shoot. Although I had spent my youth watching the sport take place, I had never had the opportunity to hunt for rail. Also I felt a bit guilty about having my dad do this. He was fifty years old; I was twenty-one. Railbird pushing is very hard work, although my dad was still in good physical condition. I had just spent three years with a lot of hard physical training. I didn't like the idea of standing in a skiff while my dad worked up a sweat showing me a good time. At first I balked but he obviously wanted to do it, so we made plans.

Conditions for our outing were ideal. Flood tide occurred in early afternoon. The weather was good, a bit on the warm side, with plenty of sunshine and wind almost calm. Dad took the skiff upriver a half mile or so and entered a breach off the west side of Upper Mauricetown Reach. The condition of the habitat was excellent. The marshes were covered by a very thick growth of reed topped with wild oats. Dad had loaned me the double-barreled 12-gauge Fox Sterling which we had used for ducks many times. I hadn't lost my skill with the shotgun; I had qualified in trap shooting in flight training. I shot the limit of twenty-five birds without wasting many shots. I was glad of that because my dad had the opportunity to witness many misses in his day. I didn't want him to include me with that group. I had the chance to see first hand what a great guide he was. I downed several birds in the thick reed. I would have never found them by myself in a million years. Dad never lost one and in fact didn't have to spend a whole lot of time looking. By the time we finished he was perspiring heavily but was grinning ear to ear and enjoying himself immensely. I was grateful that our hunt had been successful. It was the first and last time that we ever went railbirding together.

I spent a couple more days at home while Mom tried to fatten me up with her delicious homemade coconut cakes and lemon pies. We feasted on the railbirds she prepared for us, too. Then I got the idea that my dad wanted to see the river from the air. Mom was not going to be a candidate to test my new wings and my sister Irene wasn't either. Uncle Albert loaned me his car and Louise and Dad came with me to rent a plane.

We drove up to the little sod airfield located on the Delsea Drive halfway between Millville and Vineland. I showed the airport manager a commercial license, which the navy had issued to me in the final stages of flight training. Our training had more than surpassed the requirements for this civilian pilot rating so I was able to get the CAA license on request. The airport manager took me around the field a couple of times to see if I could fly. I was cleared to go after this brief check. He rented me a little red Porterfield with an 85 horsepower engine, the only plane available. It had only two seats, so my dad and Louise had to take turns. I took Louise around the field for a landing or two and she was glad to get back on the ground. I have to give my dad credit for having a lot of faith in me. He wasn't a bit afraid to go up. This did surprise me a bit because he had lived all through aviation's most dangerous years. There had been many airplane accidents since the first flight of the Wright brothers, and the cause of several of them was still unknown.

We lifted off in the little airplane and headed south, climbing to one thousand feet. We had picked a good day for the flight and from over Millville we could make out the Delaware Bay in the distance. My dad didn't say much—the noise level was high—but I did hear him remark about how crooked the river appeared. It was true. The Maurice curves back and forth like a snake within its flood plain. Although he had spent his life on the river and knew full well its twists and bends, the all-encompassing look from an airplane was worth a thousand descriptions. The tide was well up and with the heavy growth of reed in the marshes the river and its surroundings were lush and very beautiful.

We covered the miles to Mauricetown in a few minutes. On our second pass overhead Mom came out of the house and stood in the street. I circled just high enough to stay within Civil Aeronautic Administration rules. Dad had seen me slide the side window open earlier while we were still on the ground and decided it was okay to do this in flight. It appeared to him that the plane was just floating along, not really moving. Many people who go flying for the first time are subject to these same sensations. The illusion was probably heightened by the apparent backward movement of the wingtip across the surface while making turns around the house. He poked his arm out to wave at mom and the windstream slammed his elbow against the window frame. The little Porterfield was only doing 85 miles per hour but when you're not expecting it the wind speed can come as a surprise. It hurt his pride more than anything else; there was no harm done. We circled the town a few more times and then headed downriver again.

Flying at 500 feet gave us enough height to glide to farms close by if the engine failed, and we could see well from that low altitude. With the mouth of the river just over the nose we picked out the high school in Port Norris off our right wing tip. There was no activity on the school grounds, because the school was closed. That was no surprise; my class of '43 had consisted of only 22 students, and attendance had dwindled since then. I turned left to an easterly heading, then circled right in a wide turn over the villages of Maurice River and Bivalve. This gave my dad an easy view. It was the time of year when oystering was in full swing. The river's lower reaches and bay were thick with two-masted schooners. Many were moored along the river banks but some were sailing in from the bay. As we rolled out of the turn over Bivalve, I thought of the trip with my dad to the Dubois sail loft ten years before. It seemed as though a lifetime had passed since then.

We flew upriver heading for Leesburg, with Matts Landing on our right and Peak of the Moon on our left. Dad couldn't see ahead from his tandem seat directly behind me. I made alternating shallow turns right and left to permit him to see the river out the sides. We crossed over the Fish Factory reaches, circled Leesburg twice looking for the old McClain house, then headed for Dorchester with Yock Wock Reach off our left wing. The shipyards no longer contained the hulls of navy sub chasers and mine sweepers as they had in World War II. The meadow south of Mauricetown was still diked in and we circled it twice. I'm sure my dad thought about the many hours he had spent trudging the meadow on foot and rowing in the reaches surrounding it. The little red airplane measured these distances in seconds. We could see plenty of muskrat houses in the low-lying areas of the meadows. We picked out the spot near Penny Hill Reach where we had the successful duck shoot in December of '42.

We approached our house again, this time from Noman's Friend Reach. Mom was still outside; she waved to us once more as we circled. Then we flew northwesterly on the west side of the river, checking out Steep Run and Port Creek reaches and spotting where my great grandmother had lived in Buckshutem. We circled over Spring Garden and Acorn Gut. Laurel Lake shimmered below in the bright sunshine. I tried to take a mental photograph of this entire area which would last a lifetime. We stayed low and flew on as the river narrowed in the upper tidal reaches, past The Brickyard, Ferguson Farm, and the Coal Wharf. Just south of Millville, I gradually eased the plane a bit higher and made a wide shallow 360 degree turn. We took one long last look all the way downriver to the bay. My dad never stopped looking until it was behind us again.

Next day I caught the bus from Millville to the Broad Street depot in Philadelphia, walked the fifteen blocks to the 30th street station and took the Pennsylvania Railroad train to Washington, D.C. I ran into my navy pal Ensign Ernie Tremblay in the Union station there. He had just arrived from leave at his home in San Jose, California. We grabbed a bus for Naval Air Station, Patuxent River, Md., the home base of Naval Air Transport Squadron Three.

A few weeks later I was copilot on a navy R5D transport plane flying from NAS Patuxent up the east coast to NAS Floyd Bennett in New York. The weather was clear and from 7,000 feet altitude the early fall colors of Delaware and southern Jersey were beautiful in the sunshine. Far below I saw the Maurice River flowing its crooked path to the Delaware Bay. We were too high to see clearly anything as small as a rowboat. If I were betting anyone on it though, I'd guess my dad would be on the river now, pushing a railbird hunter, or setting a carp net, or maybe just rowing somewhere.

Someday I would come back—for one more time on the river. . . .

A Vincentown Wedding:
The Marriage Book of Francis Bazley Lee and Sara Stretch Eayre

Paulie Wenger

A recently discovered book holds the key to reconstructing one of the most intricate weddings in South Jersey history. During the summer of 1894, hundreds of prominent members of society from across New Jersey and Philadelphia came to the quiet village of Vincentown to witness Francis Bazley Lee and Sara Stretch Eayre wed. Though the wedding was prominent at the time for its large gathering of politicians, professors, and doctors, history has largely forgotten the spectacle. Like many Victorian weddings, few materials have survived the ceremony with one major exception. A small wedding book, hand-bound in vellum with a striking image of an angel on the front and metal silver initials on the back survives in the archives of a local historical organization. This small book, delicately designed by one of New Jersey's greatest historians, not only allows us to look at the union of two betrothed, but to improve the understanding of Victorian weddings in New Jersey.

Along the western edge of the region of the Jersey "Pines," where the fertile farms, century-old plantation houses, and progressive hamlets of Burlington County merge by slightest graduation into the terra incognita that stretches to the distant sea, lies Vincentown.[1]

At first glance, the small book does not appear overly important. Its design is simple, yet striking, with the silver initials "E" and "L" attached to the back cover. A hand-colored illuminated figure of an angel guards the book's cover. To most, it might just be another forgotten book within the piles of late nineteenth-century volumes found in a secondhand store. Yet this book holds more than just words. Not only was it used during one of the largest events ever held in Southampton Township, but it might just help connect the history behind creating one of its most important buildings.

The quaint village of Vincentown, according to New Jersey historian Francis Bazley Lee, "boasts of no remarkable past." Comparing it to the history-rich towns of Bordentown, Burlington, Moorestown, and Mount Holly, Lee writes that Vincentown "can lay no claim to national distinction."[2] Perhaps, that is why the historical event being discussed here is so important. It is an example of an event that occurs in every town, while also being much more than a simple gathering. For Francis Bazley Lee, one of New Jersey's great historians, it might be astonishing to learn that one of Vincentown's greatest historical moments came from an event that occurs in the summer of 1894: his wedding.

The wedding of Sara Stretch Eayre and Francis Bazley Lee transpired at the Trinity Episcopal Church in Vincentown on June 12, 1894. The wedding announcements, mailed out a week earlier, arrived as public notices appeared in *The Mount Holly News* and *The Philadelphia Times*. The wedding planners expected a large crowd. Before the ceremony could begin, however, these two families deemed it important for the wider public to take notice of their notable upbringing through reading the news articles. It just so happened that both Lee and Eayre descended from extremely prominent and wealthy old New Jersey families.

Francis Bazley Lee was born in Philadelphia on January 3, 1869. He was the son of Benjamin F. Lee, a clerk at the New Jersey Supreme Court

Front cover of the marriage book, depicting the angel that originally appeared in the prayer book of Anne of Brittany from the sixteenth century. Photograph by Paulie Wenger.

from 1872–1897, and the grandson of Thomas Lee, who was a member of the House of Representatives during the Jackson administration. On his mother Annabelle Wilson Townsend's side, he was noted to have descended from the Ludlams, Mays, Willets, and Somers families. From a young age, Francis engaged in the study of history. In 1890, he received a degree from Wharton School of Finance and Political Economy at the University of Pennsylvania. He also traveled extensively, including to Europe, where he "made a translation from the French of the constitution of Belgium." At the time of the wedding, Lee had just completed working as an attorney for Trenton Chancellor Edwin Robert Walker after assisting him in establishing a city sewer system. By 1894, Lee was already heavily involved in public service as a member in the board of managers at State Charities Aid Organization, Trenton's Board of Health, and worked to establish public baths.[3]

Meanwhile, Sara Stretch Eayre was born in Vincentown on April 27, 1867. She was the only daughter of Captain George Stretch Eayre and Marie Burr Bryan Eayre. Captain Eayre, the papers noted, was the "ex-commandant of the Colorado Independent Battery during the Civil War, a military organization that bore much of the fighting in the trans-Mississippi country."[4] Another notable point of interest for the newspapers was her ancestral connection to Colonel Timothy Matlack, the "fighting Quaker of the Revolution," as well as her link to the Burr family of Burlington County through her mother.[5] The Burr family, famous throughout South Jersey notes the Mount Holly News, "furnished wives to John Woolman, the Quaker philanthropist, Governor Howell, of New Jersey, and Jefferson Davis."[6] Though historical references to her interests are not available, it is likely that she engaged in the same activities as her husband.

When the wedding started on June 12, it was instantly apparent that there were too many guests present. Though they had expected many from the early arrivals when the wedding party was entertained at the nearby Coaxen Plantation of Mrs. William Irick the night before, some reports list the guests as numbering into the hundreds, with many unable to gain access to the ceremony for lack of room.[7] Even with the commotion, the Trinity Church in Vincentown was beautifully adorned with masses of palms, exotics, sweet peas, and daisies, which were banked against the alter.

Trinity Episcopal Church in Vincentown, New Jersey, where the wedding took place. Photographs by the author.

The ceremony took place at noon with the bride wearing "a bodice of white colored silk, with deep yoke of ancient point lace" along with a veil that had been passed down by her ancestors.[8] The bridesmaids wore dresses of "white silk crepe with large sleeves, yoke and collar of orchid pink satin" and carried "large bunches of pink Eckford sweet peas tied with white ribbon." As a gift to the bridesmaids, the couple gave them gold enameled pins representing four-leaf clovers with a diamond center. To the ushers, they gave gold enameled knots.[9] After the wedding, the couple hosted a reception at Sara's childhood home and then departed for their honeymoon.

For a historian's wedding, the main draw would naturally be a book. "In place of the conventional bouquet," the Mount Holly News wrote, "the bride carried in her hand a handsome illuminated marriage service book of the Episcopal Church, of original and novel design, and from that book the service was read." What made the book especially interesting was illumination "by hand from a medieval design, the colorings of which were from the Fra Angelico painting of the 'Preaching of St. Stephen' in the Vatican." Adorning the front of the book was an "illuminated figure copied from the prayer book of Anne de Bretagne, of the Souberains collections of miniatures."[10]

The wedding book is quite interesting. On the inside cover, Lee inserted the following hand-written statement as a colophon:

This marriage book was designed by Francis B. Lee; was printed by Frank Smith; the binding by Frank Sigler; the illumination of the cover and initial letters by Augustus S. Clark and the silverwork by Horace Fine—all of the City of Trenton.

The front cover figure was copied from the prayer book of Anne de Bretagne; the colourings being from the "Preaching of Saint Stephen" (La Croix).

From this book, the Rev. Mr. Lighthipe, read, at high noon, the marriage ceremony upon the Twelfth Day of June in the year of Our Lord One Thousand and Eight Hundred and Ninety-Four.

       Francis B. Lee
       Vincentown, N.J.
       June 12, 1894.[11]

While the Reverends Lewis H. Lighthipe and H. M. Barbour used the book to conduct the wedding, it also served as a guestbook and to store the wedding certificate. Although the certificate is no longer attached to the small book, there remain many notable signatures such as the couple's parents and some of their respectable guests. It is apparent that this book was viewed as a status symbol for the newly married couple, meant to represent the prestigious education of the groom, while also showing off the wealth necessary for such a luxury to exist. Marriage books such as this one were simply not cheap and this was a unique opportunity to show a bit of opulence in front of prestigious guests.

Owing to Francis's father's position as clerk of the New Jersey Supreme Court, many prominent politicians attended the wedding. These included then-current Governor of New Jersey George Theodore Werts (1893–1896), a U.S. Senator from New Jersey William J. Sewell (1881–1887, and again, 1895–1901), two former governors in Leon Abbett (1884–1887, 1890–1893) and Robert Stockton Green (1887–1890), the former secretary of the Navy under President Grant, George Maxwell Robeson (1869–1877), multiple former U.S. House Representatives like Anthony Bullock, and several prominent judges. Among the politicians were former military members, such as Generals John S. Irick (Major General in the New Jersey State Militia), William S. Stryker (Adjutant

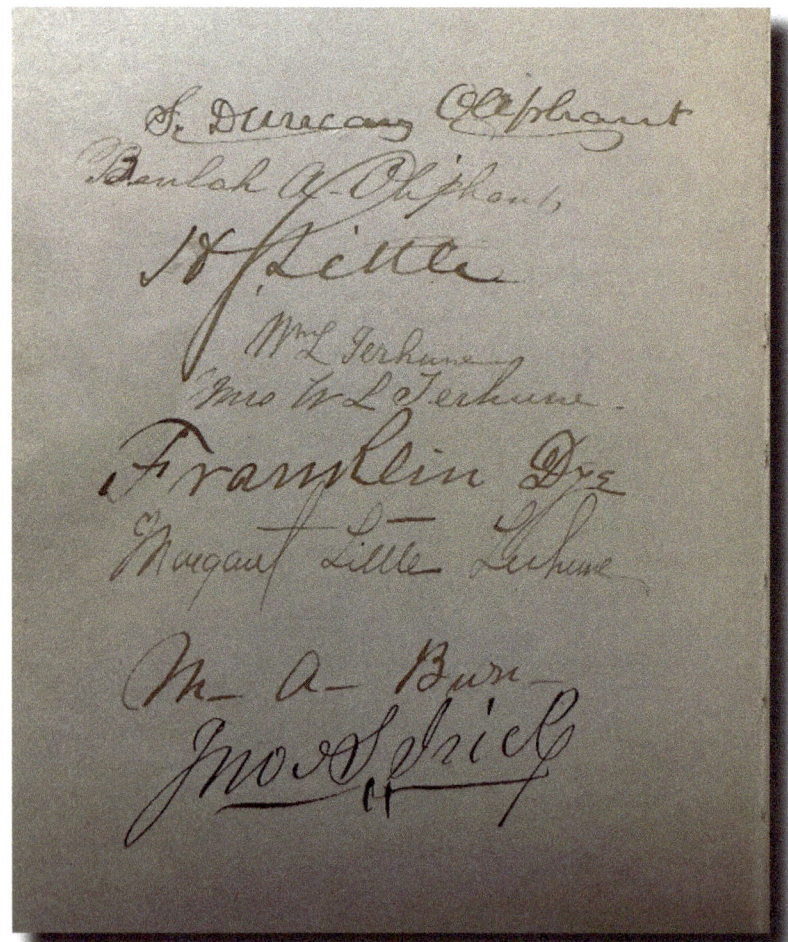

Among the famous guests to sign the book we see John S. Irick, Vincentown's greatest citizen, who served on the staff of Governor Olden during the Civil War as General for the New Jersey State Militia before it became the New Jersey National Guard in 1869 and created the Vincentown National Bank. At the time of his death, only two months after this wedding, in August of 1894, Irick was reported to be worth an estimated $500,000, roughly calculated to be more than $18 million dollars today.[25]

More famous signatures can be seen on this page with Samuel Duncan Oliphant, who served as a Brigadier General during the Civil War. Besides engaging in the battles of Alexandria, Manassas Junction, and White Oak Swamp, Oliphant is most well-known for being sent to Philadelphia to gather men from the military hospitals and transporting them to Washington in preparation of its defense. He ultimately gathered over 1,200 men. After the war, he moved to Princeton and became Clerk of the New Jersey Circuit Court for the District of New Jersey for 34 years.[26]

A Vincentown Wedding

General of New Jersey), and Samuel Duncan Oliphant (Brigadier General in the US Volunteers). Also invited were a large swath of professors from Philadelphia. These included University of Pennsylvania Professors Horace Jayne, Edmund James, and Rowland Faulkner. Other prominent individuals included stockbroker Charles D. Barney, Charles E. Green, President of the Board of Trustees for Princeton University, and Ferdinand Roebling, who was the financial leader of the John A. Roebling Company (the namesake of Roebling, New Jersey), while his brother, Washington, focused on the completion of the Brooklyn Bridge.[12]

Perhaps one of the most significant autographs in the book comes on the second signature page, where we can see the scripts of Sara's cousin, Mary S. Irick Drexel, and her aunt, Sally Stretch Irick Keen.

Mary Drexel was born Mary Stretch Irick on January 22, 1864, to Sally Stretch Irick and William Hudson Irick. As part of this prominent farming family, she was raised on the 240-acre farm, Locust Grove, located one mile outside of Vincentown. While completing her education at Patapsco Institute in Ellicott Mills, Maryland, Mary met George W. Childs Drexel, the youngest son of multi-millionaire A. J. Drexel and heir to his father's business partner and namesake, George W. Childs, co-owner of the *Philadelphia Public Ledger*.[13] After a brief courtship, Mary, at the age of 23, married George on November 18, 1891, in the same church that Sara and Francis wed. Due to the high profile of the Drexel-Irick wedding, the family funded an extension to the church that remains today. As a wedding gift, Mary's new father-in-law gave the couple a home in Philadelphia at 18th and Locust, which is now the Curtis Institute of Music.[14] Drexel, along with her husband, would go on to an illustrious career as philanthropists. The couple became prominent supporters of the Metropolitan Opera Co., and Philadelphia Orchestra, while Mary was well-known for her support of the Red Cross during World War I.

Mary Drexel is, however, perhaps most well-known in Vincentown for her endowment in 1923 to build the public library, named for her mother, which still stands as the Sally Stretch Keen Memorial Library. Perhaps it was the memories of Sara and Francis's wedding, where Mary had been a guest with her mother in the

Perhaps the most intriguing signatures in this book are those of Sally Stretch Keen and her daughter, Mary Stretch Irick Drexel. In 1923, Drexel and her husband, George W. Childs Drexel, would donate the funds to establish a town library in Vincentown, a project that cost more than $20,000. The Drexels had been married at the Trinity Episcopal Church in 1891 and perhaps it was return visits to Vincentown that ultimately led her to donate the library in her mother's name years later. The Sally Stretch Keen Library remains standing in Vincentown to this day.

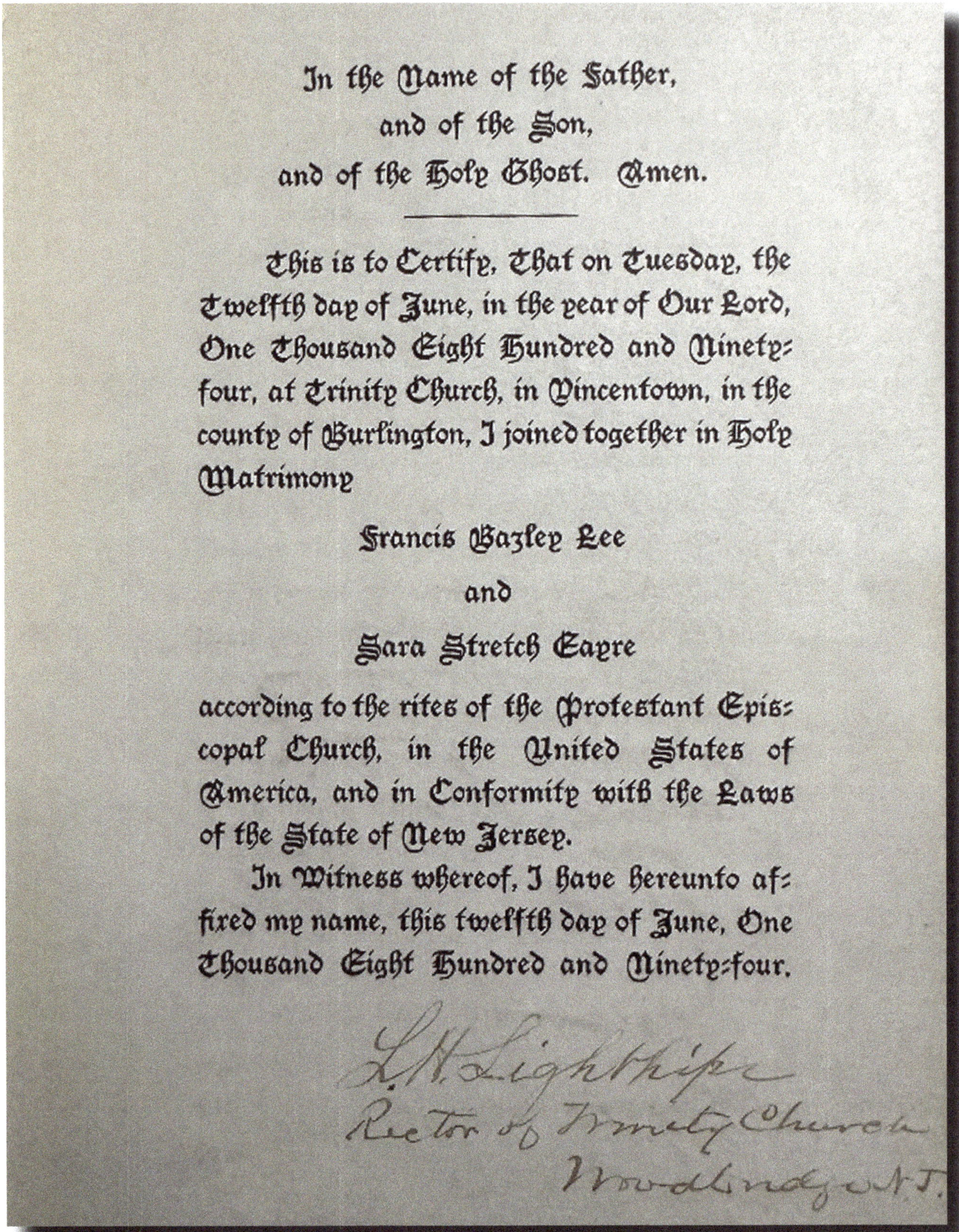

In the Name of the Father,
and of the Son,
and of the Holy Ghost. Amen.

This is to Certify, That on Tuesday, the Twelfth day of June, in the year of Our Lord, One Thousand Eight Hundred and Ninety-four, at Trinity Church, in Vincentown, in the county of Burlington, I joined together in Holy Matrimony

Francis Bazley Lee

and

Sara Stretch Eayre

according to the rites of the Protestant Episcopal Church, in the United States of America, and in Conformity with the Laws of the State of New Jersey.

In Witness whereof, I have hereunto affixed my name, this twelfth day of June, One Thousand Eight Hundred and Ninety-four.

L. H. Lighthipe
Rector of Trinity Church
Woodbridge, N.J.

This is the culminating moment in the wedding and the certification of the marriage ceremony, which the Reverends Lewis H. Lighthipe, of the Trinity Episcopal Church of Woodbridge, New Jersey, and Henry M. Barbour, of the Trinity Episcopal Church in Trenton, New Jersey, signed.

same venue where she had married, that continued to place Vincentown as a special place in Mary's heart. Sally Stretch Keen was named Sarah Stretch Eayre at her birth in 1842, which suggests the derivation of Sara's given name. Either way, the proximity of their signatures in the book denotes that they enjoyed the wedding together.[15]

In the years after the wedding, Francis continued to grow his career as New Jersey's premiere historian. One humorous story shows how high he soared in political circles. In June of 1910, *The Washington Post* wrote that Secretary of State Philander C. Knox had a doppelganger, and his name was Francis Bazley Lee. Lee had come to the capital to see his friend, whom he had met after someone had told Knox that Lee looked like his double. The *Post* wrote, "the premier member of the cabinet wrote to Mr. Lee, transmitting a large, autographed portrait of himself, and requesting a similar image of his counterpart in return. So, each obtained a photograph of the other, and the exchange led to a friendship between the two." Lee's visit in June of 1910 is described as such:

> On a recent visit to Washington, Mr. Lee called on the Secretary, but happened to appear on diplomatic day, when the representatives of foreign powers had the right of way. Nevertheless, the Secretary's double was ushered into the inner sanctum. "Yours being a foreign state, I have had you admitted as the Jersey ambassador," said Mr. Knox, greeting his counterpart. "Otherwise, the rules of the department would not have permitted me to have this pleasure."[16]

Though few news articles appeared in the papers about Sara after the wedding, it is likely that she also moved in the higher circles of society with Francis.

On May 2, 1914, Francis Bazley Lee died at Jefferson Hospital in Philadelphia from several ailments. The *Newark Star-Eagle* published his obituary and noted, "As a speaker and lecturer, Mr. Lee advanced the cause of history teaching by many addresses delivered before conventions of teachers in nearly every county in the central southern parts of the State."[17] His death elicited the praises of many figures, including a tribute from frequent opinion writer Ernest Isitt, who wrote that Lee was "a cultured, courteous, and polished gentlemen, with an utter absence of veneer, a perfect Lord Chesterfield in manner."[18] In the business world,

Cartoon of Francis Bazley Lee in which he is described as "ever busy, but [his duties] never mar his general sociability or detract from his enjoyment of life," Harry B. Salter, *Who's Who In Trenton* (Trenton: Harry B. Salter, 1908), 28.

the obituary noted his accomplishments included the president of the Trent Tile Company, director of the West Jersey Railroad Company, and member of the board of directors of the Mechanics' National Bank. The Newark newspaper enumerated his many accomplishments including his role as the receiver and managing editor of the *Trenton Times* from 1897–98; his attainment of becoming a thirty-second-degree mason; and numerous publications on Garden State history.[19]

In 1915, in recognition of his service towards developing the western section of Trenton, New Jersey, a citizen's committee appointed by the freeholders erected a memorial tablet to the new Sanhican Creek Bridge. The tablet read,

> This tablet is erected to the memory of the late Francis Bazley Lee, a distinguished citizen of Trenton, whose early and unceasing efforts were largely instrumental in the acquisition by the city for park purposes of lands lying along its river front. This avenue and bridge over Sanhican creek leading to Mahlon Stacy Park have been named in his honor.[20]

The book's pages, used in the ceremony, are illuminated in a way that mimics religious texts from the Middle Ages.

Less is known about the life of Sara Stretch Eayre after Francis's death. We do know that she never remarried before her death on November 5, 1935, and that her gravestone at the Vincentown Baptist Cemetery prominently displays her as the wife of Francis and the daughter of her parents.

From this marriage, Sara Stretch Eayre and Francis Bazley Lee had one daughter, Rhoda Lee, who appears in some of her father's writing. In 1902, Hallie Erminie Rives, notable as the author of *Smoking Flax*, dedicated her new wildly successful revolutionary romance, *Hearts Courageous*, to Francis.[21] Rives had written much of the book at the Lee family's home in Trenton, which led the family to keep a close eye on how well the story was doing.[22] One night, Francis heard the three-year-old Rhoda singing with huge enthusiasm a song that he could not place. When he asked her what the song was, Rhoda replied, "Why, papa! Don't you know that? That's 'Hearts Courageous, cleft for me, let me hide myself in three.'"[23] On November 8, 1922, Rhoda married C. Bates Compton, a 1917 graduate of the United States Military Academy at West Point, who served as a Major in the Thirteenth Cavalry during World War I. The Compton-Lee marriage took place at Rhoda's mother's house in Vincentown, likely not far from the small church that housed their own wedding.[24] Though there is no way of knowing when this marriage book left the possession of the family, perhaps it was also there at Rhoda's wedding.

Ultimately, this small book serves not only as an interesting piece of family history from a notable historian but remains an incredibly unique piece of New Jersey folk art, indicative of how Victorians within the state conducted their marriages. It details one of the greatest weddings in southern New Jersey's history and the lengths that New Jerseyians would go towards celebrating their families. And, perhaps most importantly, it shows that Vincentown is not nearly as deprived of historical memory as Francis Bazley Lee once claimed.

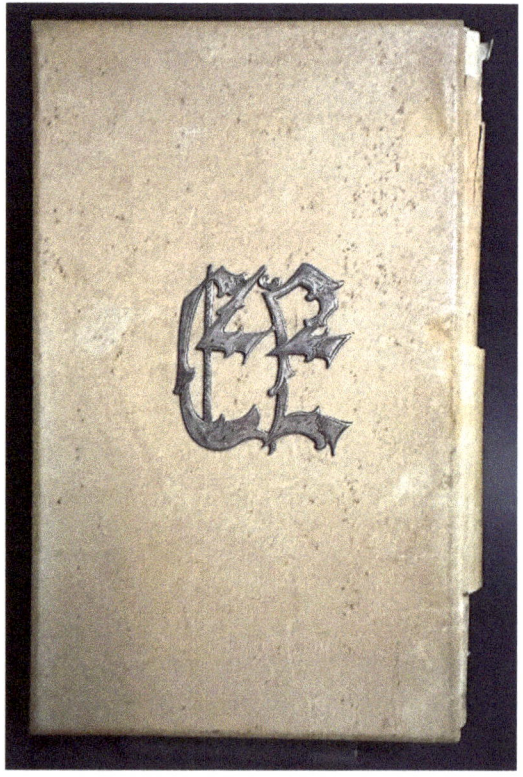

The back cover of the book. The applied delicate silver "E" and "L" represented the union of Francis and Sara. According to Lee, noted silversmith Horace Fine of Trenton was responsible for this part of the marriage book.

A Vincentown Wedding

ABOUT THE AUTHOR

Paulie Wenger is an adjunct instructor in History and Sociology at Atlantic Cape Community College. He has worked at several New Jersey museums, including the Burlington County Prison Museum, Princeton University Art Museum, and Whitesbog Preservation Trust. He is now the President of the Pemberton Township Historic Trust.

ENDNOTES

1. Francis Bazley Lee, "A Charming October Idyl: Vincentown and Its History," *Camden Daily Telegram*, October 31, 1894, 1.
2. Lee, "A Charming October Idyl: Vincentown and Its History," 1.
3. "Francis B. Lee, Historian and Lawyer, Dies," *Newark Star-Eagle*, May 2, 1914, 4.
4. "Wedding at Vincentown," *Mount Holly News*, June 19, 1894, 3.
5. Also noted was "Governor John Reed," who might be a reference to Joseph Reed, President of Pennsylvania from 1778-1781, and "other men prominent in colonial and Revolutionary times." See, "Vincentown," *Mount Holly News*, June 5, 1894, 3.
6. "Wedding at Vincentown," *Mount Holly News*, 3.
7. Coaxen Place, spelled Quaxon in newspaper reports about the wedding, refers to the home of the Coaxen Lenape tribe, which was purchased in 1835 by William Irick for $13,500 after the Lenape's land was stolen by the last New Jersey Indian Commissioner, Josiah Foster, through the creation of a fake will. See, George D. Flemming, *Brotherton: New Jersey's First and Only Indian Reservation and the Townships of Shamong and Tabernacle That Followed* (Medford: Plexus Publishing, 2005).
8. "Wedding at Vincentown," *Philadelphia Times*, June 13, 1894, 6.
9. "Wedding at Vincentown," *Mount Holly News*, 3.
10. "Wedding at Vincentown," *Mount Holly News*, 3.
11. Interesting, these names also appear in news articles about freemasons and other organizations in Trenton, which aligns with Francis later becoming a thirty-second-degree mason at the time of his death. For example, see Frank Siglev's inclusion on a masonic roster, "Among the Lodges," *Trenton Evening Times*, April 25, 1899, 4; and Augustus S. Clark's involvement with the International Order of Odd Fellows of New Jersey in "I.O. of O.F.," *Monmouth Democrat*, November 26, 1868. The statement "the colourings being from the 'Preaching of Saint Stephen' (La Croix)" refers to the illustration "The Preaching of St Stephen," completed for Paul Lacroix's *Science and Literature in the Middle Ages* (Bickers, 1878).
12. In a strange twist of fate, in 1912 Ferdinand and Washington would lose their nephew, Washington Roebling II, in the sinking of the RMS TITANIC.
13. George W. Childs was also a notable philanthropist. He donated funds for the creation of monuments to Edgar Allan Poe in Baltimore, William Shakespeare in Stratford, John Milton at St. Margaret's in Westminster Abbey. In 1884, he loaned Walt Whitman $500 to help him purchase his home in Camden, New Jersey. See, Hugh Chisholm, "Childs, George William," *Encyclopedia Britannica*, vol. 6 (11th ed.), (Cambridge: Cambridge University Press, 1911), 141–42; Jerome Loving, *Walt Whitman: The Song of Himself* (University of California Press, 1999), 428.
14. Among the other gifts received at the wedding were an elegant diamond necklace from George W. Childs, a check of several figures from Mary's stepfather, and a solid silver tea service of twelve pieces from Mrs. Childs. See, "At the Drexel Wedding," *Philadelphia Times*, November 19, 1891, 4.
15. In the years after the donation, Mary and George would continue to supply the library with additional books. They would also routinely visit Vincentown, which would be a moment of much celebration for the town's children. Often, they arrived with candy, and residents of the town would later remember that the girls would dress as boys, because they were more likely to get the candy. Mary Drexel died in 1948. Both her portrait, along with that of her mother, hang in the Vincentown Library, along with other historical memorabilia of their life. See, "Overview and History," Sally Stretch Keen Memorial Library, Accessed July 7, 2023, Overview & History | Sally Stretch Keen Memorial Library (vincentownlibrary.org).
16. "Knox's Double in the City," *The Washington Post*, June 14, 1910, 11.
17. "Francis B. Lee, Historian and Lawyer, Dies," *Newark Star-Eagle*, May 2, 1914, 4.
18. The Lord Chesterfield to which Isitt refers is Philip Dormer Stanhope (1694–1773), whose *Letters to His Son*, a reprinting of his lessons to his son, were used as a guide for how to survive the eighteenth-century world through the use of manners, not morality. See, Ernest Isitt, "Isitt Pays Touching Tribute to Late Francis Bazley Lee," *Trenton Evening Times*, May 6, 1914, 2.
19. "Francis B. Lee, Historian and Lawyer, Dies," *Newark Star-Eagle*, May 2, 1914, 4.
20. The bridge that featured the tablet unfortunately collapsed the year after erecting the memorial. It appears they refrained from replacing it. See, "Tablet to Memory of Francis B. Lee," *Camden Post-Telegram*, December 1, 1915, 8.
21. Though wildly successful as a popular novelist, Rives is most well-known for the controversial nature of her 1897 novel *Smoking Flax*, which took a favorable position on lynching.
22. In a report about the book's development, Lee writes that "Miss Rives worked tirelessly over her minutiae of historical detail. I can see her now in the state capitol at

Trenton, or in the library of Princeton pouring over maps, making memorandum, or a transcription." See, *Sioux City Journal*, January 16, 1903, 13.

23 "Out of the Mouths of Babes," *Star Gazette*, July 15, 1902, 6.

24 "C. Bates Compton and Miss Rhoda Lee Wed," *St. Louis Post Dispatch*, November 14, 1922, 19.

25 "Gen. Irick Dead," *Mount Holly News*, August 7, 1894, 3.

26 "Samuel Duncan Oliphant," The Historical Society of the United States District Court for the District of New Jersey, Accessed July 24, 2023, Samuel Duncan Oliphant | The Historical Society of the United States District Court for the District of New Jersey (historynjdc.org).

The Five Stages of *Almost* Drowning

On the night of Tuesday, January 24, 1928, Robert G. Pierpoint, James A. L. Harris, and Albert K. Blinn, the mayor, postmaster, and councilman of Wildwood, departed a town meeting and boarded a boat for what they expected would be an ordinary duck hunting trip. Approaching midnight, they anchored their boat between Stone Harbor and Avalon. Early Wednesday morning their near-drowning experience began. Stage One: Surprise—The men were awakened from their slumber as a growing storm tossed the boat. Stage Two: Action—Trying to gain control of the situation, the councilman weighed anchor; the mayor started the engine; the postmaster grabbed hold of the wheel; and the group made a break for safer seas. Stage Three: Comfort—Deciding that they had avoided the dangers, the officials dropped anchor and planned to wait the storm out until the sun rose. Stage Four: Realization and Fear—Despite their sense of safety, the boat began to fill with water, and the men realized they would not have the luxury of waiting for daybreak. As the gravity of their situation became clear, fear arose. Stage Five: Escape—When the boat thankfully ran aground on a sandbar, Pierpoint, Harris, and Blinn, valuables in hand, clambered to shore and trudged the two miles to safety. Having escaped a potential tragedy, the officials and their hunting-trip-gone-wrong would make the papers not for drowning, but for an *almost* drowning.

Summary description by Ashley Baker, Stockton Class of '25.

"Wildwood Mayor Nearly Loses Life on Fish Trip," *The Daily Journal* (Vineland, NJ), January 26, 1928, 1.
"Wildwood Officials Escape," *The Morning Post* (Camden, New Jersey), January 26, 1928, 1–2.

Wildwood Mayor Nearly Loses Life On Fishing Trip

Wildwood, N. J., Jan. 26—Mayor Robert G. Pierpont and Postmaster James A. L. Harris, of this city, and Councilman Albert K. Blinn, of Wildwood Crest, narrowly escaped death in Great Sound early yesterday morning when their boat broke from their moorings during the heavy storm and ran aground. The three officials were on a fishing trip, and when the storm became so severe, they anchored and waited for daylight. The boat began to fill, and they found it necessary to abandon it.

After salvaging virtually all their valuables, they walked two miles to the Coast Guard Station. The Guards made preparations to pump out the boat with hopes of floating it on next high water.

The Hurley House

William J. Lewis

Nowadays in the Pines, you are oft to see a wayward traveler heading down a sandy dirt road seeking out a forgotten town. The notion of finding a lost town is somehow mysterious, romantic, and exciting. But more than likely, the people who lived in that space and time lived with harsh realities. Life was often hand to mouth. Today's twenty-first-century conveniences—running water, electricity, home heating and cooling, the internet—were lacking in many Piney homesteads up until the 1960s (and later). The photographs below show a location that once was an important family homestead, a wellspring of life for the folks who raised their families there.

Our imaginations tend to fill in the blanks for us, painting pictures with bright cheery colors, whereas inhabitants of forgotten places may have experienced darker colors—perhaps various shades of black or gray. Every cloud did not have a silver lining. Many of the life stories of the poor will never be remembered.

In 1983, by a stroke of luck, a roadside vegetable stand captured the eye of photographer Joseph Czarnecki who at the time was part of a team spearheaded by the American Folklife Center. He was collaborating with several state and federal agencies to document the folklife of the residents of the New Jersey Pinelands. Czarnecki was the main photographer for the project. We are not certain how his image of that roadside vegetable stand was selected as the cover photo for the book *Pinelands Folklife*. To the locals, it depicts just a country farm stand, like so many others to be encountered on the byways of Southern New Jersey.

The photograph, featured prominently on a well-known publication, gives us a rare opportunity to look into the poor farmer's window and peer back at forgotten

1366 Veterans Way, Jackson, New Jersey, as it appeared, April 2, 2020.

Pinelands Folklife. Ed. Rita Zorn Moonsammy, David Steven Cohen, and Lorraine E. Williams. Rutgers University Press, 1987.

The Hurley House

history. Even though the farm stand and home are gone, this time, the story is not lost.

Why did this photograph make the cover? After contacting two members of the federally funded Pinelands Folklife Project, we still can only guess as to why this image was chosen to represent Pine Barrens culture. Dennis McDonald, photojournalist for the *Burlington County Times*, who also worked on part-time assignment for the Pinelands Folklife Center, stated on April 13th, 2020:

> It's a good question about why Joseph Czarnecki's photo got selected as the cover but I'm not aware of the reason. I guess they thought the farm stand with its self-serve look, as opposed to someone running one of those monster farm stands you see everywhere, was appealing. And the house behind it with that washed cedar look must have struck them as being typical of the area. The Pinelands Folklife project was huge. It had a lot of people involved in it. It must have been someone's idea of what the Pinelands looked like to an Outsider. I love the house—like others in the Pines with that weathered look. In fact, the farm stand looks like one of the types where you leave the money in the box. The variety of vegetables and stuff is neat. I have probably driven by it a million times like other farm stands throughout South Jersey. If I am not in the buying mood, I just look at it and drive by. It has a classic look. It *does* say South Jersey but not specifically the Pines to me.

Mary Hufford, the Project Director for Pinelands Folklife Center based out of Washington D.C., was the second person contacted to try to solve the mystery of *why this image*. In electronic correspondence she said,

> Regarding how the photo was chosen for the cover of *Pinelands Folklife*, I don't actually know how that was chosen. It was taken during the Pinelands Folklife Project and is a beautiful image. I have a blown-up version of that framed in my home.

Why the image was chosen may remain a mystery, but the owners of that home and their life story are captured here.

The owner of the house (which originally had a dirt floor) was William Edward Hurley Sr. whom everyone endearingly called Uncle Ed. He and his wife Margaret (née Emery) Hurley raised five of their own children along with Margaret's niece Cheryl. The children were, in order of oldest to youngest, William Jr., Harry, Frank, Dixie, and Zanetta. Behind those cedar-shingled walls the home was warmed with only a wood stove. The love of Ed and Margaret enabled the family to live happy lives.

Uncle Ed was a thrifty person. He was so thrifty his brother-in-law Joseph Emery used to say, "Ed's still got the first dollar he ever made." Joseph Emery farmed his four acres down the road south on Hawkins Road. Ed had twice the acreage of his brother-in-law, situated on Veterans Highway. The two relied on each other quite a bit, pooling resources and hands together when needed. Ed was old school and lived frugally. When he died, the kids had to dig up the yard as Ed kept all his money in glass jars. Like most of his generation, he didn't trust the banks for good reason.

Joseph Lewis, a family friend, remembers, "Ed had grown his own pink variety of tomatoes and he was smart and sharp even into his later years in life." They were called Pop's Pinks. There is a pink tomato variety in seed catalogs of today. Ed and Margaret also worked the land growing other Jersey crops that included sweet potatoes, eggplant, squash, beets, and watermelon. Their best sellers were baskets of cantaloupes and baskets of sweet

(Left) In the early days, Ed Hurley used well water to irrigate at 1366 Veterans Way. (Right) Proud farmer Ed Hurley with bumper potato crop. (The date is unknown, but certainly from the early days.) Images courtesy of the Hurley family.

William Edward Hurley Sr. and wife Margaret (Emery) Hurley.

traced the branches, and there were a lot, and read the names of the wedded, you would scratch your head at how many brothers and sisters are mixed up and married into the same family. Using the Hurleys who owned that two-story farmhouse with roadside veggie stand as an example, there were a set of brothers and sisters married to another set of brothers and sisters. Ed Hurley and Lavinia Hurley were brother and sister. Margaret Emery and Joseph Emery were sister and brother. William Edward Hurley Sr. married Margaret Emery and Joseph Emery married Lavinia Hurley.

Looking back further through the window of the past, the Hurley clan got its start off East Colliers Mills Road in New Egypt. All that is left of Edward's boyhood home is a tree stump in the middle of the farm field marking where a home once stood. Ed and his younger sister Lavinia moved to state property known as Colliers Mills WMA where their dad Charles Andrew Hurley managed the property for the state. They lived there until potatoes. He also worked at the local Agway for twenty years in addition to the vegetable roadside stand famously pictured on the cover of the *Pinelands Folklife*.

By the time the roadside stand photo was taken in 1983, the children had grown up and moved out, all but Billy Hurley, the eldest son. Billy lived in the house with his parents until Ed and Margaret retired in their 80s and they moved into their son Frank Hurley's home in New Egypt in 2005. Billy accompanied them. Of note is the fact that Frank Hurley, like his grandfather Charles Hurley, worked for the state and at one time lived in a house on the Colliers Mills Wildlife Management Area (the WMA property). He was a renowned trapper in the New Jersey Division of Fish and Wildlife.

Edward and Margaret sold their home and land to a contractor. The eight acres had four acres zoned commercial and four acres residential. Whether the property was purchased as a real estate investment or with some other intention is unclear, but the Hurley homestead fell in disrepair and was torn down. Sadly, Ed passed away in 2005 from cancer. His wife Margaret lived to a ripe old age of 90 passing in 2014.

The earlier Hurley and Emery family tree(s) take particularly strange turns as each branch out. If you

Ed and Margaret, happy couple, at home 1366 Veterans Way.

The Hurley House

they were adults. When Ed Hurley eventually married Margaret, they purchased farmland less than two miles north from Ed's dad's house at 1366 West Veterans Highway, Jackson Township, Ocean County, New Jersey. In an interesting geographic note, the families who lived on the eastern side of Hawkins Road were in Jackson Township and the ones across the street on the western side of Hawkins road were in Plumsted township.

Looking at the main trunk of the Hurley family tree conjures more confusion. Charles Andrew Hurley and Lillian (née Housekeeper) Hurley had a mess of kids after marrying and moving to New Egypt from Neptune, New Jersey. Ed and Lavinia were just two of their children. Lillian (née Burroughs, from Trenton) had two children from a previous marriage, Albert Housekeeper and Lillian Housekeeper. In order of first born there were Albert, Lillian, William "Uncle Ed," Jack, Lavinia, Genève, Bessie, and Harold. Charles Hurley's brother John Hurley married the daughter of Charles' wife with the same surname of Housekeeper.

Those large families of yesterday enabled the heavy load of daily life to seem not so heavy. Mostly agrarian based communities, the large families interacted with one another and often married into each other. To be clear, such marriages were not incestuous, but simply a pair of siblings marrying another pair of siblings. The crossroads of Hawkins Road and Veterans Highway or Route 528 was the epicenter for the Emery and Hurley families since the mid-1900s. Ed and Margaret's home was in Jackson straddling the New Egypt Jackson line. Ed Hurley's little sister lived down the road on Hawkins on the New Egypt side. Across the street from Lavinia was their Uncle Arthur, who was a Jackson resident.

And in-between Ed's home on Veterans Highway and Lavinia's home on Hawkins there was the home of Uncle Paul Emery, also on the Jackson side. Oh, and we almost forgot Lavinia's husband Joseph Emery's sister Thelma who owned a house and a trailer, part of New Egypt, located down Hawkins Road by one of the old horse tracks of Ephraim Emson towards Colliers Mills WMA. Through the years, the landscape has changed, and families have spread out, but the history remains for those that go looking.

About the Author

Filmmaker, published author, and Pine Barrens folklorist with a passion for the environment: William J. Lewis is a lifetime New Jerseyian who served in various environmental advocacy roles both, governmental and nonprofit, including founding a 501c3. Author of the bestselling book *New Jersey's Lost Piney Culture,* he can be found on multimedia platforms under the social moniker Piney Tribe.

Ed Hurley at home at home 1366 Veterans Way.

Margaret Emery Hurley at home circa early 2000s.

Figure 1. Inside his kitchen, Herb Misner hand-knits a net that will be placed inside the snapping turtle fyke. He learned how to make the nets from a book. All photographs by Dennis McDonald/American Folklife Center/Library of Congress.

Herb Misner:
Snapper Trapper

Dennis McDonald

Sixty-five-year-old Medford resident Herb Misner had been trapping snapping turtles for more than half a century when I photographed him for the American Folklife Center in July 1984. The sixty-five year-old retired auto mechanic learned to catch them from local Pineys when he was fourteen. They walked in drained bogs and poked in the mud with sticks. "When you found a turtle, you'd stand on it and they would move. Turtles always move forward; then you would know where the head and tail was. I'd reach down with my hands and pull them out of the mud," Misner said.

He now uses a five-foot, cylindrical wire mesh fyke with a hand-knit net funnel and cans of sardines inside a bait box. He sets about a dozen traps in waterways always leaving one part of the fyke above water so the turtle can breathe. He places the traps in places such as Fisher's Pond in Southampton and Lake Ockanickon in Medford although Misner set traps throughout southern Burlington County down to Little Egg Harbor. He always obtained permission from the land owners who find the turtles a nuisance.

He checks his traps daily from May to September by walking through heavy brush to get to a slow-moving stream or he uses an old Sears & Roebuck aluminum rowboat to get to others. Removing the snapper from the trap is the most dangerous part of the work. He always grabs them by the tail and places the turtle carefully inside a canvas bag. He has been bitten a couple of times but considers himself lucky that he has never lost a finger. Misner says their jaws are vise-like and their teeth are sharp as razors.

After capturing and weighing them he kept the turtles in his backyard in old claw-foot bathtubs till he was ready to transport the live snappers to local markets. He sold to local restaurants such as Old Original Bookbinders in Philadelphia and the Old English Pub in Pennsauken for snapper soup, shipping as much as 1,000 pounds at a time.

Misner didn't always sell all his turtles. Herb said his late wife, Thelma, made the best snapper soup. He recalled wonderful parties with everyone sitting under a tree in his back yard on a Sunday summer afternoon with a half keg of beer.

The information for this article came from:

Sari Harrar, "Medford Turtle Trapper Is One of a Dying Breed," *Burlington County Times* (Willingboro, New Jersey), August 23, 1984.
Rita Zorn Moonsammy, David Steven Cohen, and Lorraine E. Williams, *Pinelands Folklife* (Rutgers University Press, 1987).
Interview with Herbert Misner, Betty Gravinese, and Lou Gravenise regarding snapping turtles, Medford, New Jersey, part 1 & part 2, April 11, 1985. Credit: Pinelands Folklife Project collection (AFC 1991/023), American Folklife Center, Library of Congress.

Figure 2. Herb Misner's gnarled hands mend the fyke net used inside the snapping turtle trap.

Figure 3. Herb Misner prepares to launch his Sears & Roebuck aluminum rowboat on Fisher's Pond in Southampton, New Jersey, to check his snapping turtle traps.

Figure 4. Herbert Misner rows his Sears & Roebuck aluminum boat out to one of his traps placed in Fisher's Pond located in Southampton, New Jersey.

Figure 5. Herbert Misner rows his Sears & Roebuck aluminum boat out to one of his traps placed in Fisher's Pond located in Southampton, New Jersey.

Figure 6. The most dangerous part of catching a snapper is placing a recently caught turtle inside the canvas bag. Misner performs this task while on a boat at Fisher's Pond in Southampton, New Jersey.

Figure 7. Wearing hip waders Herb Misner removes his fyke from the side of a Pine Barrens lake in Medford, New Jersey.

Figure 8. Herbert Misner checks a captured snapping turtle that he just pulled out of a lake at Camp Ockanickon in Medford, New Jersey.

Figure 9. Herb Misner drags his fyke with a snapping turtle inside back to his truck through heavy brush. The trap was placed in a lake in Medford and the trip back to the truck was about a ½ mile.

Figure 10. Herb Misner drags his fyke with a snapping turtle inside back to his truck through high, dense brush in the Pine Barrens. The trap was placed in a lake in Medford and the trip back to the truck was about a half mile.

Figure 11. Herb Misner drags a fyke with a snapping turtle inside to his truck parked in a blueberry field in Medford, NJ.

Figure 12. Herb Misner unloads the snapping turtle trap/fyke from the back of his pickup truck in the parking lot of the Evergreen Dairy Bar in Southampton, New Jersey.

Figure 13. Herb Misner weighs a recently caught snapping turtle in the parking lot of the Evergreen Dairy Bar on Route 70 in Southampton, New Jersey. He has caught snappers weighing 45 pounds.

Figure 14. Herb Misner, second from right, shows off a recently caught snapping turtle in the back of his pickup truck to interested customers at the Evergreen Dairy Bar on Route 70 in Southampton, New Jersey.

Figure 15. Herb Misner of Medford, New Jersey, holds a snapping turtle by the tail as he removes it from his boat.

Figure 16. Herb Misner, left, and Ray Drayton, right, hold recently caught snapping turtles by their tails with the shell facing outward.

Figure 17. Herb Misner carries a snapping turtle inside a canvas bag to his pickup truck. He once had a turtle bite his finger through the bag while carrying it.

Figure 18. Common snapping turtle (*Chelydra serpentina*) in Herb Misner's backyard.

Figure 19. Herb Misner brings a snapping turtle to the surface of a bathtub full of snapping turtles in his Medford backyard. He keeps them in bathtubs till he is ready to bring them to market.

Figure 20. Herb Misner pulls a large snapping turtle from the murky water of a bathtub storage container in the backyard of his Medford home.

Figure 21. Herb Misner holds a snapping turtle on the side of a bathtub in his Medford backyard where they are stored till he is ready to bring them to market.

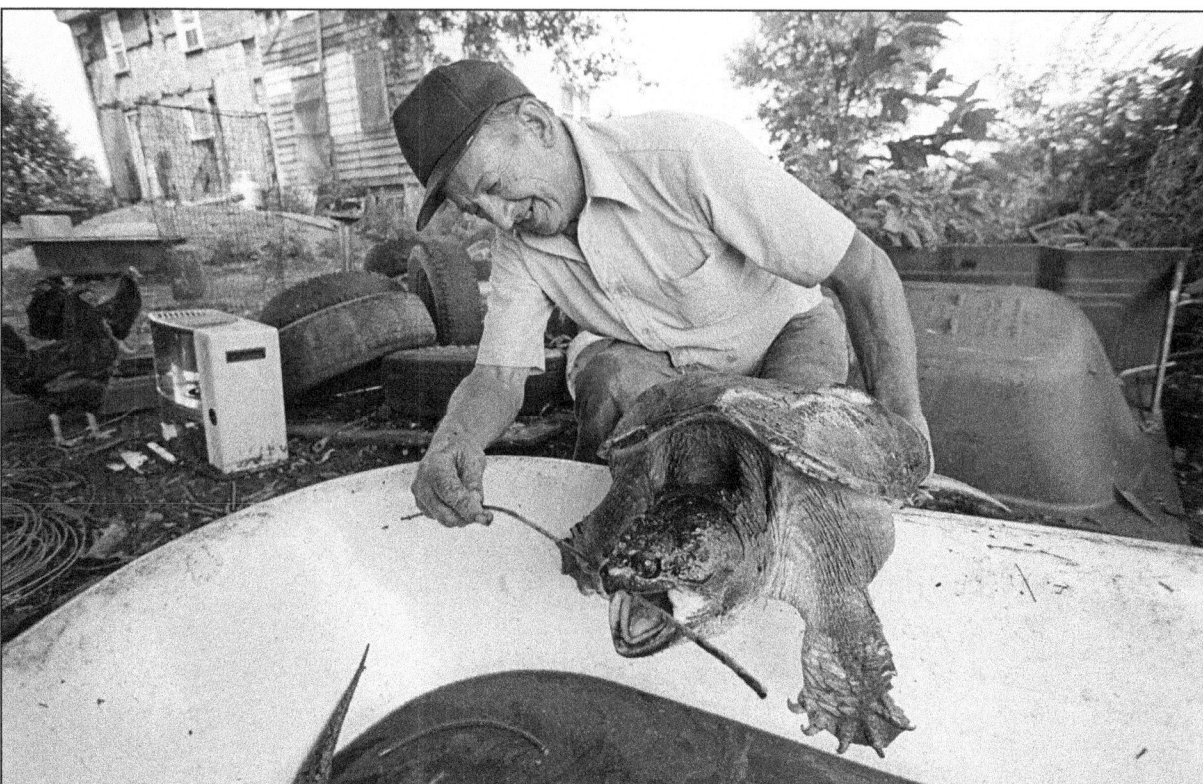

Figure 22. Herb Misner gets a snapping turtle to bare his teeth by teasing him with a piece of straw. The turtles are stored in claw-foot bathtubs in Herb's Medford backyard.

Figure 23. Herb Misner pulls a snapping turtle out of a bathtub in his Medford, New Jersey, backyard where he stores them before bringing them to market. He uses a piece of straw to get the snapping turtle to bare his teeth. Also note the turtle's sharp claws.

Figure 24. Herb Misner uses binoculars to see if there is any movement in his traps/fykes placed in Fisher's Pond in Southampton, New Jersey.

HIGHBOY RINGS DOWN THE CURTAIN: A REVIEW

Cynthia Anstey

South Jersey is rich with stories written by folks who have made this place their home. Time and space scatter these precious tales across a literary landscape. One example is a brief story entitled *Highboy Rings Down the Curtain*, published 100 years ago in 1923.

During a lecture at the Gloucester Historical Society, Jim Bergmann mentioned this book had been published in a limited edition. Bridgeton Evening News Company printed and bound only 300 copies, intended as gifts for friends of the aspiring author. Though Chamberlain's catalog of titles grew to 43, with seven transformed into Hollywood cinematic productions, *Highboy Rings Down the Curtain* could have remained forgotten, found only in several hard-to-acquire anthologies. We are able to enjoy Chamberlain's thought-provoking style today because of a collaboration between community and academia—specifically a generous contribution from William W. Leap, the publishing efforts of the South Jersey Culture & History Center, and Stockton University's Special Collections.

Stockton University students working with the South Jersey Culture & History Center enjoyed the experience of designing and editing this 100th commemorative anniversary edition. Reminiscent of the copy conserved in Stockton's Special Collections, it is a wonderful example of the student-staffed local history press at the university. The design honors the original work using a classic format. The easy-to-read Baskerville Old Face font gives the reader a sense of the story's time period, while its updated presentation provides a visually engaging story despite being a century old.

The story presents itself as a modest and simple tale regarding horses. Mr. Kindly Crewe suffers the gutting loss of a beloved horse. A second horse provides the possibility of healing Kindly's broken heart. It takes nurturing, however, to bring out the true nature of this "dappled devil," branded as "waste," just barely spared from an "ignominious and unostentatious exit."

The reader learns to appreciate Chamberlain's "literary craftsmanship." The subtlety of his writing conveys sadness, joy, excitement, and tension, which is displayed during the exchanges between the story's characters. These moments deepen the interpersonal relationships that drive the pages forward. Each character, including Highboy, bears witness to a complicated past fading into a markedly different and unknown future. For a moment, Chamberlain's *Highboy Rings Down the Curtain* offers a bittersweet commentary regarding the transformation of physical terrain and a particular way of life that would soon disappear altogether. It gives a sense that 1923 is not as far away from 2023 as we might think.

Some may find the story difficult to read as this work of fiction deals with death and grief. However, it also explores the healing potential of nurturing while Kindly, the human protagonist, deals with the weight of overbearing emotions. It considers societal change and its impact on how people live. The tale's dramatic finish marks the end of an era quite pointedly. Most importantly, it is a lovely introduction to George Agnew Chamberlain, whose life experiences ranged from U.S. consular service in Brazil and Africa to working on a ranch in New Mexico as a cowboy. In 1905 he managed *El Farol*, "the only Spanish paper as far east in New Mexico as Las Vegas or the Rio Grande Valley." Mr. Chamberlain was a "molder of fiction" whose work captures the spirit of his life and time with descriptive prose that deserves our attention.

ABOUT THE REVIWER

Cynthia Anstey is currently pursuing her Master of Arts in American Studies at Stockton University. As a former undergraduate editing intern, she can attest to the enriching nature of the experience, combining archival research, material culture, and community interaction.

Samuel C. Chester:
Southern New Jersey Photographer

Gary D. Saretzky

History professors often warn their students not to rely exclusively on secondary sources, but instead, use primary sources when available such as personal correspondence, photographs, and government documents to verify information found in histories, journal articles, newspapers, websites, and other publications. A good example of how a secondary source misled one historian involves the photographer Samuel C. Chester (1851–1937), who spent much of his long career in Camden, Cape May, and Millville, New Jersey.

Chester produced a substantial body of high-quality work and appears to have been a law-abiding family man and a skillful photographer from 1865 to about 1932. This essay will review the mistakes previously made in published accounts about him and then provide an accurate, illustrated review of his career.

Robert Taft (1894–1955) taught chemistry at the University of Kansas, where he had obtained his Ph.D. in 1925, but his avocation was art history, including the history of photography. In 1938, he published an unprecedented, thoroughly researched, history that scholars still consult today.[1] In discussing the renowned Mathew Brady (1822–1896), who organized the most comprehensive photographic documentation of the Civil War, Taft listed Samuel C. Chester as one of Brady's team of cameramen.[2] In his long endnote no. 255, Taft thanked Leon Conley of Haddonfield, New Jersey, for furnishing him with the information on Chester and cited Chester's obituary in the April 26, 1937, *Courier-Post* (Camden), that Conley no doubt had kindly sent to him.[3]

What Taft failed to realize was that Chester's obituary, entitled "Samuel C. Chester, Photographer, Dies; Man Who Took 1600 Civil War Pictures Succumbs Here at 86," was carelessly written with a misleading title. It was based on an article published in the *Evening Courier* (Camden) on January 26, 1937, for which a reporter interviewed the venerable widowed photographer, living in poverty without gas or electricity with his daughter Linnie (Melinda) Chester in North Camden.[4] In that interview, Chester stated that he made his first photographs in 1865 at the age of 14, when he lived in Millville, Cumberland County. As a youth, he habituated the premises of Millville photographer J. B. Brown and learned the collodion wet plate process by watching the professional at work.[5] When Brown asked him to keep an eye on his gallery while he was away in Atlantic City, Chester asked his friend Sam Richards to sit for him. He fixed Richards' head with a clamp called an immobilizer, prepared a collodion glass plate negative, inserted it into the camera, and made a ten-second exposure, followed by development, fixing, and washing. Upon his return, Brown's surprise at Chester's success led to a job, as will be discussed below.

In the January 1937 interview, Chester related how he and Brady's nephew Levin C. Handy (1855–1932) printed three copies each of 1,600 glass plate negatives that the War Department had purchased from Brady. Chester may have been mistaken about the purchase as it was Congress that had paid Brady in 1874 and 1875.[6] Perhaps the negatives were only stored at the War Department. In any case, this printing was likely done at Handy's own gallery, located on the second floor of a carriage house behind his home at 494 Maryland Avenue SW, Washington, DC. Chester stated that the negatives were so valuable that the War Department

Portrait of Samuel C. Chester, circa 1880. Library of Congress, Brady-Handy Collection, from glass plate negative taken in Mathew Brady's or his nephew Levin C. Handy's gallery in Washington, DC.

only let them borrow one box at a time. It is clear that Chester did not take any of these Civil War photos because he was only 14 when the war ended and did not work for Brady until about a decade later. Apparently, the obituary misled Taft when it stated that Chester "took 1600 negatives during the Civil War, among them one of General William T. Sherman and his staff."[7]

The obituary conflated Chester's photograph of Sherman and his generals with a well-known one by Brady taken more than a decade earlier in 1865. Chester, who at a still unknown date in the latter 1870s, began working with Brady and Handy, had mentioned in his interview that among his photos was a group shot of Sherman with his generals, including General Alexander McDowell McCook (1831–1903), who was Sherman's aide-de-camp from 1875 to 1880.[8] After that portrait, recalled Chester, McCook asked if he could change his clothes and leave his valise and uniform at Brady's while he went out on the town overnight.

Before McCook's return the next day, Chester put on the general's uniform and sat for a portrait, probably by Handy, for by that time Brady did little camera work himself. That photo is unfortunately not in the Brady-Handy Collection at the Library of Congress (LC).[9]

That Chester worked with Brady and Handy in Washington is incontrovertible. Although the one of Chester in uniform has not been found, another of a bearded Chester wearing a suit is in the LC Brady-Handy collection.[10] The date of the photo is unknown, but Chester was definitely with Brady in 1879 and 1880 when he was listed in the Washington city directories as a photographer at Brady's studio, 635 Pennsylvania Avenue NW. Brady also lived there and because Chester is not listed with another address, he probably resided with either Brady or Handy.[11]

In other work for Brady, according to the interview, Chester photographed engineer John Ericsson, who had designed and built the iron-clad ship *Monitor*, which engaged the *Merrimac* in the famous Civil War naval battle at Hampton Roads on March 9, 1862. Chester also claimed that he took the first picture of Thomas Edison with his phonograph in April 1878, when the inventor was in Washington to obtain patents, although Edison had already received his patent for the phonograph on February 19, 1878. He was in the capital to demonstrate his invention to the National Academy of Sciences, Congress, and President Rutherford B. Hayes at the White House.[12] At least two negatives of Edison alone were made and two with associates.[13] Although it is possible that Edison had been portrayed with the phonograph before he came to Washington, no such portrait has been found so Chester's claim of priority still stands.[14]

In another example of his work for Brady, Chester claimed in his interview to have taken the last photographs of President James A. Garfield and his family shortly before Garfield was shot

Samuel C. Chester, obituary, *Morning Post* (Camden), April 26, 1937. The text contains significant errors, including assertion that Chester took 1,600 Civil War photos.

Samuel C. Chester, Thomas Edison with his tinfoil phonograph, April 1878. Taken at Mathew Brady's studio, Washington, D.C. Brady-Handy Collection, Library of Congress.

Samuel C. Chester, President James Abram Garfield, with Lincoln chair, 1881. From glass plate negative taken at Mathew Brady's studio, Washington, D.C. Brady-Handy Collection, Library of Congress.

by disappointed office seeker Charles J. Guiteau at the Baltimore and Potomac Railroad Station. Garfield had been sworn in on March 4, 1881, and the portraits would have been made before Guiteau attacked the President on July 2 of that year. Sadly, Garfield died of his wounds, exacerbated by infections likely the result of medical treatment, in Elberon, Long Branch, on September 19, 1881.

Chester made several portraits of Garfield, including a close-up of his head and shoulders that illustrates the biography of him on Wikipedia, and two of the President standing with the famous Abraham Lincoln chair. In February 1857, the House of Representatives was refurbished and Lincoln, who had been an Illinois Congressman (1847–1849), rescued his chair and gave it to Mathew Brady, who used it for many years thereafter for sittings by important clients.[15] The Library of Congress' Brady-Handy Collection also includes Chester's portraits of Garfield's family. He photographed Garfield's wife Lucretia (1832–1918) alone and the couple's five surviving children with the same painted background that appears in one of the photos of Edison.[16]

Chester's career started in the collodion wet plate era, when hand-prepared glass negatives, after processing, were used to make monochrome purplish-brown contact prints in the sun on albumen paper sensitized by the photographer.[17] For cabinet cards, about 4 1/4 x 6 1/2 inches, and larger photos, photographers would retouch the faces on the glass negatives to remove blemishes using a retouching stand like the home-made one in the photo of Chester that accompanied the January 1937 article. Enlargements colored in oil, watercolor, and charcoal became a staple of the portrait photography business by 1870, as were inexpensive tintypes. Around 1880, like other professionals, Chester would have switched to gelatin dry plates, known by photographers as "the instantaneous process" because these glass negatives significantly shortened exposure times, as well as being more convenient, since unlike collodion negatives, they came ready to use.[18]

In 1889, George Eastman became the first manufacturer of flexible roll film, supplied for simple Kodak box cameras that significantly increased the number of amateur photographers, including women and children, and impacted the professional photography business. In the 1890s, this flexible nitrocellulose film, also called nitrate or celluloid film, enabled the first commercial motion pictures, which Thomas Edison introduced in 1894 and viewed by one person at a time in Kinetoscopes. Despite the availability of roll and sheet film, some amateurs and professionals like Chester continued using glass plate negatives until the 1920s.

The 1890s also saw a profusion of photographic printing papers. In addition to albumen, photographers made collodion and silver gelatin prints, some of which could be printed with gas or electric light on "gas-light papers." To distinguish their work from amateurs, some photographic artists in the early 1900s began offering portraits in platinum, carbon, gum bichromate and other high priced, hand-crafted alternatives.[19] With the advent of photomechanical reproduction, newspapers and magazines, beginning in the 1890s, started routinely reproducing photographs, creating a new market for professionals. In 1907, color photography became commercially feasible with the Autochrome, the first widely used color process. Others followed, including Dufaycolor transparencies and Vivex color prints, and Chester lived to see the introduction of Kodachrome for still photography in 1936.

Although Chester was not a Civil War photographer, he did have a long and remarkable career that began in Millville, Cumberland County. He was born there on September 27, 1851, to Hannah and Asbury Chester, a carpenter who grew up on a farm near Williamstown and settled in Millville in 1847. Born near Haddonfield in 1815, Asbury, the son of a Methodist clergyman, became a Methodist preacher, homebuilder, farmer, butcher, Justice of the Peace, and railroad station agent. Early on, he was known as Mayor of Millville, although his actual title was chairman of the Millville Township Committee that governed until the town was incorporated as a city in 1866. Asbury was married twice and had two children with his first wife, who died in 1849, and eight, including Samuel, with his second, Hannah (née Clunn), whom he married in 1850.[20]

Chester's mentor, Josiah Burnstead Brown, usually found as J. B. Brown, was born in Massachusetts in 1833. His early life is obscure and evidence has not been found that he was a self-employed photographer before the Civil War.[21] In the 1860 U.S. Census for the town of Burlington, New Jersey, he is listed as "Jones" B. Brown, 26, bricklayer, born in Massachusetts, living with his wife Mary C., 26, and daughter Mary J., 3, both born in Pennsylvania. The census listed his personal estate as $500, worth about $17,000 in 2022 dollars. How he learned photography remains to be discovered, but in May 1863 he paid for a $10 license to practice camerawork under the name Josiah B. Brown in the village of Pottsgrove, Montgomery County, Pennsylvania, in accordance with the Internal Revenue Act of July 1, 1862, passed to raise money for the federal government's enormous war expenses.[22] Since his wife Mary was from Pennsylvania, that might explain his presence there.

Some early carte-de-visite portraits by Brown have an imprint on the back with "J. B. Brown, Photographer, Tenth Regt. N.J.V."[23] The Tenth Regiment, New Jersey Volunteers, which was raised in Beverly in Burlington County, was stationed near Philadelphia between July and September 1863, when it was reassigned to Pottstown, about 50 miles northwest of Pottsgrove. Brown may have followed the regiment there and like other contemporary photographers, set up a tent studio at the encampment. But not long after, with his growing family (another daughter, Cornelia, was born in 1863), Brown relocated to Millville, where under the name J. B. Brown & Co., he paid for a $10 license in May 1865 and renewed it for $15 in August, a month before Chester turned 14.[24]

Brown may have initially operated from a tent as the label on the back of his ferrotype cards reads, "Brown & Co's Wigwam Photograph & Ferrotype Rooms, High Street, Millville, N.J."[25] In 1866, Brown opened a new gallery, this time without "& Co."[26] He was still in Millville as late as 1867 when he paid for a $10 license, the last year the federal government collected this fee.[27] Where he operated for the next few years has not been firmly established. He may have stayed in Millville, but he may also have been the J. B. Brown listed as a Warren, Massachusetts, photographer in the 1868 Worcester County Directory.

By 1870, Brown was in Cape May and Samuel Chester was working for him. Chester, then 19 years old, was enumerated twice in the census that year. In the village of Cold Spring, Lower Township, Cape May County, Chester was recorded as an apprentice artist living with Josiah B. Brown, photo artist, 36, his wife Mary C., 36, the three Brown children, and an English-born domestic servant, Rhoda Milin, 18. In Vineland, Chester was recorded without an occupation with his own family, including his father Asbury, 50, railroad station agent, his mother Hannah, 38, and six siblings.[28] Double counting in the census occurred because the recordings were not taken on the same day. Apparently, when the census taker came around in Cold Spring on June 28, Chester was there, but he was with his family in Vineland on August 8.

In the 1860s, Cape May in the south and Long Branch in the north were the leading Jersey Shore resorts, attracting a high percentage of their visitors, respectively, from Philadelphia and New York. (Later in the century, Atlantic City began to surpass Cape May in popularity.) Cape May, which is at approximately the same latitude as Washington, DC, became a convenient and profitable place for Brown to operate in the summer, in part because the Cape May & Millville Railroad had been completed in 1867. In addition to linking its namesakes with connections, the railroad sped travel for vacationers from Philadelphia and other departure points, although steamboats continued to offer an attractive alternative.[29]

In Cape May, Brown had a gallery at the foot of Ocean Street where it ends at the beach, not far from the current location of the Cape May Convention Center. There he made portraits, and also sold stereographic views taken in the area, including one, now at the Library of Congress, of six men and women playing croquet at a Mr. McCrary's cottage.[30] Other stereographs by Brown's Gallery featured couples with children on a large lawn in front of McMakin's (Atlantic) Hotel. It is possible that young Chester made some of the photographs credited to Brown as it was quite common in those days not to mention the camera operator if different from the gallery owner. Brown left Millville and Cape May but was still a photographer when he died in 1901.[31]

Between 1870, when Chester was listed twice in the U.S. Census and April 1878, when he photographed Thomas Edison at Brady's, Chester's whereabouts remain an opportunity for future research, with the exception of his activities in Wilmington, Delaware, around 1875–1877, although precise dates for this episode in his career have not been found.[32] In Wilmington, Chester partnered with the ambitious Thomas E. Sexton (1835–1913).[33] Sexton was born in Mercer County, New Jersey, where he was raised on a farm. When he was fifteen, his parents moved to Bordentown and by 1859 he became a daguerreotypist and photographer there for about a year before re-establishing his business in Springfield, Illinois. In 1862, he ran a livery stable for five years.[34] By 1864, however, he was also conducting a photo gallery in Wilmington, where he patented a photographic printing frame in 1866.[35] Meanwhile, Sexton managed a farm that he had purchased in 1859 near Pawnee, Illinois, and periodically he left Delaware for extended periods to live

J. B. Brown, Foot of Ocean Street, Cape May. McCrary's Cottage, stereograph, circa 1870. Marion S. Carson Collection, Library of Congress. From period when Samuel C. Chester was Brown's apprentice.

J. B. Brown, Foot of Decatur Street, Cape May. J. B. Brown and family, stereograph, 1870–1871. Dated by estimated age of Brown's youngest daughter, Rosalee, two years old in the 1870 census. Likely taken by Brown's apprentice Samuel C. Chester. Kenneth H. Rosen collection.

there or in Taylorville in the same state. In 1877, he left Wilmington permanently and went back to his farm. After a few years, he sold it and bought another farm in Springfield Township, and later retired to the city of Springfield, where he died a prosperous and well-respected man.[36]

Chester was in Wilmington by September 1875, when the Board of Education authorized him to do group photos of schoolchildren.[37] It appears likely that Sexton brought Chester into the business because he was making regular trips to Illinois and planned to go back there permanently. Chester continued operating from Sexton's at 414 Market Street after his partner left, and at some point, moved to 302 Market Street.[38] Soon thereafter, he went to work for Mathew Brady and his nephew in Washington, DC.

An obvious question is how Chester, at that time a young man without a national or regional reputation as a photographer, became associated with Brady and Handy. One possibility is that they met in 1876 during the Centennial Exhibition in Philadelphia, which included a major photography exhibit at which Brady won an award.[39] Hundreds of photographs by U.S. and foreign photographers were displayed in the Photographic Art Building, a 242 x 77-foot annex to the Art Gallery, one of the five principal buildings. In conjunction with that exhibit, the National Photographic Association, the professional organization of photographers, held its annual convention there on August 15–17. Considering Chester's proximity to Philadelphia, it seems reasonable to hypothesize that he was among that throng of photographers and may have met Brady or Handy, or both. Another possibility is that Brady, or more likely Handy, vacationed at some point in Cape May and met Chester there.

It is doubtful that Chester met Brady before 1876 as Brady had fallen on hard times after the Civil War. Brady went bankrupt and his Washington gallery, a branch of his main one in New York, was sold in 1873 for $5, subject to liens of $5,000.[40] The sale did not resolve Brady's financial problems, as he continued to be indebted, especially to Levin Handy.

However Chester became acquainted with Brady and his nephew, his work with Handy in the late 1870s led to a Chester & Handy partnership for about five years, with galleries in Cape May, Philadelphia, and Washington, DC. Although some sources date this partnership to 1882, when Chester and Handy are first listed together in the Washington, DC, directory, one of their stereo views depicting the Cape May Lighthouse is dated in pencil, August 9, 1880. The imprint on the back reads, "Chester & Handy, Photographers, Next to Stockton Bath Houses, [Southwest] Cor. Beach Avenue and Ocean Street, Cape May, N.J."[41] The partners are

Chester & Handy (Samuel C. Chester & Levin C. Handy), Corner Beach Avenue & Ocean Street, Cape May. Lighthouse, stereograph. Kenneth H. Rosen Collection. Another copy of this view seen, dated August 9, 1880.

Chester & Handy, Corner Beach Avenue & Ocean Street, Cape May. Large group at Stockton House, stereograph 1880–1885. Kenneth H. Rosen collection.

Samuel C. Chester

Chester & Handy, Cape May. Group under Cape May Pier, promenade card (4 1/8 x 7 1/8 inches), August 1885. Kenneth H. Rosen collection. Note the African American man and children in the group.

Chester & Handy, Corner Beach Avenue & Ocean Street, Cape May. Life Saving Station, stereograph, 1880–1885. Kenneth H. Rosen collection.

found in the 1881 Cape May County Directory at this address. In that year, they were not listed in the Washington, DC, directory, but in the 1882 edition, they can be found at 426 7th Street NW.[42] The imprints on their cartes-de-visite from the early 1880s mention that the Cape May business was a branch of their establishment at 907 Ridge Avenue, Philadelphia, or of Cape May with a branch at 426th 7th Street, Washington, "Next door to Ballantyne's Book Store."[43]

As did other Jersey shore photographers such as Gustavus Pach and William H. Stauffer in Monmouth County and William Long and Gilbert & Bacon in Cape May, Chester & Handy made stereo views with hotel guests, from small groups to more than fifty, who became potential buyers. In particular, they photographed gatherings on the Stockton House veranda near their gallery.[44] Not surprisingly, given the times, the guests were mostly Caucasian. An August 1885 Promenade card photo by Chester & Handy of a large group on the beach under the Cape May Pier includes one well-dressed African American man and several black children, probably his.[45] Cape May tried to attract mainly the white elite, however, and relatively few African Americans vacationed there compared to Asbury Park and Atlantic City.[46]

In addition to group photos, Chester & Handy also produced stereo views of local points of interest, e.g., a street scene with the Westmoreland Villa.[47] Others included the Cape May Life Station, one of a series of such facilities spaced at regular intervals along the shore before the U.S. Coast Guard was established. Another view shows the crowded beach and ocean with a horse-drawn passenger wagon in the foreground. On the left side in the distance can be seen a large frame with photos, apparently marketing photographic services. The pink back carries the imprint, "Chester & Handy Portraits, 907 Ridge Avenue, Phila., Pa. Branch, Cape May, N.J. Views, Samples & Machinery Photographed."[48] Chester & Handy also sold Cape May stereo views of other beach scenes, a boat on the ocean, at least four different hotels, and the street along the ocean with Denizot's New Ocean Pier on the left. They also made cabinet cards of people sitting on hotel verandas and made portraits at the studio in the cabinet card and carte-de-visite sizes.[49]

The Library of Congress holds an extraordinary Chester & Handy carte-de-visite of a photographer wearing a straw hat, with his camera and a painted backdrop of waves in the background. Under the camera body is a sign with "Chester & Handy" and the Cape May address. Someone has written, "Welcome The Dude," on the front and on the back, "Good Evening Mr. Handy. It is a Mash you want, Dick." The imprint gives the Cape May address and "Branch of 426 7th St., N.W., Washington, D.C. Groups Photographed Instantaneously Under the Sky Light." A list of names written on the back may be customers of the firm.[50]

On December 21, 1882, the *Evening Critic* (Washington, DC), reported that Mathew Brady "has associated himself with Chester & Handy, where they are prepared to make fine work, any size or style."[51] In 1883, Brady took out a full page ad in the Washington, DC, directory for this "National Portrait Co." at 1113 Pennsylvania Avenue, NW. Listed as the gallery manager with Chester and Handy as associates, Brady offered portraits by the aforementioned "instantaneous process," and sold likenesses of government officials, including the President, the Cabinet, Senators, Members of Congress, Supreme Court Justices, and other celebrities. In addition to the standard card photographs, patrons could purchase portraits on porcelain and in oil and watercolors. Although not mentioned in the ad, Brady also sold his Civil War views. The individual listing for Chester in the 1883 directory shows that he lived with Handy at 494 Maryland Avenue SW.[52]

Brady's National Portrait Co. of 1883 only lasted about a year. In 1884, Brady no longer appeared in the Washington, DC, directory, while Chester & Handy continued at their 7th Street location. Their cabinet photo of a woman, likely from 1884, is on a dark maroon card with a gilt imprint below the image and beveled gilt edges, with the back blank and gray.[53] The imprint only gives the studio's 7th Street address in Washington.[54] Another dark maroon cabinet card by Chester & Handy has been seen of a posed studio shot of ten men and women. As obvious by the maritime backdrop, it was taken in Cape May and its gilt imprint reads, "Cape May, N.J. & Washington, D.C."

In 1885, the partners were listed at Handy's on Maryland Avenue, where Handy remained for many years.[55] Subsequently, Chester continued alone in Cape May and examples of his portraiture with his imprint, sans Handy, have been found between 1886 and 1896.[56] The Cape May business was seasonal, and Chester must have felt the need to open at another location during the non-summer months. Not surprisingly, he chose his hometown of Millville, where he would return from Cape May in the fall.[57] The *Bridgeton Evening News* stated on January 4, 1888, "A large number of people are very much pleased over the advent of so good a

Chester & Handy, 426 7th St., Washington, DC. Unidentified woman with lace collar, cabinet card, circa 1884. Author's collection.

Chester & Handy, Cape May. Ten adults, cabinet card, 1886. Author's digital collection.

photographer as S. C. Chester. His arbor and winter background scene receives much praise. Mr. Chester succeeds D. W. Carpenter, High Street, Millville."[58] The next day, the same newspaper mentioned that Chester was able to make portraits day or night, implying that he had electric light in his studio.[59] Electricity had come to Millville in 1886, so Chester was able to take advantage of it when he opened on High Street at the end of 1887 or early in January 1888.[60]

The years 1887 and 1888 were important for Chester's personal life as well. On May 15, 1887, at the age of 36, he married Amelia Hunt, 22, who grew up on a farm in West Whiteland, Chester County, Pennsylvania, and was living in Springfield, Ohio. Their first child, Melinda (Linnie) Chester, was born on November 26, 1888, at their Millville home, 424 Oak Street. Their second, Charles Sumner Chester, was born in the same place on December 1, 1890.[61]

Most of Chester's extant work from the late 1880s and 1890s consists of portraits, usually in the form of cabinet cards, which had replaced the smaller cartes-de-visite and ferrotype cards (tintypes mounted to the size cartes-de-visite) as the most popular card photograph.[62] In 1866, with the waning of the early 1860s carte-de-visite craze, the cabinet card had been introduced in England and then widely adopted in the United States, although cartes-de-visite continued to be the most popular format until the 1880s.[63] Albums to store both card formats were available from photographers and stationery stores.

Unlike other collodion processes, tintypes persisted in the photographic marketplace in New Jersey after 1880, especially at the shore, but Chester did not make any that have come to this author's attention. Because no negative or printing was involved, tintypes could be processed and delivered to the sitter in about

15 minutes or less and they were the cheapest form of photography available. Chester, it seems, was more interested in the higher end of the market, those he termed the "elegant clientele," especially in Cape May. Rebuilt with what was then conservative, Victorian architecture after a huge fire on November 8, 1878, that destroyed 40 acres of downtown buildings, Cape May attracted more upscale Philadelphia area vacationers than other shore destinations like Atlantic City.[64]

Among Chester's subjects in Cape May during this period were baseball players. He made a series circa 1889 of ten cabinet cards of young men in baseball uniforms with "Cape May" across the jersey, each standing in front of a painted backdrop depicting the ocean with a sailing ship in the distance. No two poses are alike. In several, a man is catching a ball stopped in midair while in others, players hold their bats. Most of these athletes had attended Ivy League schools—Harvard, Princeton, and the University of Pennsylvania—and had been active in various leagues in the Philadelphia area.[65]

Individual cabinet card portraits of men, women, and children formed the majority of Chester's work during these years in Cape May and Millville. In posing his subjects, as did many other photographers of this era, Chester tended to present just the head and torso and the sitter looks somewhat away from the camera. The print is often vignetted to make the customer appear to be floating in a cloud.[66] Maintaining a generous camera-to-subject distance avoided making the noses look unnaturally large and left ample blank space around the image. A shorter distance would also have exaggerated any movement by the subject during the exposure. Chester made exceptions to these stylistic characteristics when he wanted to show the entire figure, such as the baseball players or a baby in a very long white baptismal dress, and then he would not use

Samuel C. Chester, Cape May. E. O. Wagenhurst, baseball player, cabinet card, 1889. Huggins & Scott Auctions, March 30–April 9, 2015.

Chester & Handy, 426 7th St., Washington, DC. Unidentified woman, cabinet card, circa 1884. Author's collection.

Samuel C. Chester

Boy with hat and dog, cabinet card, circa 1890. Author's digital collection.

Samuel C. Chester, 326 Federal, Camden. Twin babies, cabinet card, circa 1895. Author's digital collection.

Samuel C. Chester, Cape May. Young girl with big eyes, cabinet card, circa 1890. Author's collection.

Samuel C. Chester, 326 Federal, Camden. Charles Newcomb, football player, cabinet card, 1897. Camden County Historical Society. Footballs were round until 1906, when the forward pass was approved for use in collegiate sports.

the vignetter. He also occasionally had the subject look directly into the camera, as he did in a striking portrait of a young girl with big eyes at his Cape May studio. Chester also shot portraits outdoors, including a cabinet card of a family next to a house in Cape May.

Chester's career in Millville ended when he moved to 319 Federal Street, Camden, in the second half of 1893.[67] This address had hosted a long series of photographers since 1874.[68] Chester did not remain there long, as in 1895 he rented the second floor studio at 326 Federal, where he worked for almost 30 years. This gallery had belonged to photographer J. E. Smith in 1893–1894, and previously by the brothers Frederick and William Fearn beginning in 1883.[69] Chester and his family also resided at 326 Federal until the 1920s.

As mentioned above, Chester continued his summer gallery in Cape May until at least 1896 and during the rest of the year did portraits in Camden. Four Chester Camden cabinet cards of football players in the mid-1890s are in the collection of the Camden County Historical Society. The cabinet card, ubiquitous in the 1880s and 1890s, gradually yielded in the latter decade to other formats in a variety of sizes. One Chester portrait on a dark gray card, measuring about 3 x 4 inches, depicts a young woman wearing a turtleneck sweater. There is an embossed design around the photo and Chester's blind-stamped imprint with the 326 Federal Street address at lower right.[70] Another example from the early 1900s is a boy standing next to a wicker chair with the photo trimmed to an oval and mounted on a dark gray card the size of a cabinet card.[71] In 1912, Chester photographed nearly 50 employees of the Camden-based C. C. Chew Store posing in front of the establishment before they left for a picnic. This group portrait was published in the *Courier-Post*.[72] After he moved his business and residence to 612 Broadway in 1922 or early 1923, Chester continued at that location until 1924–1925.[73] One example seen from his Broadway studio is a real photo post card (RPPC) of a smiling child standing on a chair. Although information on his post-1900 commercial work is scant, apparently, he provided the typical services of a portrait photographer in this era.

Samuel C. Chester, 326 Federal Street, Camden. Young woman with turtleneck sweater, circa 1910. Paul W. Schopp collection.

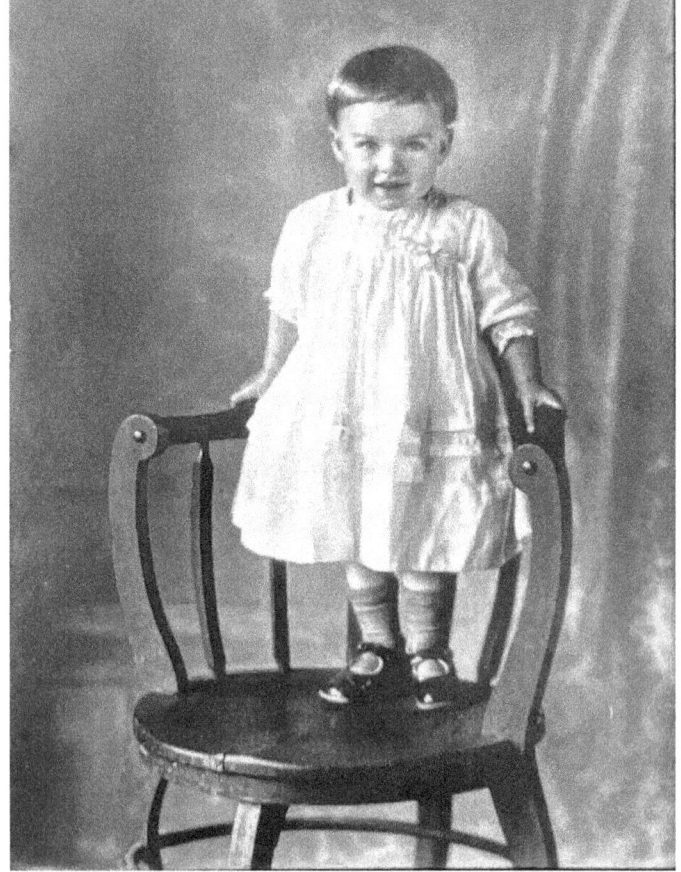

Samuel C. Chester, 612 Broadway, Camden. Child standing on chair, real photo postcard, circa 1924. Author's digital collection.

Samuel C. Chester

In 1926 and 1927, Chester no longer appears in the Camden business directory as a photographer, although he was still listed as such in the 1926 individual listings that recorded him with his wife Amelia at 500 N. 5th Street.[74] The 1928 directory indicates that he had become a watchman for Broadway Merchants Trust Co., but he probably continued to do some photography.[75] In 1929, the couple moved to their last home at 517 Fulton Place. The 1930 U.S. Census and the 1931 directory both record Chester with the same job. After Amelia died at age 69 on November 10, 1934, the aged Chester continued living at Fulton Place with his unmarried daughter until his death on April 25, 1937.[76]

In his January 1937 newspaper interview, the 86-year-old photographer pondered the history of photography and questioned, "I wonder what life will be like 86 years from now?" He reviewed the progress of photography from his youth and predicted that "television will materialize. There's no limit to what modern photography can do. The progress is so rapid. I can hardly believe they make color pictures—actually, without coloring the prints. Natural colors I mean. Three-dimensional photography? I don't know, it may come."

Considering the state of photographic technology in 2023, 86 years after Chester's interview, one must agree with him that progress has continued to be rapid, if not accelerating. Television was indeed perfected and three-dimensional holographic pictures and 3D video are now routine.[77] But Chester probably could not have imagined devices such as cell phones with cameras that have made billions of people into amateur photographers, documenting their own daily lives.

Samuel C. Chester, 326 Federal Street, Camden. C.C. Chew Store employees, *Courier-Post* (Camden), July 12, 1912, page 5.

About the Author

Gary D. Saretzky, archivist, educator, and photographer, worked as an archivist for more than fifty years at the State Historical Society of Wisconsin, Educational Testing Service, and the Monmouth County Archives. Saretzky taught the history of photography at Mercer County Community College, 1977–2012, and served as coordinator of the Public History Internship Program for the Rutgers University History Department, 1994–2016. He has published more than 100 articles and reviews on the history of photography, photographic conservation, and other topics, including "Nineteenth-Century New Jersey Photographers," in the journal *New Jersey History*, Fall/Winter 2004, a revised version of which is available at http://saretzky.com.

Endnotes

1. Robert Taft, *Photography and the American Scene* (New York City, NY: Macmillan), 1938. Available as a Dover paperback, 1964.
2. Ibid., 230.
3. Ibid., 485–86.
4. W. Oliver Kincannon, "10 Seconds to 1-200th Tells Advance of 72 Years Spent in Photography by Camden Man," *Evening Courier* (Camden, NJ), January 26, 1937, 11. Kincannon wrote that Chester did not complain about the darkness in his apartment or "the obvious poverty." The portrait of the aged photographer accompanying the article was photographed using a flash bulb. Chester lived at 517 Fulton Place, a short street that no longer exists. See http://www.dvrbs.com/camden-streets/CamdenNJ-Streets-FultonPlace.htm.
5. To prepare a collodion negative, the photographer coated a sheet of glass with collodion, a clear sticky liquid, and then immersed it in a silver nitrate solution to make it light sensitive. Exposure and development needed to be made before the negative dried, hence it was known as the "wet plate" process. Similar steps were required for ambrotypes on glass and ferrotypes (tintypes) on iron plates coated with a shiny black varnish.
6. Hirst D. Milhollen, "The Brady-Handy Collection," in Renata V. Shaw, compiler, *A Century of Photographs, 1846–1946* (Washington, DC: Library of Congress, 1980), 44–45.
7. Among other errors in the obituary, it stated that Chester was survived by a daughter Amelia, even though his daughter's name was Melinda. Amelia (née Hunt) was Chester's wife, who had died in 1934. Chester also had a surviving son, Charles Sumner Chester of East Lansdowne, Pennsylvania, and his family. In the 1940 U.S. Census for East Lansdowne, Charles, 49, an auto salesman, was living with his wife Lillian, 48, and their daughter Lillian, 24, all born in New Jersey.
8. This photo with both Sherman and McCook has not been located. Brady's 1865 portrait of Sherman and his generals, not including McCook, is readily available. Handy became an apprentice for Brady when he was 15 years old in 1870 and remained a photographer throughout his life. He inherited negatives from Brady's studio that are now at the Library of Congress.
9. McCook's biographer, Wayne Fanebust, stated that he had not seen the group photo with Sherman and McCook, letter to author, March 24, 2013. For McCook, see Fanebust, *Major General Alexander M. McCook, USA: A Civil War Biography* (Jefferson, North Carolina: McFarland & Co., 2013).
10. The negative sleeve included an annotation that Chester was of Haddonfield, New Jersey. No other reference to Chester in Haddonfield has been located by the author.
11. Chester & Handy have not been found in the 1880 U.S. Census, so it is possible he was traveling when it was taken. As discussed below, Chester & Handy were in Cape May in the summer of 1880. In 1881, they were listed in the Cape May County Directory. Chester reappeared in the Washington directories in 1882, when he was listed as a partner in Chester & Handy at 426 7th Avenue NW. In 1885, the partners were at 494 Maryland Avenue SW, where Handy was listed alone in 1878 and 1886.
12. Paul Israel, Executive Director, Thomas Edison Papers, to author, email, March 17, 2013.
13. Paul Israel to author, email, March 16, 2013. The associates were Charles Batchelor and Uriah Painter.
14. Archivist Leonard DeGraaf, Thomas Edison National Historical Park, reported that a copy of the Edison portrait credited to Brady, taken in April 1878, is the earliest in the Edison archives but he could not verify that it was the first ever made or that Chester was the photographer. DeGraaf to author, email, March 15, 2013. In the portraits of Edison alone, he sits with his machine resting on a table over a patterned rug that extends into the foreground. In one version, there is a painted backdrop behind him that also appears in other portraits by the Brady studio. In another photo, the background is blank.
15. Roy Meredith, *Mr. Lincoln's Camera Man: Mathew B. Brady* (New York: Charles Scribner's Sons, 1946), 78–79. According to his bibliography, Meredith obtained the history of the chair from a letter to him by M. H. Evans and verified by Will H. Towles, "last owner of the Brady Washington Gallery and present owner of the chair." Meredith did not provide a date for Lincoln's gift which was in 1860 according to the Walt Whitman Archive https://whitmanarchive.org/multimedia/zzz.00034.html. The distinctive chair with a U.S. shield on the wooden back may be present in a view of Towles' studio in Will H. Towles, *Towles' Portrait Lightings: A Practical Method*

for Making Photographic Lightings (Philadelphia: Frank V. Chambers, 1925), 13. The chair sold for $449,000 at Bonham's auction, October 26, 2015. https://www.antiquesandthearts.com/brady-portrait-chairbrings-449000-at-bonhams/.

16 The Garfields had seven children (five sons and two daughters). Two had died by 1876, before this photo was made. The children were Eliza Arabella (1860–63); Harry Augustus (1863–1942); James Rudolph (1865–1950); Mary (1867–1947); Irvin M. (1870–1951); Abram (1872–1958); and Edward (1874–1876).

17 Photographers usually bought paper already coated with albumen (egg white) and then sensitized it by floating it face down in a bath of silver nitrate. After drying, it could be kept in the dark for a few days without losing its sensitivity to light. For details on this process, see James F. Reilly, *The Albumen & Salted Paper Book: The History and Practice of Photographic Printing, 1840–1895* (Rochester, New York: Light Impressions, 1980).

18 A committee appointed by the Professional Photographers of America reported in January 1881 that the exposure time for the gelatin dry plate was one-tenth that of collodion and the quality was the same. The only disadvantage was that the cost for a prepared plate was higher than using plain glass and chemicals to make negatives. (Both collodion and early gelatin negatives were insensitive to red, which would print as black.) As more photographers adopted the new negative, the price came down. Taft, op. cit., 370–71.

19 In Camden, the Sherman Studio offered platinum prints. See author, "Careers in Camerawork: Six Photographers of Camden, New Jersey, 1860–1910," *SoJourn: A Journal Devoted to the History, Culture, and Geography of South Jersey* 6, no. 1 (Summer 2021), 7–25. For a Philadelphia photographer who specialized in gum bichromate, see author, "Elias Goldensky: Wizard of Photography," *Pennsylvania History* 64, no. 2 (Spring 1997), 206-272, available at https://journals.psu.edu/phj/article/viewFile/25383/25152 and "Elias Goldensky Collections," http://saretzky.com/history-of-photography-images-texts.html.

20 Samuel Chester's birth, New Jersey Births and Christenings Index, New Jersey State Archives, Volume H-2, 61 (ancestry.com). Information about Asbury Chester from U.S. Census returns and three 1949 newspaper clippings at the Millville Historical Society for which the source is not identified. In 1880, Asbury, Hannah, and four young children were recorded in the U.S. Census in Weymouth, Atlantic County. Walter B. Chester, the couple's last child born in 1872, became a Camden photographer in 1890 with Garns & Co. Walter then worked for Garns at least part time until his death at age 26 on December 20, 1897, in Millville. New Jersey Death Record, New Jersey State Archives. For Garns, see author, "Careers in Camerawork: Six Photographers of Camden, New Jersey, 1860–1910," op. cit.

21 Brown is not listed in *Craig's Daguerreian Registry* (Torrington, Connecticut: John S. Craig, 1996), nor before 1860 in Langdon's List of 19th & Early 20th Century Photographers, https://www.langdonroad.com/photographer-lists-2.

22 Cynthia G. Fox, "Income Tax Records of the Civil War Years," *Prologue* 18, no. 4 (Winter 1986), https://www.archives.gov/publications/prologue/1986/winter/civil-war-tax-records.html.

23 Carte-de-visite of a soldier, William Frassanito collection, email to author, December 10, 2014. Introduced in France in the 1850s, the carte-de-visite (cdv) is a small photograph on paper mounted on thin cardboard about 2 1/2 x 4 1/8 inches. Tintypes mounted to the back of cards the same size as cdvs with an aperture for the image are usually called ferrotype cards.

24 Ross J. Kelbaugh, *Directory of Civil War Photographers. Volume Two. Pennsylvania, New Jersey* (Baltimore: Historic Graphics, 1991), 23, 73. The license was in the sum of $10, $15, or $25 depending on the annual income of the photographer who was required to pay what amounted to an income tax.

25 Author's collection. The bottom of the front of the gem ferrotype card is imprinted "Patent Pending," in reference to Potter's patent for mounting tintypes to the back of aperture cards the size of cartes-de-visite for use in albums. Ray W. Potter's U.S. Patent No. 46,699 for Picture-Card Frames was granted March 7, 1865, and thereafter the patent date is often found on ferrotype cards.

26 *Philadelphia Photographer* 3, no. 32 (August 1866), 255.

27 New Jersey State Tax Assessment Lists, RG 58, National Archives and Records Administration, New York, Boxes 360–366. Now available at ancestry.com.

28 Cold Spring is a little more than three miles from the city of Cape May and today is best known for the tourist attraction, Historic Cold Spring Village. The Brown children in 1870 were Mary J., 14, Cornelia, 7, and Rosalee M., 2, all born in Pennsylvania. In 1870, J. B. Brown still had a personal estate valued at $500. Asbury Chester's personal estate was worth $150. Samuel Chester's siblings in the 1870 Vineland census were Clara, 17, Rebecca, 15, Emma, 9, Frank, 7, Mary, 4, and Grace, 2. Neither Brown nor Asbury Chester were recorded as owning real estate in the 1870 census.

29 Philadelphians would have taken a ferry to trains from Camden to Cape May until the Pennsylvania Railroad completed the first railroad bridge over the Delaware below Trenton in 1896. The state legislature chartered the Cape May & Millville Railroad in 1863. West Jersey Railroad leased the line in 1869. The Cape May & Millville then merged into the West Jersey in 1879.

30 Both this stereograph and a carte-de-visite seen by author of an African American woman have the "Foot of Ocean

Street" address. Chester & Handy's Cape May gallery in the 1880s was also at or near this location.

31 In the 1870s or 1880s, Brown probably partnered briefly in Millville in Brown & Beaulieu at the "New Daylight Gallery," and made a stereo view of an unidentified hotel. In 1874–1876, he made at least seven views of Vineland. He may have traveled in subsequent years, as his whereabouts have not been determined. (Stereo views by photographers named Brown, whose first name is not known, were made in a wide variety of locales.) T. K. Treadwell and William C. Darrah, *Photographers of the United States of America*, 1994, last updated 11-28-2003, National Stereoscopic Association, 108, https://stereoworld.org/wp-content/uploads/2016/03/US-PHOTOGRAPHERS.pdf. In 1894–1895, Brown photographed for the United States View Co., 1215 Race Street, Philadelphia. The 1900 U.S. Census listed him as a photographer living in Ocean City, Cape May County, with his married daughter Mary J. Hutchinson and her physician husband Dr. [Y.?] C. Hutchinson. After suffering from lung disease for two years, Brown died at age 67 of "phthisis pulmonalis" (pulmonary consumption) on April 19, 1901, in Vineland and laid to rest at West Laurel Hill Cemetery, Philadelphia. On the death record, his parents' names were Valantine [sic] and Mary Brown, both born in Massachusetts. His last address was 103 Landis Avenue, Vineland, and he had been a resident of New Jersey for five years. Pennsylvania, Philadelphia City Death Certificates, 1803–1915, https://familysearch.org and State of New Jersey. Transportation of Dead Human Body, Josiah Burnstead Brown, No. 8253, New Jersey State Archives.

32 Chester may have operated seasonally in Cape May in the early 1870s. Between 1870 and 1874, a shoemaker named Samuel C. Chester was listed in Philadelphia city directories, not likely Chester the photographer, although the shoemaker's wife's name was Amelia. In 1891, there was a locomotive engineer named Samuel C. Chester listed in the Camden directory. Three Samuel C. Chesters are in the 1900 U.S. Census for Camden: the engineer, the photographer with his family, and a 72-year-old man.

33 William A. McKay, *A Directory of Delaware Photographers 1839–1900 and Beyond* (New Castle, Delaware: Oak Knoll Press), 2018, 53.

34 John S. Craig, *Craig's Daguerreian Registry, Volume 3* (Torrington, Connecticut: John S. Craig), 1996, 513. Carte-de-visite by Sexton in Bordentown in author's digital collection.

35 U.S. Patent #54,416, May 1, 1866. In July 1867, Sexton acquired U.S. Patent #66,964 for an Improved Railroad Rail-Coupling.

36 A versatile and successful entrepreneur, Sexton at various times also ran a butcher business and a grocery store and had another farm in South Fork Township, Christian County, Illinois, where he raised horses. Briefly, he also was postmaster in Zenobia, Illinois. MacKay, 200–202.

37 *The Morning Herald* (Wilmington), September 14, 1875, 1.

38 McKay, *A Directory of Delaware Photographers*, 53.

39 *Philadelphia Photographer*, No. 156 (December 1876), 384.

40 *Daily Times* (New Brunswick, New Jersey), August 29, 1873, 2.

41 Stereo view seen on eBay, March 17, 2022. "Southwest" is from the 1881 Cape May County Directory studio address.

42 Milhollen, 44, asserts the 1882 establishment date, as does Wilson, 219. The Yale University guide to its Brady/Handy Collection states, "Around 1880, Handy entered a photographic partnership with Samuel C. Chester. They operated a studio in Cape May, New Jersey, in 1882."

43 Example from the Washington, DC, studio in author's collection.

44 The author has seen four different stereo views of groups by Chester & Handy taken at the Stockton House. The author thanks Kenneth Rosen for sharing several Chester & Handy stereo views in his personal collection. For Monmouth County, see author, "Gustavus W. Pach: A Nineteenth-Century New Jersey Photographer," *The Daguerreian Annual 2021* (Cecil, Pennsylvania: The Daguerreian Society, 2022), 158–177, and George H. Moss Jr. and Karen L. Schnitzspahn, *Those Innocent Years, 1898–1914: Images of the Jersey Shore from the Pach Photographic Collection* and *Victorian Summers at the Grand Hotels of Long Branch, New Jersey* (Sea Bright: Ploughshare Press, 1993 and 2000). The *Ocean Grove Record*, August 24, 1889, reported that Stauffer (1848–1935), who had a gallery in Asbury Park (1880–1917), took a group of about 100 guests at the Howland House, including more than a dozen New Jersey preachers. Born about 1826, William Long was based in Philadelphia (1853–1882) and was active in Cape May in the 1870s and 1880s. Conrad M. Gilbert & W. F. Bacon were Philadelphia photographers from 1875 to the 1900s, with a branch in Camden in the 1890s, when they also produced some Cape May stereo views.

45 Kenneth Rosen collection. Promenade cards (4 1/8 x 7 1/8) and Boudoir cards (5 1/4 x 8 1/2) were two of the more common larger versions of cabinet cards in the 1880s.

46 In the 1880s, Atlantic City and Asbury Park welcomed all classes and races of visitors, including Sunday excursions by black church and fraternal organizations, although like some other Jersey shore towns, they tried to segregate beaches and other facilities that attracted both African American visitors and, on their time off, black hotel workers. Segregated lodging was prohibited by the 1875 U.S. Civil Rights Act until it was found unconstitutional in an 1883 Supreme Court decision, but New Jersey passed its own Civil Rights Act in 1884, banning discrimination in public accommodations. Nevertheless,

white-only hotels probably remained typical at the shore. The manager of the traveling Fisk Jubilee Singers commented in 1885 that while performing at New Jersey resorts, "we have been treated more shamefully than we ever were in a southern state." In Cape May, the first upscale black resort, the Dale Hotel, opened in July 1911. In part, David E. Goldberg, *The Retreats of Reconstruction: Race, Leisure, and the Politics of Segregation at the New Jersey Shore, 1865–1920* (New York: Fordham University, 2017) 48, 74.

47 Mentioned in George H. Moss Jr., *Double Exposure Two: Stereographic Views of the Jersey Shore (1859 to 1910) and Their Relationship to Pioneer Photography* (Sea Bright, New Jersey: Ploughshare Press, 1995), 184. Moss listed the following as producers of stereo views of Cape May: J. B. Brown (Cape May), Chester & Handy (Cape May), James Cremer (Philadelphia), Henry H. Hall (Sea Grove, Cape May), E. F. Hovey (publisher, Philadelphia), Levi D. Johnson (Vineland), William Long (Cape May), R. Newell (Philadelphia), [George?] Williams (Cape May, "late with Brady"), and Oliver H. Willard (Congress Hall Lawn, Cape May). Other nineteenth-century producers of Cape May views include Continental Stereo View Co., Chase & Bachrach, and Spader & Nowell.

48 Stereo view seen on eBay, March 17, 2022.

49 In part, Kenneth Rosen to author, email, March 29, 2022.

50 Other subjects of cartes-de-visite by Chester & Handy in Cape May include a woman with elaborately gilded embroidered appliqué trimmed bodice and large, ostrich plumed hat; two lifeguards; a little girl with a doll; and a soldier in uniform with a long rifle.

51 *Evening Critic* (Washington, DC), December 21, 1882, 2.

52 Curiously, in the 1883 directory, Brady is also listed with Chester & Handy at 450 Pennsylvania Avenue NW.

53 Cards this style are included in the *Price List of Photographic Card Stock of the Manufacture of A. M. Collins, Son & Co.*, [Philadelphia], included in catalog, *Scoville Manufacturing Co., Manufacturers, Importers & Dealers in All Articles Pertaining to Photography* ([New York]: September 1884). Collins was the major manufacturer of photographic card stock in the nineteenth and early twentieth centuries.

54 Author's collection. Dark maroon cards were in use from 1884 to 1895, according to Gary W. Clark, *19th Century Card Photos Kwik Guide: A Step-by-Step Guide to Identifying and Dating Cartes de Visite and Cabinet Cards* (n.p.: PhotoTree, 2013), 40.

55 *Plainfield Daily Press*, August 1, 1888, stated that Handy had completed a "remarkable feat," an album of 500 photographs of federal government officials, including the President, Cabinet, Supreme Court, Senate, and House of Representatives, completing more than half of the portraits himself. It took him a year to prepare.

56 In his interview, Chester mentioned that he had photographed in Cape May for 26 years. Since he was in Cape May by 1870, this would indicate an end date of 1896.

57 *Bridgeton Evening News*, November 25, 1891, 4: "The popular Millville photographer, Chester, is on duty again at the old stand." In 1892, he returned from Cape May at the beginning of October. *Bridgeton Evening News*, October 4, 1892, 4.

58 January 4, 1888, 4. Born about 1841, Daniel W. Carpenter grew up in Homer, Cortland, New York. During the Civil War, he enlisted in the 76th New York Infantry Volunteers and was wounded in the Second Battle of Bull Run in August 1862. Later he transferred to the Marines and served as an orderly in the Naval post office in Brooklyn until he was discharged in July 1865. By 1870, Carpenter had a photography gallery in Millville, where he specialized in portraits. After selling out to Chester, Carpenter became a photographer in La Junta, Colorado, by 1891. He continued there until 1898, after which he worked in various towns in Arizona, California, and Colorado. In June 1902, he, and his wife Mary M. (née Hogate), moved to Haddonfield, New Jersey. Whether he did photography after his return to the Garden State is not known. In the 1910 census, he was listed as a brush agent in Pitman. Carpenter died there on March 3, 1913, age 71, and was buried in Cedar Green Cemetery, Plot B, Clayton, New Jersey. In part, email to author, March 17, 2022, from photo historian Carol Johnson, specialist in early Colorado photographers. *La Junta Tribune*, June 25, 1902, 1, mistakenly stated that Carpenter was located in Haddonville instead of Haddonfield.

59 January 5, 1888, 1. Photographs using electric light had been made as early as August 6, 1863, by John A. Whipple, when he photographed Boston Commons at night using exposures of 90 seconds. William Kurtz of New York began producing studio portraits by electric light in the fall of 1882, shortly after the city was electrified. Taft, *Photography and the American Scene*, 383. Kurtz' cabinet cards were imprinted "Electric Light" under the photo. The Edison Electric Illuminating Company of New York turned on electric lights in the city on September 4, 1882.

60 "Wires Under Ground," *Morning Post* (Camden), January 7, 1885, 1, reported that plans for electricity in Millville were underway. Street electric lighting was installed in Millville by October 1, 1886, by the Franklin Electric Light Co. *Morning Post* (Camden), September 4, 1886, 1. Cabinet cards with Chester's 121 High Street address are in the author's collection, although the Cumberland County Directory in 1889 and 1893 listed the address as 125 High Street.

61 Birth records of children, New Jersey State Archives. Marriage record, Samuel C. Chester, photographer born in Cumberland County, New Jersey, resident of Washington, DC, and Amelia Hunt, born in Pennsylvania, in Ritchie County, West Virginia, West Virginia State

Archives, http://archive.wvculture.org/vrr/va_view.aspx?Id=11540178&Type=Marriage. Why they married in West Virginia is undetermined. The 1880 U.S. Census, West Whiteland, Chester County, Pennsylvania, listed Amelia Hunt, 15, born in Pennsylvania, with her Pennsylvania-born parents, Jesse, 45, farmer, and Matilda, 42, as well as three siblings, Joseph, 20, Matinda, 17, and James, 12.

62 In part, Welling, 185, citing *Philadelphia Photographer*, October 1866, 311–13, 357. Note that Brady and some other New York photographers had made photographs in this format by 1865, calling them Imperial cartes-de-visite. Imperial was sometimes used thereafter to refer to cabinet cards, although the term was also used for much larger photographs, from about 7 x 10 to 11 x 14 inches.

63 John Rohrbach, ed., *Acting Out: Cabinet Cards and the Making of Modern Photography* (Fort Worth: Amon Carter Museum, 2020), 14–16.

64 "Cape May on Fire," https://www.capemay.com/blog/2003/11/cape-may-on-fire/.

65 Huggins & Scott Auctions, March 30–April 9, 2015. The auction description listed each man with affiliations and provides additional detail about the set. Not in this auction, another cabinet card with three baseball players wearing the same uniforms has also been seen by author.

66 Vignetting is the gradual diminution of tone around the figure towards the color of the paper. There were various methods in the nineteenth century to achieve this effect, either during exposure in the camera or while printing. By 1880, at least seven U.S. patents had been issued for vignetting devices. Janice G. Schimmelman, *American Photographic Patents: The Daguerreotype & Wet Plate Era, 1840–1880* (Nevada City, California: Carl Mautz, 2002).

67 Chester took out an ad for six months in the *Camden Daily Telegram*, November 21, 1893, reading, "Chester New Photo Studio, 319 Federal Street. Special attention given to children."

68 Almost a dozen previous galleries at 319 Federal in author's database, abstracted at http://saretzky.com/history-of-photography-indexes-to-photographers.html.

69 For the Fearn brothers, see author, "Careers in Camerawork: Six Photographers of Camden, New Jersey, 1860–1910." J. E. Smith was likely John E. Smith, Bordentown photographer from 1869 to the early 1900s. According to the 1891 Sanborn insurance map of 1891, the first floor of 326 Federal housed a telephone office.

70 Paul W. Schopp collection.

71 Samuel C. Chester. Portrait of a Boy. 4 1/4 x 6 1/2 inches. Instead of 326 Federal, the blind-stamped imprint erroneously reads 826 Federal. Collection of the Free Library of Philadelphia. Retrieved from the Digital Public Library of America, http://libwww.freelibrary.org/diglib/searchItem.cfm?itemID=pdcp00111.

72 July 12, 1912, 5.

73 *Camden County Directory*, 1923 and 1924; ad, *Morning Post* (Camden), January 11, 1923, 3.

74 The author thanks Bonny Beth Elwell, Library Director, Camden County Historical Society, for retrieving information from several directories in the mid-1920s that are not available online.

75 In his interview, Chester, who moved to Camden in 1892, stated that he photographed in Camden for 30 years, which would suggest 1932 as his retirement date from photography.

76 Death record, New Jersey State Archives. Chester died from chronic myocarditis with contributing cardiac asthma and was buried in Camden. A copy of this document was one of several kindly provided by archivist Bette Epstein before her retirement.

77 To ask questions of a Holocaust survivor in a holographic video, see Dimensions in Testimony, https://sfi.usc.edu/dit.

The South Jersey Culture & History Center
Local history press

The student-staffed local history press at Stockton University has produced over thirty titles related to South Jersey, along with this twelfth issue of *SoJourn*. Titles cover many topics including the history and culture of the Pine Barrens, the environmental history of South Jersey rivers, architecture, Jewish farming communities, literature, and more. For an up-to-date catalog, please visit stockton.edu/sjchc/publications/

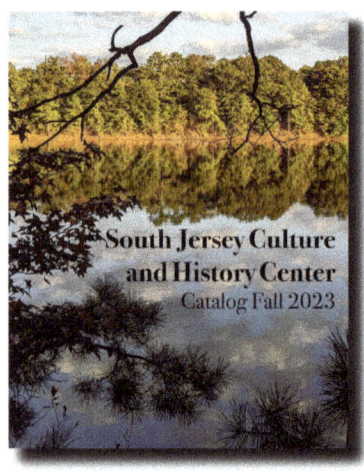

Recent Publications

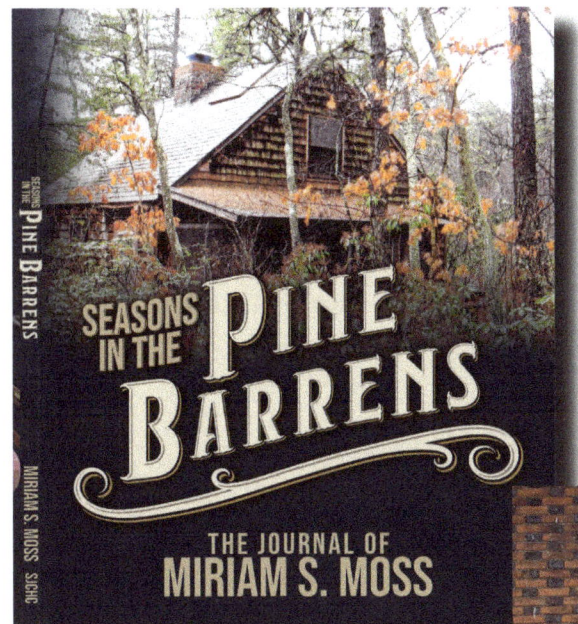

Frank Wending and Gabrielle Shockley, editing interns, hard at work. Henry, to the left, oversees their efforts. All titles available at Second Time Books. Most available on Amazon.

The Cape May Lighthouse today.

The Cape May Lighthouse:
A Sight of South Jersey

Amanda Sciandra

Located at the confluence of the Atlantic Ocean and the Delaware Bay in Cape May, the Cape May Lighthouse is one of South Jersey's great landmarks. Although it may appear as many other lighthouses, the innovation behind this structure, especially at the time of its construction, sets it apart. Constructed in 1859 by the Army Corps of Engineers, the Cape May Lighthouse is the third lighthouse to be constructed at the southern tip of New Jersey. Unlike the first two lighthouses, which were lost due to erosion by the sea, the 1859 lighthouse remains operational to this day.

Standing roughly 157 feet tall, the Cape May Lighthouse offers a 360-degree view of the Cape May peninsula. The lighthouse features a spiral staircase of 199 steps, initially ascended without the aid of a railing until its installation in 1865. The lighthouse contains many innovative features, including the use of porthole windows throughout the structure. These portholes provided light for the keepers and offered a view in each direction. The lighthouse also features floor vents, which help control the airflow throughout the structure.

Perhaps the most unique feature of the Cape May Lighthouse was its Fresnel Lens. Created by French physicist, Augustin-Jean Fresnel, the Fresnel Lens is a beehive-like structure consisting of 656 ground glass prisms. The Cape May Lighthouse's Fresnel Lens is the largest in existence and has a 19-mile range. This lens projects a flash of light every 30 seconds, which was how ship captains could recognize the Cape May Lighthouse at night as every lighthouse has its own flash time. During the day, the lighthouse is differentiated by its beige tower and red top.

The Cape May Lighthouse c. 1906. Courtesy of the Paul W. Schopp collection.

One of the floor vents within the lighthouse.

The lighthouse's spiral staircase.

View from one of the lighthouse's porthole windows.

The Fresnel Lens, currently located in The Museum of Cape May County.

Collectively, the Cape May Lighthouse cost $40,000 to build, $15,000 of which was spent on the Fresnel Lens. This lens was finally put into action on Halloween, October 31, 1859. Today, the original Fresnel Lens is on display at The Museum of Cape May County. As for the lighthouse itself, it has been fully restored and open to the public since 1988. The state of New Jersey leases the structure to the Mid-Atlantic Center for the Arts & Humanities (MAC), a non-profit organization dedicated to the preservation of the Cape May area. With its innovative features, unique history, and breathtaking views, the Cape May Lighthouse is certainly a site to see.

Want to Visit?

Location: 215 Light House Ave, Cape May, NJ 08204.

Hours of Operation: Friday-Sunday 12:00pm-4:00pm.

(Top Right) the beach and World War II bunker as seen from the top of the lighthouse. (Bottom) Cape May as seen from the top of the lighthouse.

A Visit to the NASW Museum

Cory Krause

As I walk through the open hangar doors, the natural piney scent of crisp October air surrounds me and fills the large, open military hangar. Behind me, the soft, pillowy aroma of fresh pancakes wafts through the air and fills me with warm nostalgia. The walls left and right are lined with interesting exhibits displaying a mix of local and WWII stories. My eyes dart to the large watchtower that guards the entrance of the hangar. *That's a bit smaller than I remember it*, my now adult mind thinks naturally as I reflect on my previous visits here as a child—a child who swears that tower was ten times as large, and remembers how fun but exhausting it was to climb to the top. My mind bounces around the room as I see all the different military vehicles and exhibits, wanting to read them all but not knowing where to start. Planes, engines, boats, helicopters, drones, and more fill the large hangar, each with a display paragraph that explains the vehicle's history and significance.

Some of these exhibits give faces to the names on the street signs and grade schools in my community, while others introduce me to people I've never heard of

Front view of the beautiful museum hangar. Museum hours are 9am–4pm everyday.

A memorial for local fallen soldiers, celebrating the lives of those who lost their lives defending this country.

A Visit to the NASW Museum

View from the museum parking lot of the wonderful Flight Deck Diner wafting the scent of pancakes in the air. The Museum and Flight Deck Diner are located at 500 Forrestal Rd, Cape May, NJ 08204.

before. All these people are remembered and thanked for their service.

This is the Naval Air Station Wildwood Museum, located at the Cape May Airport in Lower Township, Cape May County. This WWII training ground is a piece of local history that is too often missed by the tourists of Cape May County. It is now owned privately, bought for $1 in 1997 from the county (yes, you read that correctly), and restored from the ground up. Its mission is to remember the forty-two brave young aviators who lost their lives training as dive bombers during WWII. If you visit the NASW, you'll have the chance to learn the stories of these military men from people such as Austin Myers, the museum's communication manager, and volunteer Stephanie who are passionate about the Museum's rich history and purpose.

As Tom Kinsella, my professor, and I visited, Austin, our knowledgeable guide, told us a funny story that a WWII trainee shared with him many years ago. The young trainee met up with his unit for early morning flight drills; they were standard drills, nothing out of the ordinary. Upon takeoff, the young pilot brainstormed the best way for him to prank his fellow pilots. As he went through takeoff procedures, he discovered a peanut butter and jelly sandwich in his bag. The young pilot smirked as an idea formed. Once they reached about a thousand feet, the young pilot tossed the peanut butter and jelly sandwich out the window toward the plane behind him, thinking he'd scare his fellow trainee and make everyone laugh. Instead, the jelly inside the sandwich froze almost immediately upon hitting the open air, flew backward, and hit the turbine of the plane behind him. A puff of black smoke shot up from the large plane and the young pilot's heart sank, thinking,

Image of one of the training crashes.

Cory Krause engrossed in a cool movie at the NASW museum.

A Visit to the NASW Museum

A plane exhibit in Hangar #2 of the museum.

Oh my goodness, what have I done! Luckily, the plane's turbine sputtered another time or two, and then back to life, and the flight continued, with no harm done. Years later, both of the pilots were able to laugh at this story.

As a future educator, I am pleased to know that the seventeen- and eighteen-year-olds of past generations did ill-advised things, not just today's seventeen- and eighteen-year-olds (whom I thoroughly enjoy in the classroom). Austin shared this story and many others during our day at the museum. Some stories were about romance, some about family, some were humorous. Austin enjoys sharing these stories with all the museum's patrons as a way to honor and remember the veterans who served at this training hangar. I am sure he will be happy to share them with you on your visit!

Amanda Sciandra, author of "The Cape May Lighthouse: A Sight of South Jersey," and Cory Krause, author of "A Visit to the NASW Museum," graduated from Stockton University as Literature majors in 2023. Both wrote their pieces in order to entice readers to visit these outstanding historic sites.

Absecon Club

Paul W. Schopp

The all-male Absecon Club formed sometime during the nineteenth century and likely after 1854 and the arrival of the Camden & Atlantic Railroad onto Absecon Island. The song lyrics indicate that the membership comprised young men when they first associated to form the club. At the time the author drafted the lyrics, the members were all old and gray. The final stanza suggests the membership was dwindling and soon there would be but one remaining. Contemporaneous newspapers contain a scant few references to the club, and most describe clay pigeon shooting contests during the late 1880s and early 1890s in which the members competed against other area clubs like the Pleasantville and the Atlantic City gun clubs. The club maintained its own clubhouse on Absecon Bay and yachts could tie up at the club's dock or moor in its anchorage.

The names of those who held membership in the club are almost completely unknown. In April 1896, *The Philadelphia Inquirer* reported, "ATLANTIC CITY, April 9.—Harry Disston, son of Horace Disston, the wealthy saw manufacturer of Philadelphia, fell from the rigging of his yacht at Absecon Club House anchorage to-day and broke his leg." An article appearing in the July 18, 1897, edition of *The Sunday News-Dealer* (published in Wilkes-Barre, Pennsylvania) provides the name of one member when it reported "The *Philadelphia Item* gives currency to this vile slander on the person of one of the most popular members of the Absecon Club: 'The extraordinary high water reported at Atlantic City on Sunday is said to have been caused by Coroner's Physician Morton taking his annual bath.'" Dr. Thomas J. Morton served as the coroner's physician for the City of Philadelphia. The social status of Disston and Morton suggests that the club membership comprised men of stature and means.

The lyrics published here, copyrighted 1903, are the last reference to the club found. Newspaper mentions appear to end in 1897. The lyric's author, initialed T. F. P., was most likely Theodore F. Pidgeon, a resident of Chestnut Hill, an affluent neighborhood in the northwestern edge of Philadelphia. Born in 1838, Pidgeon obtained a position with the Philadelphia & Reading Railroad and rose through the ranks to become the transportation company's cashier, a position of prominence. During his lifetime, he fulfilled various positions in social and civic organizations. In 1879, his fellow masons elected him as secretary of Lodge No. 51, F. and A.M. Four years later, he served as president of the civil officers of the corps of Washington Grays. Pidgeon was a captain in Company G, First Regiment, First Brigade of the Pennsylvania National Guard; by 1904, he had risen to the rank of colonel and commanded the Washington Grays. The April 13, 1891, edition of *The Philadelphia Inquirer* provides further clues about Pidgeon's prowess at writing song lyrics: "Upon the conclusion of his speech Brother Peabody sang the 'Centennial Song of Lodge 51,' the words of which were written by Past Master Theodore F. Pidgeon and adapted to the air of 'Tenting on the Old Camp Ground,' the entire company joining in the chorus." Pidgeon retired from the railroad in December 1909 after 42 years of service. The Pidgeon family initially occupied a summer cottage on South Carolina Avenue in Atlantic City, but by 1899, they relocated to a cottage on Connecticut Avenue.

Pidgeon metered his *Old Absecon Bay* lyrics to be sung to Stephen C. Foster's *Old Folks At Home*, also known as *Swanee River*. Foster composed this number in 1851 as a minstrel song. Since 1935, this piece of music has served as the official state song of Florida.

If anyone has more information on the Absecon Club, please send an email to one of SoJourn's *editors for publication in a future issue as an addendum to this piece.*

OLD ABSECON BAY.

(AIR—Old Folks at Home)

DEDICATED TO "THE BOYS" OF THE ABSECON CLUB

BY T.J.P.

Copyrighted, 1903.

Down by Absecon near old ocean,
    Where breakers roar;
There's where the youngsters pledge devotion
    To old friends evermore.
There's where we play on our vacation—
    There's where we stay,
'Till skeeters lance our vaccination
    By old Absecon Bay.

Oh! Oh!! the story of our glories—
    Oh! the many tales!
If fishes were as big as stories,
    Then all we caught were whales!
Mermaids and Serpents—our creation,
    Fresh ev'ry day,
Caught on the hook of 'magination,
    Dreaming on shore by the Bay.

CHORUS.

Here in sight of the old, old ocean
    With lov'd ones to-day,
Once more we pledge our staunch devotion
    To the old Absecon Bay.

When first we built our habitation,
    By the old Bay,
We all were joyous with animation,
    Now we are growing gray;
But with our hearts as young as ever,
    And our spirits gay,
We never will grow old, no! never!!
    Down by Absecon Bay.

For many, many years we've mingled
    By the old Bay,
But one of us may soon be singled—
    Called home, far, far away;
Then sadly with our hearts a-welling,
    On the last day,
Our prayers breathing—with tears telling
    Love for our friend of the Bay.

CHORUS.

And now vacation days are o'er,
    We're going away,
Hoping to meet again in clover,
    By the old Absecon Bay.

Call for Articles

The South Jersey Culture & History Center at Stockton University publishes annual issues of *SoJourn*. We actively seek community members, avocational historians, and scholars to contribute essays on topics related to South Jersey. Illustrations to accompany these articles are a plus. Articles should be written for laypersons who are interested and curious about South Jersey topics, but do not necessarily have expertise in the areas covered. Potential authors may contact the editors for advice on style details or just follow the style in this issue. Journal editors will be happy to guide any would-be authors. In certain instances, Stockton editing interns may be assigned to assist authors with writing.

Sample topics might include:
Biographical sketches of important but forgotten local people; the development or succession of a community's roads, bridges or buildings; local transportation (focused by mode, area or era) and what changes it wrought in the served communities; history of community businesses and industries (wineries, garment factories, agriculture, boat building, clamming, etc.); old school houses, old hotels, or meeting halls; narrative descriptions of local geographical features; essays concerned with folklore, music, arts; and reviews of new local interest publications. Photo essays and old photograph and postcard reproductions are welcome with applicable captions. In short, if a South Jersey topic interests you, it will likely interest *SoJourn*'s readers.

Parameters for submissions:
• Submissions must pertain to topics bounded within the eight southernmost counties of New Jersey (Burlington & Ocean Counties and south)
• Manuscripts should be approximately 2,000–5,000 words long (6 to 16 pages of double-spaced text and 9 to 20 pages including images)
• Manuscripts should conform to the *SoJourn* style sheet, available here: https://blogs.stockton.edu/editing/files/2023/02/SoJourn-Style-Sheet-for-Editors.pdf/
• Manuscripts should be submitted in digital format (Word- or pdf-formatted documents preferred)
• Images should be submitted as high-resolution tiff- or jpeg-formatted files (editors can assist with digital conversion of photos if necessary). 300 dpi resolution, or higher, preferred
• Complete and appropriate citations printed as endnotes should be employed (see style sheet)
• Original submissions only. Copyright licenses for all images must be obtained by the author or should be copyright-free figures and/or figures in the public domain
• If essays are accepted, authors should submit a short 50 to 100 word autobiographical statement
• Articles need to be more than just a chronology of the given topic. The author should be able to properly contextualize the subject by answering such questions as: a) why is this important?; b) what is the impact on the local or regional history? and c) how does it compare to similar events/personages/changes/processes in other localities?

Call for submissions:
Submissions are accepted on a rolling basis. Send inquiries or submissions to Thomas.Kinsella@stockton.edu or Paul.Schopp@stockton.edu.

Notes and Queries: Finally, we invite readers to submit brief notes of interest or queries about topics of South Jersey history to either of the two editors named immediately above.

www.ingramcontent.com/pod-product-compliance
Lightning Source LLC
Chambersburg PA
CBHW060931170426
43193CB00026B/2997